D1327331

Town and Countryside

Town and Countryside

The English Landowner in the National Economy, 1660–1860

Edited by

C. W. CHALKLIN & J. R. WORDIE

London
UNWIN HYMAN
Boston   Sydney   Wellington

Published by the Academic Division of
Unwin Hyman Ltd
15/17 Broadwick Street, London W1V 1FP, UK

Unwin Hyman Inc.,
8 Winchester Place, Winchester, Mass. 01890, USA

Allen & Unwin (Australia) Ltd,
8 Napier Street, North Sydney, NSW 2060, Australia

Allen & Unwin (New Zealand) Ltd in association with
the Port Nicholson Press Ltd,
Compusales Building, 75 Ghuznee Street, Wellington 1, New Zealand

First published in 1989

British Library Cataloguing in Publication Data

Town and Countryside: the English landowner
in the national economy, 1660–1860.
1. Great Britain. Real property.
Development. Role of landowners
I. Chalklin, C. W. (Christopher William)
II. Wordie, J. R. (J. Ross)
333.3'8
ISBN 0–04–445353–1

Library of Congress Cataloging in Publication Data

Town and Countryside: the English landowner in the national
economy,
 1660–1860/edited by C. Chalklin and J. R. Wordie.
  p. cm.
Bibliography: p.
Includes index.
 Contents: Introduction / J. R. Wordie – A country gentleman and
his estates, 1720–1768 / Janie Cottis – The purchase and management
of Guy's Hospital estates, 1726–1806 / B. E. S. Trueman – A
progressive landlord / E. A. Wasson – Estate development in Bristol,
Birmingham and Liverpool, 1660–1720 / C. W. Chalklin – Liverpool
Corporation as landowners and dock builders, 1709–1835 / Jane
Longmore – The development of the Crown and Corporation estates
at Reading, 1828–1860 / S. T. Blake – A Devon family and their
estates / P. J. Keeley – Aristocrats and entrepreneurs in the Shropshire
mining industry, 1747–1803 / J. R. Wordie.
 ISBN 0–04–445353–1 (alk. paper)
 1. Landowners – Great Britain – History. 2. Great Britain –
Economic conditions. I. Chalklin, C. W. (Christopher W.) II.
Wordie, J. R. (J. Ross)
HD594.T68 1989   88-38117
333.3'0942–dc19   CIP

Phototypeset in 10 on 11 point Times by Input Typesetting Ltd,
London and printed in Great Britain by the University Press,
Cambridge

Contents

Notes on Contributors

Janie Cottis

Dr Janie Cottis read history at St Hugh's College, Oxford, before training in archive administration at the Bodleian Library. In 1984 she obtained a PhD from the University of Reading. Formerly an assistant archivist at the Oxfordshire County Record Office, she is now Archivist at Magdalen College, Oxford, and a part-time tutor and lecturer for the Oxford University Department of External Studies. Her main research interest is the agrarian history of the seventeenth and eighteenth centuries.

B. E. S. Trueman

Dr Brian Trueman took his BA, MA and PhD degrees at the University of Nottingham, and is currently Senior Lecturer at Worcester College of Higher Education. He has published articles on the administration of Hereford Cathedral during the eighteenth century and the management of Guy's Hospital estates in the same period. He has also done work for Guy's on the history of its Herefordshire property to 1961. His present research interests include work on agricultural developments in Herefordshire during the first part of the twentieth century.

E. A. Wasson

Dr Ellis Wasson took his BA and MA degrees at Johns Hopkins University, and his PhD from Cambridge (Trinity Hall). From 1976 to 1986 he was Chairman of the History Department and Dean of Faculty at the Rivers School in Weston, Massachusetts. Since 1986 he has been headmaster of Shady Side Academy in Pittsburg, Pennsylvania. He has contributed to *Albion*, the *Historical Journal*, the *Agricultural History Review* and the *Journal of British Studies*. He has also recently completed a book, *Whig Renaissance, 1782–1845* (New York, 1988).

C. W. Chalklin

Dr Christopher Chalklin took his first degree from the University of New Zealand at Canterbury, and the degrees of BA and BLitt from the University of Oxford. He trained as an archivist at the Bodleian and worked at Kent Record Office from 1960 to 1963. He is currently Reader in Economic History at the University of Reading, and was awarded the degree of LittD by the University of New Zealand in 1986. His publications include *Seventeenth Century Kent* (1965) and *The Provincial Towns of Georgian England* (1974). He has contributed to several journals, including *Urban Studies*, *The Agricultural History Review*, and *The Journal of Transport Studies*. He is currently working on the public financing of building projects in eighteenth-century England.

Jane Longmore

Dr Jane Longmore read history at Lady Margaret Hall, Oxford, and received her PhD in 1983 from the University of Reading. Since 1979 she has taught at the Universities of Sussex and Reading and St Mary's College of Higher Education, Strawberry Hill, London. Her original research interest was the social and economic development of eighteenth- and early-nineteenth-century Liverpool, but she is currently working in the fields of Anglo-Irish relations 1880–1921 and of British social policy 1834–1948.

S. T. Blake

Dr Steven Blake read history at the University of Reading and received his PhD, also from Reading, in 1976. He was employed as a research assistant in the University of Leeds School of Economic Studies in 1974–5 and since 1975 has been Keeper of Social History and (since 1983) Deputy Director of Cheltenham Art Gallery and Museums. He has published a number of books and articles on the history of Cheltenham, and in particular on the building history of the town between 1789 and 1860, into which his researches are continuing.

P. J. Keeley

Dr Patrick Keeley read history at Manchester before obtaining a DPhil at Oxford for his study of the Northcote family. His main research interests are in the social and economic history of Devonshire in the early modern period, and in the early history of the industrial revolution. He is currently working for an Australian mineral resources company, and is continuing research into the rural economy of Devonshire between 1500 and 1800.

J. R. Wordie

Dr Ross Wordie took his first degree at Queens' College, Cambridge, and completed his PhD at Reading University in 1967. After three years at the University of Wales he returned to Reading, where he has been Lecturer in Economic History since 1970. He has contributed to the

Economic History Review, *The Agrarian History of England and Wales* and *Research in Economic History*. He has published *Estate Management in Eighteenth Century England* (London, 1982), and is currently research-ing into the history of the pre-parliamentary enclosure movement in England.

Preface

Not since J. T. Ward and R. G. Wilson published their *Land and Industry: The Landed Estate in the Industrial Revolution* (David & Charles, 1971) have we seen a collection of essays devoted to the role of the landowner in the history of England's economic development. In recent years, what might fairly be described as a plethora of volumes on the landed classes in general has poured from the presses,[1] but these have dealt with the economic functions of the landowners only in passing and in general terms, providing us with few new working examples of what the landed classes actually did to promote economic growth. Rather, these examples have been provided by a much smaller number of books dealing with individual landed families.[2] The purpose of this present collection of essays is to add to that smaller fund of specific, grassroot examples of landed enterprise in the economic field, and to throw more light onto the neglected but important subject of corporate landownership, and corporate enterprise, which was particularly important in the field of urban development.

The papers in this collection are all based upon primary sources which have not before been published, but in the cases of Drs Chalklin, Trueman, Wasson and Wordie there are obvious links with previously published work which will be of some interest to those who wish to trace the connections. Five of the eight contributors to this volume are teachers at or doctoral graduates from the University of Reading, where a great deal of research into the urban and agricultural history of England has been proceeding quietly for many years. Too little of this research has seen the light of day so far, but the aim of this collection of essays is to remedy that situation to some small degree.

C. W. C.
J. R. W.

Notes

1   G. E. Mingay, *The Gentry* (London, 1976); D. Spring (ed.), *European Landed Elites in the Nineteenth Century* (Baltimore, 1977); P. Roebuck, *Yorkshire Baronets, 1640–1760* (Oxford, 1980); D. R. Mills, *Lord and Peasant in Nineteenth-Century Britain* (London, 1980); M. L. Bush, *The English Aristocracy* (Manchester, 1984); L. Stone and J. C. Fawtier Stone, *An Open Elite? England, 1540–1880* (Oxford, 1984); J. Cannon, *Aristocratic Century: The Peerage of Eighteenth-Century England* (Cambridge, 1984); J. V. Beckett, *The Aristocracy in England, 1660–1914* (Oxford, 1986).

2   T. J. Raybould, *The Economic Emergence of the Black Country: A Study of the Dudley Estate* (Newton Abbott, 1973); E. Richards, *Leviathan of Wealth: The Sutherland Fortune in the Industrial Revolution* (London, 1973); C. W. Chalklin, *The Provincial Towns of Georgian England*, (London, 1974); R. A. C. Parker, *Coke of Norfolk: A Financial and Agricultural Study, 1707–1842* (Oxford, 1975); T. W. Beastall, *A North Country Estate: The Lumleys and the Sandersons as Landowners, 1600–1800* (London, 1975); D. Cannadine, *Lords and Landlords: The Aristocracy and the Towns, 1774–1967* (Leicester, 1980); J. R. Wordie, *Estate Management in Eighteenth Century England* (London, 1982).

1 Introduction

The landed classes of eighteenth-century England made a positive contribution to the economic development of their country in many direct ways, as this collection of essays will show. But they also made an indirect contribution through their role as legislators, policy makers and setters of social trends. Very few members of these classes could be described as profound economic thinkers, but they moved with the thought of their times and the policies which they pursued, whether by good judgement or merely by good luck, undoubtedly had a highly beneficial effect upon the nation's economic development. This less tangible aspect of the landowners' role as a ruling class is therefore worthy of consideration at this point, before our more specific examples of the contributions of individuals are presented. A short survey of the economic structure of eighteenth-century England will help to explain the role of the landed classes within that structure in politico-economic terms, for economic and political issues were inextricably linked in the eighteenth century, just as they are today. In particular, the role of the landed classes in determining the fiscal structure of the country deserves examination.

During the eighteenth century, two schools of economic thought existed side by side in Europe: one was propounded by a group of politicians and economists whom history has labelled "the mercantilists",[1] while members of the other school were proud to describe themselves as Physiocrats, the proponents of the first clearly defined and self-conscious economic philosophy in the history of the world.[2] In many respects, the ideas of the Physiocrats were similar to those of Adam Smith, who indeed built and expanded upon them. They shared with Adam Smith a firm belief in the removal of all state-imposed economic restrictions, thereby allowing the "natural laws" of economics to operate, for the common good of all classes. Indeed it was a leading member of the physiocratic school, Vincent de Gournay (1712–59), who first coined the famous injunction, "laissez faire et laissez passer".[3] Despite his debt to the Physiocrats, however, Adam Smith did not hesitate to attack them vigorously in *The Wealth of Nations* over the one issue on which he differed from them. The Physiocrats believed that the land and its agricultural produce were the only sources of real wealth.[4] Adam Smith profoundly disagreed with this contention, stressing instead the vital roles of industry and commerce within a national economy and, in this respect at least, siding with the advocates of the "mercantile system" who had themselves been the object of his attack in the remainder of his famous treatise.[5]

Mercantilist thought directly contradicted the ideas of the Physiocrats, for mercantilists not only believed strongly in state controls, but also held that the promotion of industry and commerce was the surest road to riches. To the eyes of mercantilists, investment in agriculture appeared to yield rather poor returns. Output levels could be raised only very slowly, a law of diminishing returns would tend to operate, and the limits of agricultural production would soon be reached, if only because the quantity of land available for farming was itself ultimately limited. This was not to say that the agricultural interest should be entirely neglected or deliberately penalized, but rather that no great hopes for spectacular economic growth were to be placed in this sector. On the other hand, trade and commerce generated wealth in a form that could be increased very rapidly, and seemingly without limit to all practical intents and purposes. Had not a very small country like Holland become one of the richest in Europe by trade alone? The same argument could be applied to industry. Industrial wealth too could be multiplied rapidly, and in theory indefinitely. It could come to the rescue of the agricultural sector if the latter failed to meet the food requirements of a growing population, for a high level of industrial exports would generate a trade surplus in terms of international credit, which could be employed to buy in extra food from the cheapest world market. Industry and commerce could, therefore, ultimately provide all of the wealth and resources that a nation would ever require, and prove a bottomless cornucopia of consumer goods and job opportunities that agriculture alone could never supply.

The mercantilists' contention has been borne out to a great degree in European economic history since the eighteenth century, but it is now also evident that agricultural output can be expanded to an extent that the mercantilists would never have believed possible, and the agricultural sector has remained of vital importance within the European economy, sustaining the European population from its own resources, and even producing embarrassing surpluses.

Looking back upon the great divide between mercantilist and Physiocrat over the question of the relative importance of the land, history has tended to favour the mercantilist point of view, but in one sense at least, both sides were right. Neither party to this eighteenth-century debate would have denied that land, and the ownership of land, was of vital importance to industry, no less than to agriculture. Eighteenth-century Englishmen were well aware of what to them was a self-evident connection. One of the most obvious links between industry and the land was the mineral ores which the land produced, and here the relevance of England's unique legal and political traditions immediately becomes apparent. Unlike any other country in Europe, in England the Crown failed to establish exclusive rights to the minerals that lay beneath the land of its subjects. A long series of court cases, which began in 1566 with The Queen v. the Earl of Northumberland in the Exchequer, progressively weakened the rights of the Crown and in practice coal at least, as the cheapest mineral, was freed from royal claims by the late sixteenth century. The position of other minerals remained ambiguous, but after their resounding triumph in 1688, the landed classes lost no time in clarifying the situation. Two statutes, passed in 1689 and 1694, gave landowners exclusive rights to all minerals found beneath their soil, with the exceptions only of gold and silver.[6] These rights were to obtain even if the owner's land was tenanted, but reasonable compensation had then to be paid to the tenant involved if mining took place. Thus, landlords held a power of veto over the release of coal or mineral ores into the national economy. A few chose to exercise this right, as in the case of the seventh Duke of Bedford, who refused to allow the mining of ironstone from his Oxfordshire lands, but such refusals were rare.[7] On the contrary, there were more examples of landlords exploiting their minerals directly than cases of landlords who refused even to allow others to exploit their minerals for them. Coal and iron, it is generally agreed, were "the sinews of the Industrial Revolution" and if landlords as a class had followed the Duke of Bedford's example then England's road to industrialization would have been a stony one indeed. In the same way, landlords were in a strong position to prevent the building of roads, canals and, later, railways across their property if they so wished, not only in their proprietorial capacity, but also through the strong legislative influence which they exercised, either in person or with the help of their friends and relations in Parliament. These points are obvious enough, but the landed influence upon the course of industrial development went deeper, and was much more subtle than this. There are political and philosophical dimensions to the question which are well worth examining.

It is often forgotten that England's Industrial Revolution was launched not with steam power, but with water, horse and human power, and that it began not in large factories but in small workshops. Above all, it began not in the towns but in the countryside. By 1795, only 150 Boulton & Watt steam engines had been erected in the whole of Great Britain, with other would-be manufacturers checked by the operation of Boulton & Watt's patent until 1800.[8] Even at the close of the Napoleonic wars in 1815 the steam-powered factory was still a very rare phenomenon in Britain beyond the borders of Lancashire and the West Riding of Yorkshire, and most of Britain's industry was still to be found in the countryside. The links of our early industry with the non-mineral produce of the land remained close: for example, the industrial machinery of the eighteenth century was built mainly of wood, with iron in a supporting role only, as tipping, binding and reinforcing material. Even the boilers of early steam locomotives were clad with iron-bound timber as late as the 1830s.[9] Water power was provided through wooden water wheels, along wooden shafts, to wooden cogs and gearing. Timber supply was therefore of vital importance to many branches of early large-scale industries, in the woollen and silk mills, for example, or in Richard Arkwright's great water-powered cotton mill at Cromford on the Derwent. Mining operations, too, depended heavily on timber supplies for the manufacture of winding gear and pit props. The water power itself was drawn from the swifter, upper courses of England's streams, high in the hills near to their sources. The links between early industry and the land remained close and direct, since the land supplied so many raw materials essential to those industries, such as timber, wool, flax and leather. Indeed, the produce that grew above the soil was of greater importance as an input to early industrial enterprises than the minerals yielded from beneath its surface, if only because such produce included animal and human fodder. Horse power and human power were of even greater importance to early industrialists than water power, and so close were the links between land and industry that farming enterprises were often to be found as a closely integrated part of large-scale industrial ventures, especially mining ventures, as we shall see in the case of Shropshire. The discovery of these close links between farming and industry should come as no surprise when we look back to England's pattern of industrial development in the seventeenth century, when industry was small in scale, and rural in location: the nailors of Birmingham, the lead miners of the Pennines, the woollen workers of the West Riding, all kept one foot on the land, and ran smallholdings in tandem with their industrial enterprises. The "dual economy" was the rule among small manufacturers.[10] As industry grew in scale, larger farming enterprises were needed to support it, and we can see in Shropshire some evidence of "home farms" for rural industries emerging. The economic philosophy behind this arrangement was the same as that which justified a home farm near the country seat – it was more economical to provide your own food supplies for a large establishment than to buy them in from outside.

The physical links between land and industry in eighteenth-century England were, therefore, close and direct, with industry heavily dependent upon the land and its produce and, at least indirectly, extensive in its land use. But England's infant industries also depended upon the land in a political sense. No single factor has a greater bearing on the success or failure of a nation's economic development than the economic policies pursued by its government. Even the adoption of a policy of non-intervention with the workings of the economy, in order to let natural forces take their course, could be a monumentally important decision for a government to take, fraught with potential disaster. Examples of this may be seen in the seventeenth-century histories of Poland and Spain, where the governments of both countries refused to protect their native industries at a time when their neighbours were adopting aggressively mercantilist policies. In the eighteenth century, the Spanish government changed its attitude and Spain experienced a degree of economic recovery. Poland, however, remained set in her old ways, and continued into decline and eventual political extinction in 1795, as a result of her economic weakness.[11] Like Poland, Holland too suffered from economic decline in the eighteenth century, and for much the same reasons. The Dutch adhered rigorously to free-trade policies in an age of aggressive mercantilism, relying on their skills as traders and bankers, but neglecting their industrial base.[12] On the other hand, interventionist government policies could also be harmful: common among these in early modern Europe was a tendency to discriminate against the most economically successful members of a community on the grounds of racial or religious prejudice, exacerbated by jealousy of their success. Thus the Moriscos were evicted from Spain in 1608, the Huguenots were driven out of France in 1685, and the Jews were persecuted in Catholic Poland. Moreover, in all three countries, foreign policies and taxation structures contributed to the decline of industry.[13] Misguided foreign policies were also instrumental in the downfall of the Dutch, while over-heavy taxation and obtrusive regulation of industry led to the economic decline of many German and Italian principalities.[14] Another way in which governments could severely damage the economic prospects of their countries was to discriminate against their towns and industries for the seeming advantage of their landed ruling classes, as in Russia, Poland and Spain.[15] The striking of a correct balance of policies in the turbulent economic climate of early modern Europe was not easy. Governments needed to be interventionist to a degree in that mercantilist age, but not to excess, and they had, moreover, to be interventionist in the right ways.[16] England was fortunate in the eighteenth century to be blessed with a government that was, for the times, both benevolent and intelligent. It created in England a suitable climate for economic growth by passing no harmful legislation, but on the contrary was positively encouraging with both its legislative programme and its general attitude. The nature of this government, and of the class that composed it, are therefore worthy of close examination. So too is the economic philosophy which informed their policy decisions.

In eighteenth-century England, this philosophy was mercantilism. But Robert Walpole or Jean Baptiste Colbert would have been puzzled to hear themselves described as "mercantilists". In their day the term had not been invented, and what we would call mercantilism they would have called plain economic common sense.[17] To be educated in the field of economic theory in those days was to be a mercantilist, and the precepts that they followed they believed to be self-evidently beneficial to the commonwealth. The doctrine held sway without challenge from Queen Elizabeth's day until the emergence of the Physiocrats, who consciously set out to preach an alternative economic philosophy. Their ideas, however, made no impact whatsoever in England, and even after they had been taken up, transmogrified and given resounding credence by Adam Smith they sank in only very slowly in Britain, exercising no influence on government policies before 1800. In the eighteenth century, therefore, mercantilism ruled as the universally accepted and self-evidently "correct" economic policy to adopt. To borrow a phrase from later times, "there *was* no alternative". It was so obviously a case of plain common sense that the doctrine did not even need a name. What were the consequences of all this?

The ruling class in England was a small and closely knit group, with a keen awareness of a community of interest. According to Gregory King and Joseph Massie, they made up only 1.2 per cent of all the families in England and Wales in 1688 and 1760, and only 1.4 per cent of all families in 1803, according to Patrick Colquhoun,[18] but it was into their hands that all political power was concentrated. Indeed, if we consider only the heads of the 18,000 noble and gentry "families" listed by Massie, or the heads of the 27,000 similar families recognized by Colquhoun, then the size of the effective ruling elite drops to only 0.03 per cent of the population. Eighteenth-century England was certainly no democracy, and neither was it a republic: in name it was a monarchy, but in practice it was far more of an aristocracy. George III succeeded in reviving monarchical power for a time between 1770 and 1783, but his efforts ended in failure, and for the remainder of the eighteenth century, at least from 1714, it would be fair to say that the ruling classes of England ruled the king as well as the kingdom. The ruling classes were the landed classes: so closely was the ownership of land associated with the holding of political power that the two terms were synonymous. Even the exercise of voting rights was dependent upon the occupation of land in the English counties. Within town walls the franchise varied from place to place, but was not infrequently linked with the occupation of specific freeholds there as well.[19] In any case, the franchise was largely an irrelevance. Few towns or counties made a free choice when it came to the return of their two Members of Parliament: nearly all had fallen under the sway of a group of local landed magnates, while some were controlled by just one or two powerful individuals for parliamentary purposes. Uncontested elections were therefore very common, and the general rule was only one candidate for each seat, with that candidate nominated by the local landed interest.[20] Even when contests did take place, they represented merely the clash of one gentry grouping with another.

The selection of national economic policies was, therefore, not simply a matter for government ministers alone: they had to consider the prejudices of the landed classes as a whole, because of their complete domination of the all-powerful Houses of Parliament, and (in so far as it thought about economic policy at all) this landed class was mercantilist in its economic outlook. Its views were well represented in the person and policies of Robert Walpole. Although nominally a Whig, Walpole was careful to pander to Tory prejudices in matters of religion, foreign affairs and taxation policy so as to secure some measure of Tory and independent support in the Commons. To this end he kept Britain out of Europe's wars for as long as he possibly could, and therefore kept her taxes low. By means of skilful tariff policies, he protected English industries but at the same time expanded the volume of the nation's overseas trade, and hence the flow of customs revenue to the exchequer. The Tories applauded this increase in trade, for it meant that the land tax could bear a smaller share of the burden of taxation. So successful were Walpole's policies that in the 1730s, at the height of his power, 76 per cent of the government's revenue was being raised from customs and excise duties, and only 24 per cent from land, assessed, and other taxes. These proportions varied somewhat over the course of the eighteenth century, but in the 1790s revenue from customs and excise returns was still providing 65 per cent of all state taxation at the national level.[21] Now that W. A. Cole has made so bold as to give us national income estimates for each decade of the eighteenth century, it has become possible to produce Table 1.1 below, which indicates how comparatively lightly the landed classes were taxed at the national level, both in relation to their income, and relative to the community as a whole. It also shows that the whole national tax burden in England was not heavy relative to national income, at least by our modern terms of comparison.

Table 1.1 Taxation in Britain, 1700–99

Decade	A *Average annual GNP for decade* *(£m.)*	B *Contribution of agriculture* *(£m.)*	C *Land and assessed taxes* *(£m.)*	D *C as % of B*	E *Total taxation* *(£m.)*	F *E as % of A*
1700–9 (war)	51.0	20.2	1.8	8.9	5.1	10.0
1730–9 (peace)	49.3	18.1	1.1	6.1	5.8	11.8
1750–9 (war and peace	64.9	22.9	1.8	7.9	7.4	11.4
1770–9 (war and peace)	88.7	33.8	2.0	5.9	11.1	12.5
1790–9 (war)	164.7	57.5	3.6	6.3	21.0	12.8

Sources: P. Mathias, *The First Industrial Nation* (London, 1969), p. 462; W. A. Cole, 'Factors in demand', in R. Floud and D. McCloskey (eds), *The Economic History of Britain since 1700*, 2 vols (Cambridge, 1981), Vol. 1, p. 64.
Notes: All of the figures given represent average annual sums for the decades specified. Columns A and B are after Cole, columns C and E after Mathias. Cole's national income estimates are, of course, very approximate, and are for England and Wales only. The taxation figures, on the other hand, include the taxation paid by Scotland and should, perhaps, be discounted by some 10 per cent on these grounds from 1710 onwards. Scotland had about 17 per cent of the population of England, but a good deal less than 17 per cent of the wealth, especially of the taxable wealth. For example, customs and excise revenues in the 1750s provided 72 per cent of all taxation returns, but in 1755 the volume of Scottish trade was only 5 per cent of the volume of English trade (Dean and Cole, *Economic Growth*, p. 43). Therefore, admitting all the shortcomings of the statistics, we may estimate that the burden of national taxation in England and Wales varied at between 10 and 12 per cent of the national income between 1700 and 1800.

A more important question than the overall scale of taxation, however, is that of who paid the taxes that were levied. Early modern England was not without its forms of taxation that later generations were to describe as "progressive". Examples were the hearth tax, the window tax and the land tax, the largest shares of which were paid by the richest members of society. In the eighteenth century, however, the emphasis moved away from these forms of taxation, and from parliamentary grants which again had been paid by the richer classes, and towards indirect taxation on consumer goods through the levying of customs and excise duties on such items as malt, beer, salt, soap, coal, candles, leather, tea, cocoa, wine, spirits and tobacco. These taxes were mainly, although not entirely, "regressive", because they fell on goods which accounted for a large proportion of the expenditure of the poor, but only a small proportion of the outlay of the rich. An examination of England's tax structure in the eighteenth century does something to dispel the myth of a responsible landed aristocracy dutifully taxing itself in the national interest.[22] But the situation could have been worse: at least there was no immunity from taxation for English nobles, clerics or office holders, not even the theoretical immunity extended to those classes in France and Spain. The English ruling classes did at least pay a share, if not their full share, of national taxation. They were, however, lightly taxed in proportion to their incomes: even more lightly taxed than Table 1.1 would suggest, for it shows land and assessed taxes as a percentage of *landed* income only, ignoring the other sources of income which many members of the landed classes enjoyed, from office holding, investment in the funds, share dividends from trading companies, industrial and commercial ventures and even, in some cases such as that of Thomas Gilbert mentioned below, income from professional fees. These classes were therefore left with considerable cash surpluses on current account as a rule, which many chose to invest in productive enterprises or in banks rather than spending it on conspicuous consumption or putting it into the funds. Eighteenth-century British taxation policy favoured the rich, that is to say those with the greatest marginal propensity to save, or to invest. But a key factor to note is that this taxation policy favoured the rich merchant or industrialist even more than the rich landowner. True, the goods in which they traded were in some cases subjected to excise, on items like soap and bricks, while imported products like wine and tobacco were subjected to customs duties. But the additional charges on these goods were cheerfully passed onto the unhappy consumers, so that while the volume of such goods sold may have declined somewhat in consequence, the profit margins reaped upon them were little affected. Neither were these profit margins subjected to any kind of taxation. There was never any form of company taxation levied in eighteenth-century England, nor a profits tax, and no form of personal taxation on incomes until 1799.[23] The justification for this position rested upon three assumptions. First, it was assumed that what was vaguely thought of as "the commercial sector" paid its share through customs and excise levies. Secondly, miners and manufacturers, whose produce was not excised, were known to pay rent for the land they occupied, and it was assumed that an element of this rent went towards the cost of land taxes, tithes, etc., even if these dues were actually paid by the owner of the land. But while the rent of land made up a large proportion of a farmer's costs, they were only a small part of those of a manufacturer. Finally, it was well understood that mining and manufacturing were high-risk activities, on which many adventurers lost money. If their profits were to be taxed, then what of their losses? The risk-taking entrepreneur was to be encouraged: that had been the main point of most monopoly granting in the seventeenth century. Therefore the great bulk of industrial goods produced, such as the ironware of Abraham Darby or the pottery of Josiah Wedgwood, was subjected to no excise duty. Nor was there any form of minimum-wage legislation for industrial employees, although local magistrates were empowered to regulate industrial as well as agricultural wage levels under the Statute of Artificers of 1563. Neither was industrial plant subjected to any form of imposition, escaping even such local forms of taxation as the tithe levy and an equitable contribution to the poor rates.[24] Local levies such as these could constitute a heavy burden upon those who were fully liable to them, as is well illustrated by the outgoings of one Thomas Griffin, who tenanted a 295-acre farm in Staffordshire in 1775. In that year he totted up his outgoings as follows:[25]

	£	s	d
Rent	181	2	1
Constable lewn	1	5	0
Land tax	9	17	4
Window tax	2	13	0
Church levies	0	10	6
Poor levy	15	17	0
Tithes	26	0	0
Total	237	4	11

Griffin's whole tax bill came to £56 2s 10d, a sum equivalent to 31 per cent of his rent. Most of this money, however, had gone to pay local rather than national taxes. Only £12 10s 4d, about 22 per cent of the whole, had gone for land and window tax. Moreover, the remaining 78 per cent of his tax bill that went on local levies could have been even larger, for it included no highway rate, which was another onerous burden in most parts of the country.[26] It would be entirely wrong, however, to conclude from these figures that local taxation was some three times heavier than national taxation on the whole. First, the figures above give no indication of how much Griffin had paid in customs and excise duties during the year. In the 1770s, land and assessed taxes were a mere 18 per cent of national taxation receipts, which would have made Griffin's national tax bill some £69 8s 0d a year assuming that he paid pro rata. This would seem to be a very large sum of money, but if we accept Professor McCloskey's estimate of rent as being one-third of produce,[27] then the whole value of Griffin's output would be £543 6s 3d per annum. £69 8s 0d would represent 12.8 per cent of this output, which would make Griffin only an average national taxation payer. According to Table 1.1, national taxation ran at some 12.5 per cent of national income in the 1770s. Compared to this, Griffin's local taxation, at £43 12s 6d a year, would seem to be the lighter burden, but we must remember that it included no highway levy, and that the cost of poor relief was set to rise sharply – by some 200 per cent on a national scale during the last quarter of the eighteenth century.[28] By 1800, the burdens of local and national taxation may have been approaching a parity, and were extremely onerous upon those who had to bear their full weight. But not everyone, of course, did have to bear their full weight. We should remember that, as a target for local taxation, Thomas Griffin was a sitting duck. Other members of the rural community, who were not tenant farmers, paid far less or nothing at all towards local rates. Their numbers would include the landless labourers and the many poor, but also local merchants, tradesmen and manufacturers.

But what of the role of consumers? The taxation policies of England's ruling elite clearly favoured the investing and producing classes, but did they also have the effect of dampening down demand by overburdening the poorer consumer classes? Overall, it must be admitted that the wage and fiscal policies of eighteenth-century British governments did nothing to stimulate mass demand. The indirect taxes imposed upon many consumer goods raised their price, and left the poor with that much less money to spend on the products of industry. Their wage rates were liable to determination by justices of the peace who were not, of course, impartial arbitrators: they were themselves members of the employing classes.[29] In any case, it was rarely necessary for a JP to impose a wage upon labour lower than that recommended by natural market forces. The market rate was, in all conscience, low enough. Real wage levels had indeed crept upwards with painful lassitude from 1700 to 1750, but thereafter they went into decline again, to strike a new low point by the end of the century. A downward pressure upon wage levels was exerted relentlessly by a persistent surplus of population over the number of jobs available. Eighteenth-century governments saw it as no part of their duty in any way to guarantee full employment, and if Gregory King's estimates are to be believed, then the underemployed labour pool in the England of 1688 amounted to more than half of the population.[30] Some 2,825,000 people, described as vagrants, paupers, cottagers, servants and labourers, belonged to family units which were indigent, unable to match their yearly expenditure to their income and therefore requiring, presumably, help from the parish on at least an intermittent basis. Even allowing for some exaggeration in King's figures, the existence of a large pool of unemployed and underemployed labour in his time cannot be doubted, and this must have served to depress real wage levels.

Although population growth was slow from 1650 to 1750, allowing the situation to ease somewhat, English population levels tripled in the following hundred years up to 1850, re-creating an old problem. This problem existed, however, for the employed rather than the employing classes. It meant that mass demand from the working classes was indeed suppressed, but this became a problem for producers only at a later stage, within a fully matured industrial economy, when mass-production techniques were brought into operation, demanding mass consumption for the maintenance of their economic viability. The rural, workshop industries of eighteenth-century England were still far from the mass-production stage: rather, hand crafting with the assistance of some simple powered tools was still the rule, even in 1800. A satisfactory level of demand for the products of this kind of industry was not necessarily mass demand – middle- and upper-class demand would do very well, and demand of this kind flourished in eighteenth-century England. If we consider only the rentier and professional classes, those with a high level of income as individuals, then it appears from the estimates of Massie that they made up only 6.8 per cent of all families in England by 1760, but disposed of 22.2 per cent of the national income. Moving on to Colquhoun's estimates for 1803, it would appear that these groups had grown to make up 10.3 per cent of all families, and to dispose of a 29.5 per cent share of the national income.

In addition, many individuals within the categories described by Massie and Colquhoun as manufacturers, farmers and traders would also dispose of high incomes.[31] D. E. C. Eversley has calculated that only 20 per cent of a given population would need to have the spending power of heavy consumers in order to sustain the level of industrial growth and output reached by England in the year 1780, and his arguments are very convincing in common-sense terms.[32] A depressed mass market would not be a serious deterrent to economic growth in the early stages of England's Industrial Revolution.

The labouring classes of eighteenth-century England were, therefore, in general not favoured by the legislature, but there was one way in which the economic policies of England's ruling class might be said to have benefited the poor. This was in relation to the corn laws, and the export bounties provided for grain. The first Corn Bounty Act of 1672 laid down specific rates of subsidy to be paid on grain exports: "for every quarter of barley or malt, ground or unground, two shillings and sixpence, for every quarter of rye, ground or unground, three shillings and sixpence, for every quarter of wheat, ground or unground, five shillings."[33]

In considering the purpose of this statute, we can once again see the mind of England's ruling class at work. The measure was essentially a selfish one, passed by a parliament of landlords who were anxious to ensure that their tenants could continue to pay their rents at existing levels, even although grain prices were displaying a downward trend. The export of grain would, they hoped, create more of a shortage at home. This would raise the price of food for the poor, but would also put more money into the pockets of landlords. The whole operation would be paid for out of the public purse, but this purse in turn would increasingly be filled by the levy of indirect taxation upon popular consumer goods, taxes that would be paid mainly by the poor themselves. English landlords had every reason to rub their hands with glee over this prospect. The Corn Bounty Act was a thoroughly selfish, irresponsible and class-biased piece of legislation. From the point of view of the mass of the English people, it had only one saving feature, and this was its justification in terms of mercantilist thought. An aggressively xenophobic philosophy, one of the principal objectives of mercantilist policy was always the doing down of the foreigner. Another was the ruthless promotion of exports, even with the assistance of export bounties if necessary. (How little do the policies of nations change.) Both objectives were served by the Corn Bounty Act. Its justification lay in the theory that a surplus of grain production in England could be tolerated, providing that this surplus was regularly exported. This would cajole the foreigner into sending us gold in exchange, thereby contributing to the all-important favourable trade balance, and the building up of a bullion store at home, two shibboleths of the mercantilist faith. At the same time, the foreigner would be lulled into a dependence upon our grain supplies. Then, in the unhappy event of a widespread harvest failure, such as occurred all over western Europe in 1709–10 for example, England would cut off her grain exports. The luckless foreigners would starve, but this was no more than they deserved. They would probably be Frenchmen or Spaniards in any case, and so their demise would be no bad thing. England would enjoy a grain sufficiency at home, and this would prevent such squalid inconveniences as bread riots in the streets, which might have resulted in some damage to the property of important people. In moral terms, this second argument in favour of the Corn Bounty Act was scarcely more worthy than the first, motivated again by selfish considerations on the part of the landlords. But from the point of view of the common people, it did at least have the merit of making famine at home less likely: "Famine's Prevention by a Happie Discoverie", as the agricultural writers of the day were fond of putting it.[34]

As a piece of self-interested class legislation, the reasoning behind the passing of the first Corn Bounty Act was impeccable, at least in the light of then current economic knowledge. But English landlords of the day understood little of the economics of perfect competition, or the possible existence of backward-sloping supply curves. The result of overlooking these factors was that, ironically and in spite of themselves, the interested parliamentarians had passed a piece of legislation which proved to be of more benefit to the poor, the merchants and the industrialists of England than they could ever have envisaged at the time.

Because every marketing farmer in England found himself in perfect competition with every other farmer and because there was, at that time, no possibility of nationwide agreement between them to reduce the grain supply collectively, each farmer had to settle for the prevailing market price. An oligopoly of suppliers might have succeeded in forcing up prices by restricting output, but for the individual farmer under a system of perfect competition, the only way in which he could increase his personal income was by raising his own level of output. Therefore when wheat prices fell in early-eighteenth-century England as the result of, among other things, a run of good summers in the 1730s and 1740s, each individual farmer attempted to maintain his income in the face of falling prices by raising his own production levels. This development produced the seeming paradox of a backward-sloping supply curve, with supply increasing as prices fell. Whatever the profits of this policy to individual farmers, their actions were collectively self-defeating, but not unusual among producers in a system of perfect competition, who could not easily diversify into the production of other goods.[35] A move into stock-rearing or dairying was not at all easy for the cereal farmer whose acreage and farm buildings were geared for grain production, but there was a move towards the growing of more wheat in the southern and eastern counties, since this was the cereal crop which gave the highest cash return per acre.[36]

As a result of these economic forces taking their effect, in conjunction with the introduction and spread of many agricultural improvements after 1672, runs of good summers, and a continuing very low rate of population increase, the policy of encouraging grain exports succeeded in a spectacular way, beyond the wildest dreams of those who had framed the legislation for a bounty. Between 1750 and 1754, grain exports averaged 1,080,000 quarters a year, enough to provide bread and ale for an additional 2 million people over those years, or an extra one-third of the then population of

England (which stood at about 6 million). Between 1697 and 1765 a total sum of £6,058,962 was paid out in export bounties, £2,628,503 of it between 1746 and 1765.[37] It was indeed only this very high level of grain exports, and the payment of the generous bounties that went with it, that saved many a southern grain farmer and his landlord from bankruptcy as a result of excessive over-production and falling prices.[38] For a few years in the middle of the eighteenth century, England was bidding fair to become one of the granaries of Europe, thanks in some measure to the direct efforts of individual improvers like Sir Mark Stuart Pleydell, of whom Dr Cottis writes below, but thanks also to the legislative framework in which they operated. The result of these developments was, in effect, the introduction of a cheap food policy in England during the first half of the eighteenth century, and this proved to be of some benefit to the poor. The painfully slow rise in real wage levels that took place at this time was the result not of an increase in money wages being paid by employers, but rather of a fall in the price of the basic foodstuffs being consumed by the poor.

To say this is almost to bring a happy ending to the story, at least up until 1750, but not quite. It was still no part of the government's policy to introduce job-creation schemes or to help with the unemployment problem in any way, beyond their fervent belief that a religious adherence to sound mercantilist principles would eventually result in the emergence of more "real" jobs. The continuing existence of a large pool of unemployed and underemployed labour within this pre-industrial economy therefore served to keep wages down. But the existence of a low-wage economy was entirely in line with government policy, for a firm belief in low wages was a basic tenet of the mercantilist faith.[39] This would keep down costs to manufacturers, and so they would be able to sell their manufactured products abroad more easily, forcing the foreigner to pay for them in bullion, etc. etc. The poor should be kept employed, of course: this would keep them out of mischief, reduce the poor rate, and increase the volume of manufactures for export. But they should be employed at low wages, as befitted their station in life. The contradiction between the dual ideals of full employment and low wages did not occur to the eighteenth-century mind, nor was there any reason why it should have done so. Since a condition of full employment was never reached in eighteenth-century England, the question never arose. From the 1750s, population levels began to rise, real wages fell, and the problems of poverty and unemployment increased in severity once more, except for those fortunate few who found themselves in areas of rapidly expanding industry.[40]

The reality of the situation was, therefore, that eighteenth-century government economic and fiscal policies favoured the richer classes, the investing classes, and the employing classes. These policies also, through the medium of the corn export bounties, helped to ensure a low-wage economy. The maintenance of a low-wage economy was further supported by the persistance of a pool of the underemployed, and by the post-1750 population rise. Low wages and a labour surplus were a hardship for the poor, but they were also an advantage for the manufacturing and commercial classes in England who employed labour. This was especially true of an age when much of the power used in manufacturing industry was still human power, and when wage costs were a very high proportion of total costs. Even the lack of mass demand from this wage-earning sector was hardly a disadvantage to the early manufacturers, as has been shown above.

In short, her landed and ruling classes produced in England an economic, political and social environment which was highly conducive to the development of industry, and highly advantageous to the merchant and industrialist. The advantages which these people enjoyed may be summed up under five headings.

First, Parliament's corn bounties produced what was in effect a cheap-food policy in England, thereby enabling manufacturers to pay their workers lower wages. Secondly, the ruling classes were wise to embrace a mercantilist economic philosophy in the seventeenth and eighteenth centuries. Given the fact that they lived in mercantilist times, these were the only safe and prudent policies to adopt, as the fortunes of Poland, Spain and later Holland clearly showed. The adoption of such policies meant that English manufactures were protected from imported foreign goods by tariffs, but enjoyed the advantage of low or negligible import duties on their essential raw materials, such as cotton and dyestuffs. Their own manufactured exports were carefully kept free of export duties, and as a result of this it was the export-oriented industries which grew most rapidly in eighteenth-century England. According to Deane and Cole, who may have been guilty of exaggeration, these industries more than quintupled their output levels between 1700 and 1800, while the purely home-based industries grew by only 50 per cent. Later, leading sectors in the Industrial Revolution, such as cotton and woollens, were also heavily export-oriented.[41]

Thirdly, the fiscal framework of England, at both the local and national levels, was highly advantageous to merchants and manufacturers, and so too were the legal provisions for wage regulation.

Fourthly, the all-important attitude of the ruling classes towards industry and commerce was also very favourable. They fostered an exaggerated respect for property and wealth, including the property and wealth of industrialists. They lived and moved in what was already a thoroughly capitalist world, where money ruled. Those who could earn money also earned respect, while those who lost it were objects of contempt, however high their social standing.[42] The possession of money could be translated into real social standing through the purchase of land. The winning of acceptance into the magic circle of old-established landlords was more difficult and took longer – perhaps another generation or two before parvenu families could fully integrate themselves, but accepted they ultimately were. In the meanwhile the social caché attached to the ownership of substantial amounts of land was enough to satisfy most aspiring industrialists, especially when coupled with the knowledge of the eventual acceptance of their families into landed society.[43] But even merchants and industrialists without large quantities of land were by no means treated with contempt by the ruling classes – on the contrary, they were admired and even envied for their money-earning prowess. To prove that they were without prejudice against the commercial classes, landed and noble families frequently intermarried with them, in many cases mindful of the fact that their own families had been established in remoter times by commercial or professional forebears.[44] Moreover, England's landed elite further demonstrated their approval of the industrial classes by actually rolling up their sleeves and mucking in with them at the business of making money from industry or commerce. Few took this process to the lengths of the third Duke of Bridgewater, but this eccentric peer was, in the sense of a caricature, highly representative of the attitude of his class towards industrial enterprise.[45]

Finally, a full range of raw materials, transport facilities and credit institutions was made available to the English industrialist, again all largely by the courtesy of the landed and ruling classes of the realm. They also made available for exploitation the coal and mineral ores beneath their lands, or even extracted these themselves. They actively promoted the building of turnpike roads, canals, and later railways. They encouraged overseas trade, if only for the customs revenue which it supplied, and also the coasting trade. Through their savings and by prudent financial management in government, they ensured that abundant capital for investment was made available to industrialists at low rates of interest.[46]

The closeness of the links between land and industry in the early stages of our Industrial Revolution are seldom pointed out as clearly as they should be. When the full extent of the landed classes' direct and indirect support for industry is spelled out, however, it can be seen that the industrialists of England would need to have been duffers indeed to have failed in spite of all the advantages with which England's ruling elite had strewn their path. Here was an "incentive" economy beyond the wildest dreams of Margaret Thatcher. There was no alcabala in eighteenth-century England – and no VAT! If England was uniquely well qualified to serve as the birthplace of the world's first industrial revolution, then this was very largely because of the attitudes adopted by her ruling classes. It is now well known and generally accepted that our Industrial Revolution was, in the main, self-financing. Our industrialists pulled themselves up by their own boot-straps, steadily ploughing back their profits: the investment in industry of mercantile and landed capital made up only a small proportion of the whole. In the eighteenth century, the initial capital investment required for plant was very small, and the industrialist's main problem lay in the field of "cash flow", i.e. finding enough working capital for the regular payment of raw material and wage costs.[47] But there was very much more to the making of an industrial revolution than the question of who was to provide the working capital for industries, as has been demonstrated above. In any case, when it came to the provision of an infrastructure, such as the building of roads and canals, the input of merchant and landed capital investment was very much higher.[48]

Since the political and landowning structure of England was of such crucial importance to her economic development, the question of how landed estates were acquired and managed is not without significance. This subject is touched upon in two of the essays that follow, by Drs Cottis and Trueman. The former provides us with a representative account of the building up of an average squire's estate, but the latter deals with a more neglected aspect of English landownership, namely the acquisition of property by corporate bodies. This was an ongoing process in eighteenth- and early-nineteenth-century England, as Oxbridge colleges and the great public schools steadily increased their landholding. Endowed charities, varying in scale from Guy's Hospital at one end of the range to a humble row of village almshouses at the other, were also in the market for land in the eighteenth century. Town corporations too were eager to purchase land around the town perimeters, and sometimes substantial quantities were secured as in the cases of Liverpool, Bristol and Reading, discussed below. It was also during the eighteenth century that the long process of the sale of Crown and Church lands was eventually halted, and even reversed. With the creation of the civil list in 1697 and Parliament's assumption of the financial responsibilities of government, the Crown was freed from those pressures that had previously forced it into land sales. As for the Church, the processes of enclosure and tithe commutation, both of which gathered pace after 1750, provided individual clerics with landed property in compensation for their lost rights of commoning or tithe collection. The amount of land held by the Church therefore actually increased between 1750 and 1836.[49]

The total amount of land held in corporate hands during the eighteenth century has never been measured. As a proportion of all land, it must have been small, perhaps no more than 5 per cent of the whole surface area of England, but a higher proportion of the country's good, productive farm land.[50] Indeed, it could be argued that corporate land possessed an importance out of proportion to its surface area, since much of it lay within or near towns, and so assumed a greater importance as the basis of urban development, as in Liverpool and Reading. But even that corporate land which remained in the countryside had special significance. Once land had passed into corporate hands, it vanished forever from the land market, more surely than the land of even the most strictly entailed private estate. This was not only because a corporation lived for ever, fearless of death or disasters such as a failure of the male line. It was also because a corporately held estate was, as a rule, much better managed than all but the very best run privately held estates. The degree of effort, serious-mindedness and responsibility that the trustees of corporate bodies applied to their task of management was quite remarkable, all the more so in view of the low level of remuneration that they were usually offered for their efforts. The integrity of trustees was no less even when private estates were placed temporarily in their hands, to have their fortunes restored.[51] The lands of Guy's Hospital, for example, were not only purchased with great care by its trustees, but also managed by them in an exemplary manner thereafter. Dr Longmore's paper clearly shows how the trustees of corporate land could be every bit as enterprising and innovative as private landlords, while Dr Young has demonstrated that the woodlands of Winchester College were managed in a highly efficient way, which was no doubt indicative of standards of management over the rest of the Winchester estates.[52] Moreover, corporate bodies were not only good managers, but also benevolent landlords. It was well known that they sought out good tenants rather than high rents, and that they granted long leases. This provided their tenants with both the security and the confidence to invest in their land, and also the money to do so, thanks to lower rent levels. This meant that the tenants of corporate estates were more likely to be prosperous, and in the vanguard of agricultural improvement. One such tenant was so prosperous that he entirely disgusted William Cobbett, whose strictures upon carpets, bell-pulls and crockery sets are often quoted. But he also noted: "The farm, which belongs to Christ's Hospital, had been held by a man of the name of Charrington, in whose family the lease has been, I hear, a great number of years." It is very doubtful whether farmer Charrington would have been so prosperous as the tenant of a private landlord.[53]

Efficient and significant as the corporate owners were, however, the great bulk of the land of England of course lay in private hands, mainly in the form of great estates. Small landowners with under 300 acres each cannot have held more than 25 per cent of the land between them by 1790.[54] The position reached reflected the success of the great estate owners in "rounding off" and extending their own properties, at the expense of the smaller landowners, from 1600 onwards. There were indeed many good reasons why the small owners of England should have been ready to sell out, especially between 1650 and 1750, to set themselves up as tenant farmers or to leave farming altogether, at the very time when the great landowners were in a good position to buy.[55] The way in which the great estates were built up by purchase, inheritance, marriage and strict settlement is now well understood, and has been fully explained.[56] Less closely examined, however, has been the way in which the owners of these private estates managed to accumulate a steadily greater degree of power and control over their tenants, and how they later came to use this power to force the pace of agricultural change. The process was carried out in two stages, first by an attack upon copyholds, and then by an attack upon leaseholds. Copyhold was an ancient form of tenure, deriving from the customary rights of manorial tenants in medieval times. Manorial customs varied from place to place, and so too did the security of tenure that customary tenants enjoyed. Those with strong customary rights of inheritance and small fixed rents took a copy of the relevant entries in the rolls of their manorial court, which specified their terms of tenure. As rising prices diminished the real value of their fixed rents, these copyholders became as secure as freeholders, and manorial lords found that the expense of collecting their small "quit rents" exceeded the returns from them. Accordingly, many cut their losses and sold their copyhold tenants the freeholds of their farms. Ironically, however, many of the descendants of these emancipated copyholders were later to sell their freehold farms back to the very same great estates that had sold the freeholds to their forefathers a few generations before. In any case, it was more usual for manorial custom to favour the landlord, who could levy "rent uncertain" or "fine uncertain" when the tenancy passed from father to son, "uncertain" meaning as much as the landlord pleased. With such strong bargaining weapons, the manorial lord was able to pressure his customary tenants into accepting the more modern and "progressive" arrangement of the lease, at first for a term of three named lives, but later amended to a term of years. As agricultural prices began to move upwards with increasing speed after 1750, landlords sought to ensure that rents would keep pace with prices, and so granted their leases for shorter and shorter terms of years. By the end of the Napoleonic wars in 1815, the truly progressive landlord was not granting leases for years at all, but instead only tenancies "at will", which were subject to the giving of six-months notice by either party to the bargain. No entry fine was charged to new tenants, but a full economic rent was paid.

Changes in leasing policy of this nature served to increase the degree of control that landlords exercised over their tenants. The shorter leases for terms of years that were characteristic of the second half of the eighteenth century contained leasing covenants, with positive instructions on farming practices. The final stage in landlord control came with tenancies at will, however, reinforced by the appointment of skilled, dedicated and professional estate agents. These men were empowered to speak in the landlord's name, and were charged with the duty of raising rents.[57] They were bound to force the pace of agricultural change for this end, and poor tenants, lazy tenants or recalcitrant tenants now faced the threat of six months' notice if they did not comply with the agents' directives. Potentially, the nineteenth-century English tenant farmer was in a weaker position than his eighteenth-century predecessor, but not all landlords were harsh and grasping. Many preferred to lead by example: one such was Earl Spencer, who was progressive not just in the field of agriculture, but in his political views as well. Dr Wasson suggests below that these two characteristics often went together.

One of the most important ways in which the landlords contributed to agricultural progress was through their policy of promoting enclosure and consolidating farms, to produce a larger median farm size in England. The two processes were of course closely linked, and both were aided by the introduction of shorter leases, or no leases at all. The motives of the landlords in bringing in these changes were again selfish ones. Nobody wanted to preside over a gaggle of small, inefficient, open-field tenants who were bad at paying their rents, and in general a disgrace to the estate. Far better to enjoy a much smaller number of large, prosperous tenants, who had the capital to equip and run their farms properly, who were literate and well-read in the latest progressive advice, and who paid their rents on time as a point of pride. Besides, enclosed land returned a much better level of rent per acre than did open field; therefore enclosure and consolidation became the norm. Even in the case of old enclosed land, where the fields tended to be small and irregular, consolidation could still take place with the help of shorter leases.[58]

Once again, however, selfish motives on the part of landlords resulted in policies which were conducive to the public good. The new, larger farms were economical in their use of labour, fixed capital and working capital, since these inputs could now be deployed with maximum efficiency. They were not, however, economical in their use of land: the small, intensively cultivated peasant plots of France and Germany returned a higher yield per acre, because each acre was supported by much higher labour and capital inputs. The glory of the English system lay in the lower unit costs at which each bushel of grain could be produced. Although fewer bushels were produced that way, the system was more cost-effective, and it had two important social consequences.

First, it reduced the grain supply relative to what the position would have been if the land had been divided up into a large number of small peasant holdings. This raised the price of grain, and put more money into the pockets of farmers and landowners, those essential middle-class consumers whose demand levels triggered the Industrial Revolution. It also obliged landlords to pay higher wages, but they were the great gainers by this bargain, since their large farms were very labour efficient, and a tripling of population levels between 1750 and 1850 meant that there was always an abundant supply of the cheapest possible labour, clamorously on hand.

Secondly, a more important point, the English system limited access to the land as the population grew. The owner-occupying class of English farmers was a small one by the early years of the nineteenth century, sharing a mere 10 or 12 per cent of the land, a proportion not altered by the time of Bateman's survey of 1883.[59] Even this small band were hardly "peasants" in the continental sense of the word. Among other differences they tended not to divide their land among their sons, but rather passed on an intact holding to a single heir, aping their betters' custom of primogeniture. This left the rest of England's land in the hands of private and corporate *rentier* landlords, whose policy on farm sizes and labour economies has already been explained. Slightly more people were taken onto the land to cope with the increased demand for food in that age of demographic revolution, but the increase was a small one. The census figures for Britain reveal 1.7 million people working on the land in 1801, and only 2.1 million in 1851, an increase in no way proportional to the near doubling of population which took place over the same period. In this way, the English system did not drive people off the land by a programme of enclosure – this programme had been virtually completed by 1800 in any case. What it did do, however, was to prevent people from *getting onto* the land as population grew. In this way, the English system, devised and operated by English landlords, *made available* a labour supply for industry, although it did not *create* it. In one sense, therefore, the Marxists have spoken truer than they knew, although of course they were quite wrong about the role of enclosure.

This ready supply of cheap labour for industry must have helped England's Industrial Revolution on its way, but we should not forget that the Industrial Revolution also helped the toiling masses who served it.

England's population rise would undoubtedly have taken place even if there had been no Industrial Revolution to support it, for the rise was part of a European-wide phenomenon that affected many countries with no industrial base at all. One need look no further afield than Ireland for an example of this. In these less happy lands, where there was no industry to employ the extra hands, the growing numbers were crowded onto the land. Holdings were subdivided, and the outcome was always great hardship and sometimes disaster, as in the Irish case.[60] In England, however, the economic policies adopted by her landed classes helped to save the nation from disasters such as these.

In 1812, buildings accounted for almost 15 per cent of the national capital stock of Great Britain, compared with the 20 per cent share of industrial and financial capital.[61] Increasingly, this building stock was located in the towns, and so by this criterion alone, the role of landlords as urban developers would be an important one, even if we were to disregard the many other economic functions of towns in a modern economy. In this area, however, it is once again important to distinguish between the landlords' role as originators and enablers of a project, and actual investors in that project once it was launched. In some cases, the landlords were both originators of and investors in urban development. The role played by the highest-ranking, titled aristocracy of eighteenth- and nineteenth-century England in the development of London is well known, and leaves abundant evidence behind in the form of familiar landmarks; Russell Square, Portland Place, Cavendish Road, Regent's Park and the great Grosvenor Estate to mention only a few. But the history of these developments has been well documented elsewhere.[62] Less well known is the role of the landed classes in the development of provincial towns, although work is proceeding in this field. It reveals them to have been, on the whole, less active promoters of urban development in provincial towns than they were in London, but the picture varied from place to place, and more research is needed before a fully accurate assessment of their role can be made. In one respect, however, their role in urban development remained a vital one. A great deal of strategically situated land on the outskirts of growing towns was owned by England's gentry and aristocracy. Had they failed to co-operate with the natural process of urban expansion, displaying the same contempt for towns shown by the landlords of Russia, Poland or Spain, then England's towns could have been strangled, or forced to adopt grotesquely distorted growth patterns. Once again, the politico-economic dimension deserves consideration here. England's towns of the Middle Ages had won charters of independence for themselves, first from the hands of local lords, and later from the Crown itself, an independence of which they had been fiercely proud. From Elizabethan times onwards, however, the tide began to turn, and the towns of England fell once more under the sway of local landed magnates, returning in a sense to the situation of Norman times. Local gentry appointed to town corporations, and nominated the two MPs who would serve for the town: indeed they themselves in fact took over the "representation" of the towns in Parliament.[63] One of the reasons why so many of them owned land in and around the towns was that the land had been acquired, originally at least, as a means of increasing their political control over the town.[64] Once again, however, this power was not abused, but rather used wisely and benevolently to foster the growth and development of the handsome towns of Georgian England. The expansion of Nottingham, for example, was facilitated by the passing of a series of enclosure Acts, which opened up the common land around the town for urban development. The Dukes of Newcastle and Rutland also helped the town on its way by selling their land in and around the borough to developers in the 1780s and 1790s.[65] Other gentry and titled families who played a key enabling role in urban development were the Pulteney, Haynes and Gay families at Bath, the Colmore, Bradford and Gooch families at Birmingham, the Byron, Mynshull and Mosley families at Manchester, and the Earls of Sefton and Derby at Liverpool. As a rule, these landowners leased rather than sold their land to developers and builders, and usually they laid down certain stipulations as to the nature of the building that was to take place, by means of leasing covenants. In addition, it was quite usual for the aristocratic landowners to lay out street plans, mindful of the fact that building taking place on their land would reflect upon them: they then handed over the actual process of investment and building to others lower down the social scale – builders, tradesmen, attorneys and other petty bourgeoisie.[66] On the whole, this system worked remarkably well. The handsome towns of Georgian England were, by 1820, salubrious and a credit to their designers. It was only towards the middle years of the nineteenth century that the quality of urban life in England began to deteriorate just as, significantly, the influence of the landed classes on urban development began to fall away.

In some cases, however, landowners were much more deeply and directly involved in the building of towns than were the families mentioned above. Some towns and parts of towns were almost the single-handed creation of individual gentry and noble families, who invested their own money heavily in urban development. Notable examples are the Cavendish family at Buxton, Barrow and Eastbourne, the Palk family at Torquay, the Ramsdens at Huddersfield, the Calthorpes in Birmingham, and the Tapps-Gervis-Meyrick family at Bournemouth. Nor should the contribution of corporate landowners be overlooked, for the role played by the corporate landowning bodies in Bristol, Reading and Liverpool, discussed in the following essays, was by no means unusual. At Birmingham the trustees of Birmingham Grammar School and the Lench Trust helped the town on its way, at Hull the municipal corporation and the Dock Company were instrumental in developing the town, and at Portsea the town could scarcely have grown at all without the co-operation of Winchester College and the Portsmouth Corporation. At Newcastle and Bath, too, the town corporations were instrumental in forwarding development.[67]

The importance of the part played by English landowners in the promotion of national economic growth has perhaps been underestimated in the past. The aim of generalizing about their role in this way has been to underline their significance in the forwarding of England's agricultural, industrial, commercial and urban development between the years 1660 and 1860. Specific examples of how this was done are given in the essays below.

J. R. W.

Notes

1 The broad principles of mercantilism are too well known to need further recounting here, but a full and detailed treatment of the doctrine may be found in the following works: E. F. Heckscher, *Mercantilism* 2 vols (London, 1935); D. C. Coleman (ed.), *Revisions in Mercantilism* (London, 1969); W. E. Minchington (ed.), *Mercantilism: System or Expediency?* (Boston, Mass., 1969), D. C. Coleman, "Mercantilism revisited", *Historical Journal*, vol. 23, no. 4 (1980), pp. 773–91.

2 A good English-language treatment of the Physiocrats is to be found in E. F. Genovese, *The Origins of Physiocracy: Economic Revolution and Social Order in Eighteenth Century France* (Ithaca, NY, 1976). Their manifesto was Francois Quesnay's *Tableau Economique* (1758).

3 *Dictionnaire de Biographie Française*, vol. 16 (Paris, 1985), entry GOURNAY, col. 812. See also G. Vaggi, *The Economics of Francois Quesnay* (London, 1987), pp. 5, 22.

4 C. Beutler, *La Physiocratie à l'Aube de la Revolution, 1781–1792* (L'Ecole des Hautes Etudes en Sciences Sociales, Paris, 1985), pp. 53–144.

5 A. Smith, *The Wealth of Nations* (1776), Bk IV, ch. IX, 'Of the agricultural systems, or of those systems of political economy which represent the produce of the land as either the sole or the principal source of the revenue and wealth of every country".

6 E. Plowden, *The Commentaries or Reports* (London, 1818 edn.), pp. 310–40. E. Bainbridge, *The Law of Mines and Minerals* (London, 1878 edn), pp. 122–8. W. Blackstone, *Commentaries on the Laws of England*, 4 vols, (London, 1829 edn), Vol. I, pp. 294–5.

7 M. L. Bush, *The English Aristocracy: A Comparative Synthesis* (Manchester, 1984), pp. 189–90.

8 P. Mathias, *The First Industrial Nation* (London, 1969), p. 135; A. E. Musson and E. Robinson, "The early growth of steam power", *Economic History Review*, 2nd ser., vol. 11, no. 3 (April 1959), pp. 418–39.

9 J. Rowland, *George Stephenson, Creator of Britain's Railways* (London, 1954), pp. 64–5, 144–5.

10 D. Defoe, *A Tour Through the Whole Island of Great Britain*, 11 vols (London, 1928), Vol. 11, pp. 161–3, 195–200; W. H. B. Court, *The Rise of the Midland Industries, 1600–1838*, (Oxford, 1953), pp. 98–104; W. H. Chaloner, "The agricultural activities of John Wilkinson, ironmaster", *Agricultural History Review*, vol. 5, pt II (1957), pp. 48–51; D. G. Hey, "A dual economy in South Yorkshire", *Agricultural History Review*, vol. 17, pt II (1969), pp. 108–19; J. C. Hunt, *The Lead Mines of the Northern Pennines in the Eighteenth Century* (Manchester, 1970), pp. 145–61.

11 H. Kamen, *Spain in the Later Seventeenth Century, 1665–1700* (London, 1980), pp. 67–194, R. Herr, *The Eighteenth Century Revolution in Spain* (Princeton, NJ, 1958), pp. 120–53; A. G. Enciso and J. P. Merino, "The public sector and economic growth in eighteenth century Spain", *Journal of European Economic History*, vol.8, no.3 (1979), pp. 553–92; N. Davies, *God's Playground: A History of Poland, Origins to 1795* (Oxford, 1981), Vol.I, pp. 512–46.

12 E. H. Kossmann, *The Low Countries, 1780–1940* (Oxford, 1978), pp. 1–47; C. R. Boxer, 'The Dutch economic decline', in C. M. Cipolla (ed.), *The Economic Decline of Empires* (London, 1970), pp. 235–63.

13 J. V. Vives, *An Economic History of Spain* (Princeton, NJ, 1969), pp. 412–55; W. C. Scoville, *The Persecution of Huguenots and French Economic Development, 1680–1720* (Berkeley, Calif., 1960), pp. 434–47; W. F. Reddaway *et al.* (eds), *The Cambridge History of Poland*, 2 vols (Cambridge, 1950–1), Vol.I, pp. 567–8, Vol.II, pp. 75–6; C. Abramsky *et al.* (eds), *The Jews in Poland* (Oxford, 1986), pp. 26–7.

As is ever the case, the expelling countries paid heavily in economic terms for their intolerance. Those who opened their doors to the "huddled masses" were the very great gainers.

14 C. H. Wilson, "The economic decline of the Netherlands", *Economic History Review*, 1st ser., vol.9, no.2 (May 1939), pp. 111–27; H. Holborn, *A History of Modern Germany*, 3 vols (New York, 1964), Vol.II, pp. 43–4, 256–8; E. Sagarra, *A Social History of Germany, 1648–1914* (London, 1977), pp. 56–70,143; R. T. Rapp, *Industry and Economic Decline in Seventeenth Century Venice* (Cambridge, Mass., 1976), pp. 138–67; E. W. Cochrane, *Florence in the Forgotten Centuries, 1527–1800* (Chicago, 1976), pp. 173, 349–50, 429–53; D. Caspanetto and G. Ricuperati, *Italy in the Age of Reason, 1685–1789)* (London, 1987), pp. 2–44.

15 R. Pipes, *Russia Under the Old Regime* (London, 1974), pp. 191–220; O. Halecki, *A History of Poland* (London, 1983 edn.), pp. 165–213; C. Sanchez-Albornoz, *Spain: A Historical Enigma* (Madrid, 1975), pp. 875–919.

16 Our modern dialect includes a pithy phrase which well describes the hazards of selecting a wise economic policy in those times. Translated into seventeenth-century parlance, it might read, "E faith, t'was wondrous easie to skid into ye midden heap".

17 But mercantilists they certainly were. See C. W. Cole, *Colbert and a Century of French Mercantilism* (New York, 1939); E. C. Lodge, *Sully, Colbert, and Turgot* (London, 1931), pp. 145–68; H. T. Dickinson, *Walpole and the Whig Supremacy* (London, 1973), pp. 93–112.

18 P. Mathias, "The social structure of the eighteenth century: a calculation by Joseph Massie", *Economic History Review*, 2nd ser., vol.10, no.1 (1957), p. 45.

19 See T. H. B. Oldfield, *A Representative History of Great Britain* (London, 1816).

20 L. Namier, *The Structure of Politics at the Accession of George III* (London, 1929), Vol.I, pp. 175–91; J. B. Owen, *The Eighteenth Century, 1714–1815* (London, 1974), pp. 94–122; J. Brooke, *The House of Commons, 1754–1790* (Oxford, 1964), pp. 17–18, 52–3, 85–96, 125–6.

21 See M. Jubb, "Economic policy and economic development", in J. Black (ed.), *Britain in the Age of Walpole* (London, 1984), pp. 120–7; and B. R. Mitchell and P. Deane, *An Abstract of British Historical Statistics* (Cambridge, 1971 edn), pp. 386–7.

22 P. Mathias and P. K. O'Brien, "Taxation in Britain and France, 1715–1810", *Journal of European Economic History*, vol.5, no.I (Winter 1976), pp. 601–50; J. H. Plumb, *Sir Robert Walpole: The King's Minister* (London, 1960), pp. 235–9; P. K. O'Brien, "The political economy of British taxation, 1660–1815", *Economic History Review*, 2nd ser., vol.41, no.1 (Feb. 1988), pp. 1–32.

23 W. Kennedy, *English Taxation, 1640–1799* (London, 1913), pp. 141–50.

24 E. J. Evans, *The Contentions Tithe* (London, 1976), pp. 17, 76–7; W. S. Holdsworth, *A History of English Law*, Vol. 10 (London, 1938), pp. 286–99; E. Cannon, *The History of Local Rates in England* (London, 1912), pp. 78–101.

25 J. R. Wordie, *Estate Management in Eighteenth-Century England* (London, 1982), p. 193.

26 S. and B. Webb, *English Local Government*, Vol.V, *The Story of the King's Highway* (1913, 1963 edn), pp. 33–42, 51–8, 93–104.

27 D. N. McCloskey, "English open fields as behaviour towards risk", *Research in Economic History*, vol.I (1976), pp. 136–40.

28 Mitchell and Deane, *Abstract*, p. 410.

29 R. K. Kelsall, *Wage Regulation under the Statute of Artificers* (London, 1938); D. M. Woodward, "The assessment of wages by the justices of the peace, 1563–1813: some observations", *Local Historian*, vol.8, no.8 (1969), pp. 293–8.

30 J. Thirsk and J. P. Cooper, *Seventeenth-Century Economic Documents* (Oxford, 1972), p. 781.

31 Mathias, "Social structure", p. 45.

32 D. E. C. Eversley, "The home market and economic growth in England, 1750–1780", in E. L. Jones and G. E. Mingay (eds), *Land, Labour and Population in the Industrial Revolution* (London, 1967), pp. 255–9.

33 Thirsk and Cooper, *Documents*, p. 163. The statute referred to a Winchester quarter: in the case of wheat, one quarter weighed 448 pounds, or one-fifth of a ton.

34 J. Forster, *England's Happiness Increased, or a Sure and Easie Remedie Against All*

Succeeding Dear Years, by a Plantation of the Roots Called Potatoes (London, 1664), p. 18.

35 G. R. Allen, "Wheat farmers and falling prices", *Farm Economist*, vol.7 (1954), p. 339.

36 J. Thirsk (ed.), *The Agrarian History of England and Wales*, Vol.V, *1640–1750* (Cambridge, 1984), Pt 1, pp. 216–7, 336–7.

37 R. B. Westerfield, *Middlemen in English Business, 1660–1760* (New Haven, Conn., 1915), p. 162.

38 John Paleston, a Wiltshire landowner, wrote to his brother on 22 June 1734: "By all accounts in this part of the kingdom, gentlemen's estates would have been thrown up but for ye great exportation of corn that hath lately been". Clwyd Record Office, D/GW/534.

39 One or two dissenting voices were heard on this issue, such as those of Josiah Child and William Petty, but they passed unregarded by the mainstream of mercantilist thought. See T. Hutchison, *Before Adam Smith: The Emergence of Political Economy, 1662–1776* (Oxford, 1988), pp. 39, 121, 245–6.

40 E. W. Hunt and F. W. Botham, "Wages in Britain during the Industrial Revolution", *Economic History Review*, 2nd ser., vol.40, no.3 (Aug. 1987), pp. 396–8.

41 P. Deane and W. A. Cole, *British Economic Growth, 1688–1959* (Cambridge, 1969), pp. 31, 78.

42 E. Gregg and C. Jones, "Hanover pensions, and the 'Poor Lords' 1712–13", *Parliamentary History*, vol.I (1982), pp. 173–80; R. A. Kelch, *Newcastle, a Duke without Money* (London, 1974), pp. 85–6, 129, 138–52; J. V. Beckett and C. Jones, "Financial improvidence and political independence in the early eighteenth century: George Booth, 2nd Earl of Warrington", *Bulletin of the John Rylands Library*, no.65 (1982), pp. 17–23.

43 L. Stone and J. C. Fawtier Stone, *An Open Elite? England 1540–1880* (Oxford, 1986), pp. 111–30.

44 E.g. The Manners, Cavendish, Russell, and Leveson-Gower families, who ended as the Dukes of Rutland, Devonshire, Bedford and Sutherland respectively. See D. M. Thomas, "The social origins of marriage partners of the British Peerage in the eighteenth and nineteenth centuries", *Population Studies*, vol.26 (1972), pp. 101–12, and N. Rogers, "Money, land, and lineage: the big bourgeoisie of Hanoverian London", *Social History*, vol.4 (1977), pp. 444–6.

45 B. Falk, *The Bridgewater Millions* (London, 1942), pp. 79–112; H. Malet, *Bridgewater, the Canal Duke, 1736–1803* (Manchester, 1977), pp. 94–101.

46 T. S. Ashton, *The Industrial Revolution, 1760–1830* (Oxford, 1948), pp. 11, 21–2.

47 H. Heaton, "Financing the Industrial Revolution", *Bulletin of the Business History Society*, vol. II, no.1 (1937), pp. 1–10.

48 W. Albert, *The Turnpike Road System in England, 1663–1840* (Cambridge, 1972), pp. 97–108, J. R. Ward, *The Financing of Canal Building in Eighteenth Century England* (Oxford, 1974), pp. 143–60.

49 Evans, *Contentious Tithe*, pp. 8, 17, 94–101. See also R. J. P. Kain, *An Atlas and Index of the Tithe Files of Mid-Nineteenth Century England and Wales* (Cambridge, 1986), *passim*, and V. M. Lavrovsky, "Tithe commutation as a factor in the gradual decrease of land ownership by the English peasantry", *Economic History Review*, 1st ser., vol.4, no.3 (1933), pp. 273–89. Lavrovsky expressed surprise at finding that tithe owners were compensated by "one seventh to one fifth or even one quarter of the arable land to be enclosed, and one ninth or one eighth of the meadow and pasture land" (p. 275). But this was entirely fair. Ten per cent of the land would in no way be an adequate compensation for the loss of ten per cent of the produce of the land, obtained with no work input by the tithe owner, especially in the case of arable land.

50 J. Bateman, *The Great Landowners of Great Britain and Ireland* (London, 1883), p. 515, gives corporate owners 4.4 per cent of the cultivated acreage, but his survey was incomplete and of doubtful accuracy. See A. Offer, *Property and Politics, 1870–1914* (Cambridge, 1981), pp. 125–32.

51 For examples of private estates being restored by trustees, see R. A. C. Parker, *Coke of Norfolk: A Financial and Agricultural Study, 1707–1842* (Oxford, 1975), pp. 1–11; T. W. Beastall, *A North Country Estate: The Lumleys and the Sandersons as Landowners,*

1600–1800 (London, 1975), pp. 108–10; T. J. Raybould, *The Economic Emergence of the Black Country* (Newton Abbott, 1973), pp. 120–1.

52 See Dr B. E. S. Trueman's essay below, and also his earlier article, "Corporate estate management: Guy's Hospital agricultural estates, 1726–1815", *Agricultural History Review*, vol.28, pt 1 (1980), pp. 31–44. See also J. D. Young, "The Woodlands of southern England, 1700–1914" (unpublished PhD thesis, University of Reading, 1984), pp. 206–81.

53 W. Cobbett, *Rural Rules* (1830, Everyman's Press Edition of 1957), pp. 265–6. See also J. R. Wordie, "Rent movements and the English tenant farmer, 1700–1839", *Research in Economic History*, vol.6 (1981), pp. 220–5.

54 F. M. L. Thompson, "The social distribution of landed property in England since the sixteenth century", *Economic History Review*, 2nd ser., vol. 14, no.3 (1966), pp. 505–17.

55 See Thirsk and Cooper, *Economic Documents*, pp. 143–4, 181–6; H. J. Habakkuk, "La disparition du paysan Anglais", *Annales*, vol.20, no.4 (1965), pp. 649–63; A. H. John, "The course of agricultural change, 1660–1760", in W. E. Minchinton (ed.), *Essays in Agrarian History* (Newton Abbott, 1968), pp. 223–53.

56 C. Clay, "Marriage, inheritance, and the rise of large estates in England, 1660–1815", *Economic History Review*, 2nd ser., vol.21, no.3 (1968), pp. 503–18; L. J. Bonfield, *Marriage Settlements, 1601–1740* (Cambridge, 1983); B. English and J. Saville, *Strict Settlement: A Guide for Historians* (Hull, 1983).

57 D. Spring, *The English Landed Estate in the Nineteenth Century: Its Administration* (Baltimore, 1963), pp. 55–134; Wordie, *Estate Management*, pp. 53–74, 214–26.

58 J. R. Wordie "Social change on the Leveson-Gower estates, 1714–1832", *Economic History Review*, 2nd ser., vol. 27, no.4 (1974), pp. 593–609.

59 G. E. Mingay, *Enclosure and the Small Farmer in the Age of the Industrial Revolution* (London, 1968), p. 16.

60 F. E. Huggett, *The Land Question and European Society* (London, 1975), pp. 87–123; L. M. Cullen, *An Economic History of Ireland since 1660* (London, 1972), pp. 100–33; R. Price, *A Social History of Nineteenth-Century France* (London, 1987), pp. 143–96.

61 Deane and Cole, *Economic Growth*, p. 271.

62 D. J. Olsen, *Town Planning in London in the Eighteenth and Nineteenth Centuries* (Yale, New Haven, Conn., 1964); S. Jenkins, *Landlords to London* (London, 1975); F. H. W. Sheppard (ed.), *The Survey of London*, Vol. XXXIX, *The Grosvenor Estate in Mayfair* Pt.I, "General History" (London, 1977), pp. 1–72.

63 P. Clark and P. Slack, *English Towns in Transition, 1500–1700* (Oxford, 1976), pp. 13–14, 126–40.

64 For example, the Leveson-Gower family purchased land in and around Newcastle-under-Lyme, and the Anson family made purchases at Lichfield. Wordie, *Estate Management*, pp. 234–52.

65 R. Mellors, *Old Nottingham Suburbs Then and Now* (Nottingham, 1914), pp. 30–6; M. I. Thomis, *Old Nottingham* (Newton Abbott, 1968), pp. 52–68.

66 C. W. Chalklin, *The Provincial Towns of Georgian England* (London, 1974), pp. 74–112, 228–48.

67 S. Pollard, "Barrow-in-Furnace and the Seventh Duke of Devonshire" *Economic History Review*, 2nd ser., vol.8, no.2 (1955), pp. 213–6; C. Stephenson, *The Ramsdens and Their Estate in Huddersfield* (London, 1972), pp. 20–32; D. Cannadine, *Lords and Landlords: The Aristocracy and the Towns* (Leicester, 1980), pp. 41–61, 81–93, 229–238; Chalklin, *Provincial Towns*, pp. 74–9, 84, 113–39.

2 A country gentleman and his estates, *c.* 1720–68: Sir Mark Stuart Pleydell, Bart., of Coleshill, Berkshire

JANIE COTTIS

Few gentry landowners of the early eighteenth century can have left estate records as copious and revealing as those of Sir Mark Stuart Pleydell, Bart., of Coleshill in the Berkshire Vale of White Horse. Some twenty-five volumes, largely in his own hand, have survived, together with hundreds of loose documents. They cover a period of fifty-five years from 1713, when Pleydell came of age, to 1768, the year of his death.[1]

Pleydell was a contemporary of Thomas Coke, first Earl of Leicester, but Pleydell's estate papers provide an interesting counterbalance to Coke's, illustrating the immense difference in aims and methods between those of a high-income, high-spending great landowner whose lands lay on improvable sands, and a country squire of modest means and parsimonious habits who nevertheless wished above all to restore the quality of his rich grazing lands on clay. In 1732 Pleydell's income from inherited landed estates was less than $2,000 a year, with a further £700 in reversion from lifeholds, whereas Coke's gross income from rents in 1730 was just over £11,500 a year.[2] Both had lost heavily in 1720 as a result of the South Sea Bubble, with Pleydell probably losing more, in proportion to his income, than Coke; like Coke, Pleydell avoided investing in the stock market after this chastening experience.[3] But whereas by the 1730s Coke was receiving well over £2,000 a year from the Dungeness lighthouse and his office of Postmaster-General, Pleydell had virtually no income from non-agricultural sources. He was never a Member of Parliament, and his wife's income, due in part from her father's West Indian estates, proved difficult to collect.[4] Therefore, although both were intent on improving their estates, their resources were very different, and Pleydell cannot be judged by the same standards as Coke.

The value of Pleydell's estate papers lies chiefly in the detailed picture given of the personal dealings of a middle-range landowner with his tenants, especially the tenants on rack-rented dairy bargains. There is nothing resembling the orderly financial summaries drawn up annually at Holkham.[5] Even Pleydell's so-called ledgers turn into commonplace-books recording leasing agreements, breaches of covenant and the character of tenants as well as receipts and expenditure. But this is a significant modification, for Pleydell was concerned above all with controlling farm management by means of the lease. It is this that makes him stand out from other gentry owners of the mid eighteenth century.

Professional land stewards were rarely employed before 1750, even on great estates. Most of the gentry, like Pleydell, managed their own estates with the help of a manorial steward and a bailiff to collect the rents and act as go-between. Since, however, the great age of demesne farming was long past and the era of the model home farm had scarcely begun, most landlords were content to maintain the level of rents, safeguard the fertility of the land in a minimal fashion, and enforce the accepted husbandry practices of the neighbourhood. Some were improvers insofar as they provided capital for enclosing and reorganizing common-field farms, reclaiming wastes, or providing new buildings and expensive long-term dressings such as marl, but very few were interested in experimenting with new techniques or imposing progressive methods through lease covenants. Christopher Clay writes that, before 1750, "landlords scarcely ever seem to have attempted to use lease covenants as a means of making their tenantry change their ways in a progressive direction", and this situation changed little in the following twenty-five years.[6]

Sir Mark Pleydell's leasing agreements and accompanying memoranda provide clear evidence that here was a landlord who was one of the exceptions to Clay's rule. Pleydell has left little estate correspondence, because he rarely left home for any length of time, but he personally negotiated leases of enclosed lands, often recording the various stages in reaching the final agreement. The evolution and implementation of his policies regarding grass management on tenanted dairy farms are of particular interest. These policies developed slowly and were based on his own experience. They were in some respects idiosyncratic, but once he had become convinced of the superiority of permanent grass pastures, and the right way to establish them, he went to considerable lengths to convince his tenants that the system and methods that he was advocating would be best for both landlord and tenant.

The Pleydell Estates

In 1732, the year when he was created baronet, Mark Stuart Pleydell was the owner of estates in three western counties. From the Pleydells he had inherited lands at Shrivenham, Bourton and Watchfield in Berkshire, at Duntisbourne, Ampney Crucis and Slimbridge in Gloucestershire, and at Lyneham, Broad Blunsdon, Chiseldon and Minety in Wiltshire; they ranged in size from large manorial estates to a few closes. The family seat, however, and the heart of his estates was at Coleshill in Berkshire, and this manor, with a moiety of the adjoining manor of Great and Little Coxwell, came to him as a result of his grandfather Thomas's marriage with Mary Pratt.[7] Although they were scattered across three counties, all his possessions except Slimbridge lay within twenty miles of Coleshill House, a superb building designed by Sir Roger Pratt in the Jonesian style. This was by far the largest house in the Vale of White Horse in the 1660s, when it was built, and was one of the first country houses to be built in the classical style on the new block layout which supplanted the courtyard plan.[8] In 1732 it was still unsurpassed in the Berkshire section of the Oxford Heights, later known as the "Golden Ridge" because of its many fine houses. Unlike many of his neighbours, therefore, Sir Mark had no need to embark on expensive building projects.

The Pleydells have been justifiably cited as a classic example of a family which rose largely through the accidents of marriage and inheritance, and especially as a result of the Pleydell–Pratt alliance of 1666.[9] But the Pratt estates were no longer as considerable as they had been in the mid seventeenth century. Sir George Pratt, Mark Pleydell's great-grandfather, had been a lavish spender and a generous friend to the king and others, and had spent lavishly on the building of Coleshill House, with the result that two of his manors had to be sold at his death in 1673 to pay outstanding debts. His widow, too, died in debt and two of the demesne farms at Coleshill, as well as the Great Farm at Great Coxwell, were therefore sold in 1700 to her grandson, George Pratt Webb.[10] Moreover, at the time of Mark Pleydell's marriage in 1719, there were several obstacles in the way of his inheritance. Although his father had been the sole child of the Pratt–Pleydell marriage, Thomas Pleydell died young and his widow Mary, the Pratt heiress, later remarried and produced another son, the aforesaid George Pratt Webb. The consequence of this was that while Mark Pleydell's father, another Thomas, inherited Coleshill House and the manorial title, the greater part of the enclosed demesnes at Coleshill were devised to George Pratt Webb. These lands of Webb's were entailed, but even if he were to die childless Mark Pleydell would only receive a share in them, as joint heir with his cousin, Thomas Eyre of Huntercombe in Buckinghamshire. A further complication and reduction in Mark's prospects resulted from his own mother's early death, his father's remarriage, and the birth of his half-brother, Thomas Forster Pleydell.[11] Thus the advantage gained by low fertility and high mortality, those prevalent elements in contemporary demography, had been to some extent counteracted by second marriages which produced sibling co-heirs.

In the early 1720s, then, Mark Pleydell and his wife were lodging in his father's house, and living on about £500 per annum.[12] But within ten years this income trebled through a combination of predictable and fortuitous inheritances. His father died in 1727, and in 1731 both his kinsman George Pratt Webb and his half-brother Thomas Forster Pleydell died childless: Mark Pleydell was chief heir to his father, heir to Thomas Forster Pleydell and joint heir, with his cousin, to Webb's entailed estates. All three events were obliquely referred to by Pleydell in one of his ledgers, where he jotted down a list of "Purcha[se]s and other Accessions or Lucky Events".[13] The two latter were probably classed among the "lucky events". In 1732 he was created baronet, confirming his position among the leading Berkshire gentry, where great estates were few.

However, as owner of some 3,500 acres and co-owner of a further 600 acres at Coleshill and perhaps 2,000 in the Coxwells, Pleydell was only in the middling category of landowners.[14] Furthermore, the greater part of these lands were his in name only, as reversionary owner of many life-leaseholds and copyholds of inheritance. Thus one of his main tasks, as landlord, was to consolidate and if possible to extend his estates, and another was to convert customary and lifehold estates into estates for a fixed term of years at rack rent. Costs might be reduced by consolidating tenancies and by making the estates more compact through selling off the more scattered branches and buying up lands closer to his seat, while the enclosing of common-field estates would give him greater control of farm management, and should ultimately lead to a rise in rents.

Pleydell was an astute purchaser of land, and invested much of his surplus income, or "new capital" as he called it, in buying land, or the freehold or tithes of existing estates. The most pressing need, in 1731, was for the reunification of the Coleshill estate. This was to a large extent achieved in 1738, when Pleydell bought Thomas Eyre's moiety for £6,000.[15] But he never regained Webb's freehold lands at Coleshill and Great Coxwell, and no record has been found of any attempt to do so. In all, at least £20,000 was laid out on land purchases in Berkshire, Gloucestershire and Wiltshire during his lifetime, with the 1730s and 1750s seeing the greatest activity. Some of his acquisitions were the result of opportunism, arising from the difficulties of mortgagees.[16] Others were made in order to free his estates of irksome payments or restrictions; among these were Sly's farm in Duntisbourne and the manor of Duntis-bourne Abbots, following a legal battle over commoning rights.[17] Among his more substantial purchases were Widhill Manor near Cricklade and Little Park at Wotton Bassett. Although these lay in parishes where he previously owned no lands, they were enclosed dairy farms, each situated conveniently near one of the main roads to Swindon, and would have proved almost irresistible to him at a time when dairy bargains were his consuming interest. Besides, his only grandchild and heir, Jacob Bouverie, was the son of a Wiltshire landowner, and these estates would make a fine addition to the inheritance of the future Earl of Radnor and Baron Pleydell–Bouverie of Coleshill.[18]

A professional land agent might have recommended the sale of some of Pleydell's more distant minor estates: those at Slimbridge, for example, which lay 40 miles distant from Coleshill. But Pleydell was greatly attached to his ancestral inheritance, and reluctant to part with any of his lands. Apart from his youthful sale of some Shrivenham estates to buy the South Sea stocks he never willingly parted with any, although some additional lands in Shrivenham were sold in 1734 to Lord Barrington, his neighbour, after a long-standing dispute over copyholds in their respective manors.[19] In 1734 he was able to claim that, apart from the Shrivenham sales,

no Lands or Tythes belonging to the Family of the Pratts or to the Family of the Pleydells have ever been Sold out by any of the Ancestors of the said Sr. Mark except Such Sales as were made from the Estate of the Pratts by Sr. George Pratt and the Lady Pratt and her Trustees in Pursuance of her Will.[20]

Pleydell, his lifehold and common-field tenants

In describing Pleydell's leasing policies there is an important distinction to be made between his tenants on rack-rented, enclosed farms, and those cultivating common-field lands, usually with lifehold tenancies granted by copy of court roll or by lease for ninety-nine years determinable on three lives. When drawing up guidelines for lease covenants in 1744, Pleydell acknowledged that for copyholders only the simplest of agreements could be prepared, "because all other matters are directed and overruled by the Custom, and even a Collateral Agreement would affect only such of the Lives as signed it". In the case of life leaseholders, he thought that his basic printed lease form could be used, but that the supplementary covenants, designed for rack-rented leases, would be "improper" for life tenants.[21]

A survey of Sir Mark's tenants, taken in 1735 and including all his estates except the joint Coxwells manor, indicates that more than two-thirds of his tenants were lifeholders by copy or by lease, but they held only about a quarter of the non-freehold land.[22] This meant that a disproportionate share of the cost of rent-collecting and negotiating about repairs and taxes was being expended on a relatively small acreage. At Great Coxwell and Little Coxwell nearly all the inhabitants had secure tenancies, mainly copyholds of inheritance or long leaseholds for 1,000 or 2,000 years, granted mainly before 1620. There were some fifty of these at Great Coxwell, as against one leaseholder for nine years and two cottagers holding at will. Sir Mark was well aware that in those circumstances the revenue from the manor was scarcely worth the trouble of collecting it. In 1733 he summarized the drawbacks of this estate as:

> the Expense of a Dinner and Beer at the Annual Court in October, and Collecting the Quit Rents. Servants' time, horse hire, entertaining the tenants at my house and some abatements. . . . The Quits fall short and Godfrey's is extinct, and uncertain on what spots to distrein for any one, great No. of buildings in proportion to the rents. Large repairs and no wood whatever to support them.[23]

The policy advocated by Edward Laurence in the 1730s was for landlords to convert copyholds into leaseholds for lives, and leaseholds for lives into leases for 21 years or less.[24] A regular annual income from rack-rented land was preferable to an occasional windfall from entry fines and, besides, reversionary lifehold estates were a bar to land improvement and enclosure, which ultimately raised the value of the land. These changes in tenure had made considerable progress in the Vale of White Horse, as in other southern and western counties. On a few estates an advanced stage had been reached by the 1730s, as for instance at Shellingford, where Robert Packer was "determined to enclose his estate as soon as he can buy in the lives now in being thereon". But in other manors such as Uffington, part of Lord Craven's estate, there were too many tenants to make a buy-out policy feasible at this stage. And in a few places impoverished gentry owners were enfranchising their customary tenants, enlarging the already considerable freehold element of this fertile region.[25]

Like most of his neighbours, Pleydell favoured a gradual approach, which was less disruptive and less expensive than an active policy of buying up copyholds and leases, which survived on the Pleydell estates in such considerable numbers. Coleshill was the manor in which the strongest case could be made for accelerating the conversion of tenancies: it was Pleydell's home estate and it was moving piecemeal towards enclosure. Some conversion from copyhold to lifehold appears to have been made between 1691 and 1735 here, probably by Thomas Pleydell. Most of the leaseholders for lives, however, had messuages or cottages with little or no land attached, and Pleydell made no attempt to force them out by raising fines. Instead he used the very reasonable Newton method of calculating the fine due, and he even insisted that the good health of the incoming lives be proved. Some life leaseholds were renewed by him and during the 1740s, when tenants were hard to find, he even obtained the consent of some tenants that they would hold for life or for 99 years, although such bargains did not always appear in the printed leasing agreement.[26]

Sir Mark Pleydell made no attempt to convert Coleshill copyholds into leaseholds for lives, and his only purchase of such a tenancy was in 1735, when for £60 he bought out an absentee tenant with a messuage and a half-yardland.[27] Copyholds here were for lives, at fine certain, with widow's free bench, and in 1733 he sought legal advice on the possibility of extinguishing the widows' and executors' estates, but such a change in custom would not have been allowed in law at that date.[28] From 1727 Pleydell's policy was to wait for copyhold lives and common-field life leaseholds to fall into his hands. From this date until 1768 he kept a check on the "lives in being", and made a note of tenants who suffered from a serious illness such as palsy or cancer. The satisfaction with which he recorded the end of a line makes uncomfortable reading. The Jatt copyhold, for example, was nearing extinction in 1745, when informants notified Pleydell that

John [Jatt] and Henry son of Jno. are just dead, and Stubs says that Edw[ar]d, son of Jno., had not been heard of by his Father many years and tho[ugh]t dead, and Robinson adds, "there is an end of the[e]m all." Jno.'s wido[w] is in a Madhouse, where she has been this 30 years. [Later] S[ai]d wido[w], name[e]d Alice, dyed 24 Apr[il] 1756 at Finchampsted.[29]

These tenants, however, were for the most part absentee *rentiers* whom Pleydell had probably never seen and for whom he cannot have felt any paternalistic concern. Some lived miles away at Challow, Minety, Longworth or Wantage; one was a London indigo maker at Aldermanbury. One of the Slimbridge lifeholders had been transported to Barbados, where he became overseer of a plantation but had not been heard of since.[30] By 1768 only eight copyholds and lifeholds with common-field lands attached were extant at Coleshill, compared with eighteen in 1735. This prepared the way for enclosure by agreement by Pleydell's successor, Viscount Folkestone, who inherited in that year.[31]

Common-field lands were the other major obstacle to an integrated leasing policy. In the pastoral vales of north-west Berkshire, north Wiltshire and the Vale of Gloucester there had been a considerable degree of early enclosure. Great Coxwell and Shrivenham had been completely enclosed in the 1650s by agreement confirmed in Chancery; all the Pleydell lands at Lyneham, Longworth and Minety were also enclosed by 1720. Surviving common-fields were mainly residual and not closely regulated; often the pastures had been enclosed, as they had been at Coleshill and Bourton, leaving the arable and meadow commonable. Nevertheless, the surviving commonable arable could be a considerable irritant. At Duntisbourne there were tiresome disputes over commoning, while at Watchfield tenants had adapted the field system to allow for more intensive cropping, to an extent that Pleydell considered harmful to the land.[32]

Sir Mark's tactics on this front, even in those townships where he was principal landowner and manorial lord, where constrained by lack of the substantial capital that would have been needed to bring about complete enclosure. Only one township where he owned land was enclosed during his time as owner; this was Broad Blunsdon, where an agreement to enclose was confirmed by Parliament in 1750, but Pleydell was only a minor owner with fifty enclosed acres there and nine of common meadow.[33] For the most part, given that his resources were limited, he preferred to buy land with his surplus capital, and wait for the falling-in of lifehold tenancies to ease the path to enclosure.

The policy followed at Coleshill exemplifies his gradual and piecemeal approach. As early as 1726, before inheriting from his father, he secured the consent of the homage, duly recorded in the court book, that he might "enclose and keep in severalty all or any part of his own freehold lands in common field, he abating and allowing commons in proportion to what he shall enclose".[34] He was soon singling out suitable pieces for enclosure and from 1727 this policy was combined with the consolidation of tenancies so as to advance steadily towards enclosure by agreement, or more accurately by the extinction of secure tenancies with commoning rights. As mentioned earlier, this process was nearing completion by 1768, the year of his death, and a lease granted in that year bound one of his tenants to submit to Pleydell's agreement with the common-field tenants and to lay down the open lands "as soon as enclosed" with grass seeds. It was a simple matter for Viscount Folkestone, his heir, to buy out the remaining lifeholders, only two of whom were "yeomen of Coleshill", with annuities granted because he was "now enclosing the common fields of the said manor".[35]

At Duntisbourne, piecemeal enclosure took the form of block enclosures in certain furlongs, with landlord and tenant sharing the cost. There was a series of enclosures from *c.* 1722 to 1733, affecting about 100 acres of Pleydell land, and further agreements and enclosures took place between 1754 and 1760 following Pleydell's purchase of the manorial title.

Sir Mark's largest tenant at Duntisbourne, a life leaseholder, advised him in 1721 that it would cost upwards of £100 to enclose Nutbene Farm, but that she considered this money would be well spent, since "an Acre worth 15 pence may be St. Foin and Inclosure be improved to 20 shillings". Since it cost him over £36 to enclose twenty acres in 1733, her estimate of cost was too sanguine; nor did the land values rise as steeply as the forecast. The difference in value was considerable nevertheless, for in 1733 the best sainfoin at Duntisbourne was said to be worth 10*s* an acre, the old sainfoin 5*s*, and tillage "Inclosed from the field" also at 5*s*, while the common arable, when sown, was valued at only 2*s* 6*d*, with sheep commons in the fallow field valued at 1*s* 3*d* for 2½ sheep per acre. But this rise in value was not sufficient to offset the cost of a parliamentary award, which was not obtained until 1780.[36]

Pleydell suffered a considerable set-back at Watchfield, by the rejection of a parliamentary Bill for private enclosure, introduced in 1732. Here he pressed for enclosure, hoping that, as impropriator of the great tithes, he would be given a generous allotment of land by the commissioners, free of costs and charges. "Tythe of Arable is worth quarter of the rent, tythe of Medow one tenth," he wrote in 1727, " . . . therfore in case of an inclosure I ought to have a fourth part of the Arable and a tenth of the Medo[w]."[37] The opposition voiced at the outset by a few tenants on the grounds of expense did not prevent a Bill from being introduced, but Pleydell's claim for almost one-fifth of the total allotment led to separate counter-petitions from a group of landowners, the Vicar and Viscount Barrington, all of whom complained that Pleydell was asking for an unfair distribution of land, counter to their own interests. This combination of numbers, power and prestige was sufficient to defeat the plan, which had almost certainly been instigated by Pleydell himself, and Watchfield remained open and commonable until 1792.[38]

As an alternative to enclosure, the best that could be achieved was greater control of common-field husbandry. This, too, was accomplished only gradually, because the common-field farmers were anxious to adapt their fields and rotations, so as to sow a greater proportion of land in compensation for the low corn prices of the period. By doing so they risked over-ploughing their land, unless stock-crop ratios could be adequately increased with the aid of sown grasses, pulses and roots. Watchfield was a typical example of this trend. Here the two large arable fields had for a long time been modified by cultivating the best sands near the village as every-year land, and by defining four permanent hitchings which were sown three years in four. But by 1725 the farmers were also sowing new "casual hitchings" of up to 100 acres a year, and Pleydell strongly objected to these even though, as tithe owner, he ostensibly stood to gain by the increased production. It was not until 1748–50, however, that the Watch-field farers agreed to re-divide the fields into quarters, laying down exhausted parts of each with sainfoin for twenty-four years, undersowing the spring corn with clovers and rye grass, and allowing for turnips to be sown in severalty. By 1756 Pleydell was also asking the homage of the Coleshill and Coxwell manors to permit turnips and clover to be sown in the open arable for sheep feed.[39]

Pleydell and the tenants with leaseholds for years

In 1735 Sir Mark Pleydell had eighteen tenants on farms leased for 21 years or less. They ranged in value from a close at Shrivenham rented at £3 a year to a farm at Coleshill rented at £300. Even on the home estate of Coleshill there were a number of modest bargains, more so than on the estates of Pleydell's neighbours: the median rent at Coleshill in 1735 was £65, compared with £79 on Viscount Barrington's farms at Beckett in 1723 and £170 on the Packer estate at Shellingford in 1737.[40] The Pleydell leases rarely state the acreage, but the size of the enclosed farms at Coleshill was probably little changed from 1691, when one was below 50 acres, four from 50 to 100 acres, two from 100 to 200 acres and one was over 200 acres. The largest farm, of 435 acres in 1734, was at Duntisbourne, but this was largely arable and common-field.[41] At least a dozen more farms were acquired or converted to leasehold for lives between 1736 and 1760.

There was a noticeable tendency towards engrossing on the Pleydell estates, especially in the 1740s. Engrossing was a prominent feature of English agriculture in the first half of the eighteenth century and especially so in Berkshire and Wiltshire, according to Mordant.[42] At Coleshill the two Midlease farms had been merged by 1742 and in the same year Old Hayes was joined with other closes to become the United Bargain. At the same time there was some rearranging of closes and farms. Similar cases of engrossing and rearranging can be found at Shrivenham and at Duntisbourne.[43]

The 1735 survey shows that leases of from four to eight years predominated, especially in leases granted in 1731 or after, but this was a temporary feature due to the joint inheritance of Coleshill and Coxwell farms. Leases granted before 1731 tended to be for longer periods of 15, 18 or 21 years, and after buying out Thomas Eyre in 1738 Pleydell reverted to a policy of longer lease terms. From 1738 to 1760 only three leases for a short term of 6 to 8 years were granted, but three times that number were granted for 9, 10 or 12 years, and four times as many were for terms of 14 to 21 years, with 21 years as the largest single category. No doubt Pleydell was anxious to ensure that farms did not lie untended for want of tenants during the decades of depression, and the longer terms also suited his aim of long-term improvement. In the 1760s there was a revival of the short lease of three years, but it is difficult to judge whether these were an indication of more buoyant times for landlords, as prices and rents rose, or whether Pleydell was simply conscious of his advancing years and reluctant to saddle his heir with too many tenants on relatively long leases.[44] It could also be claimed that by this date Pleydell was seeking to control his tenants more effectively, and may have chosen the indirect threat of triennial lease renewals, or refusals, as a weapon.

Where tenants held enclosed lands on lease for a fixed term of years there could in theory be complete freedom of negotiation between landlord and tenant as to conditions of tenure and husbandry practices. This is why such farms were known as "bargains". But the bargaining power of each side depended on current economic circumstances and local husbandry practices.[45] Pleydell made lease negotiations his prime concern and drew up a set of twenty-nine rules for covenants in 1735. These were refined and enlarged in 1744, when he became one of the first landlords to devise a printed lease, ordered 300 at a time from Aris of Birmingham.[46]

From 1744 onwards, the drawing up of a lease for Pleydell tenants involved four clear stages. First came the selection of a tenant, followed by a preliminary settlement regarding the rent, term of years and liability for taxes and repairs. Next, the printed leasing agreement would be signed by both parties. The printed text incorporated thirty-four basic covenants of a standard type which nevertheless allowed for some variations; these were known as the heads of agreement. On every lease, however, there was an empty half page on which Pleydell could add a selection from the forty or so supplementary covenants drawn up in 1744, or indeed any other conditions that he and his tenant had agreed upon. This part of the leasing agreement is usually the most indicative of Pleydell's evolving policies, and it gave scope for new ventures undreamed of in 1744. Only after all these stages had been concluded came the execution of the indentures on stamped parchment.

Selection of tenants and preliminary settlements

The choice of tenant was the first and most important element in the bargaining process. It is significant that Sir Mark's only direct reference to an agricultural treatise was a quotation from *The Farmers Maxims*, in which the aims of the "Bad Tenant" were said to be "1st and before all things to hurt his Land, 2ndly and next to hurt his Landlord, 3rdly and lastly to help Himself – & thus the Helping himself, being deferred to the last, never cometh at all".[47] Some tenant families had long-standing connections with their farms, amounting to sixty years or longer. More than once a lease was granted to the widow and son of a former tenant. Knowledge of the lands clearly counted for a good deal and perhaps personal acquaintance with the landlord over a long period made it harder for him to turn a tenant out of his farm.[48]

When a new tenant was needed, however, his abilities and financial standing were carefully investigated, as can be seen from the memoranda in Pleydell's draft lease book. When William Phillimore, for example, wrote to Sir Mark in 1764 asking for the tenancy of a small farm in Slimbridge he cited in his favour his family's long connection with Pleydell and his ancestors, but Pleydell required more than this from someone he did not know personally. Fortunately for Phillimore, James Matthews was able to inform Pleydell that he had been told at Gloucester by one of the richest inhabitants of Slimbridge that Phillimore owned a freehold estate worth £30 a year, that he had recently bought another valued at £10 a year, and that his "character, substance and parts are all remarkably good". If nothing was known about a prospective tenant even more corroboration would be needed: as with Stephen Finch, whose good character was endorsed by six referees, their opinions being relayed to Pleydell in 1755 via two of his informants.[49]

From the 1750s an increasing population of the Coleshill tenants came from outside the parish. Possibly the agricultural depression of the 1730s and 1740s forced Pleydell to look farther afield, but a more important factor was the accelerated pace of change in Pleydell's methods of grassland management. It was the native farmers who resisted the innovations and caused Pleydell to comment in his "Journal of Haining" that "the Coleshill Farm[e]rs are the foolishest men in three Counties".[50] One of the imported tenants was Jonathan Barnes of Hannington, who with his son and son-in-law held a succession of Pleydell leases. Barnes was fully in accord with his landlord's ideas and in 1762 was asked for his advice regarding Sir Mark's longhaining experiments. From a small tenancy of £40 a year at Broad Blunsdon he then advanced in 1763 to Midlease bargain at Coleshill at £87 a year and finally in 1767 to the large and recently-purchased Widhill farm in Wiltshire at an annual rent of £600.[51]

As Pleydell became increasingly interested in grass management, a tenant's readiness to co-operate in his experiments became a more important attribute than his character or capital. In character, Pleydell preferred men of the "sober, civil and substantial" type said to abound on the neighbouring Barrington estate; Pleydell tenants were not permitted to sell ale or strong liquor, and a fondness for drink was carefully monitored. Yet a favoured tenant such as Amos Wilson of Coleshill was allowed great latitude. Wilson was reported to be drunk and idle in 1755, drunk and mad in 1758, yet his lease was renewed in 1757 and 1763. In 1766 he nearly murdered the landlady of the Swan Inn at Faringdon, but Pleydell's account of this incident concludes, "I don't find him remarkable for Toddy, any more than w[ha]t shall casually happen", and he continued to lend him money and tolerate substantial arrears of rent.[52]

A more important and positive aspect of Pleydell's flexible attitude to his tenants was his willingness, in later years, to lend capital to stock their farms, as he thought it essential that farms should be fully stocked. As Professor Mingay has observed, few landlords in this age was prepared to lend working capital.[53] In some parts of the country, however, it was accepted practice for dairy farmers to rent their cows, and in 1738 a prospective tenant suggested that Sir Mark might invest £300 in stock and regard the tenant as his bailiff. The idea lay dormant until 1742, when a small allowance of cattle was made to Joseph Herring "on his taking Midlease".[54]

From 1748 Pleydell regularly offered interest-free loans to tenants. This policy was closely linked with that of encouraging dairy farming on improved permanent pastures, since he wished to ensure that the restored sward would be adequately dunged. The first loan supplied cattle, sheep, hay and cash to the value of £344 14s 8d to Amos Wilson for Brimstone bargain at Coleshill, a farm which Pleydell had been at pains to improve since 1738.[55] The loans continued, and gave Pleydell extra leverage in negotiating husbandry covenants. In 1756–7, for instance, he loaned £251 to William Sayer, allowing generous repayment terms:

1. He shall repay the said Principal as it shall best suit his own conveniency, and when the whole is paid and a full stock left on the premises and no more than two years' rent shall remain due I'll allow him ten per Cent on the said Principal.
2. It is my intention to improve the premises until they are a good bargain at the rent: and in case the allowances already made him by this Lease to make good the damage he shall suffer till they be so improved shall be insufficient I will from time to time make him further allowances to be settled by two indifferent persons. And I hereby direct my Heirs to conform themselves to these my intentions.[56]

The condition attached to this offer, however, was that Sayer should keep all closes perpetually in grass and fed only with cows, a scheme of husbandry which was by no means universally popular with Pleydell's tenants. The loan system worked well, proving to be a way of helping intelligent young farmers to become established. Pleydell continued to grant loans after the depression was over, and as late as 1767 he loaned £400 to Jonathan Barnes to stock the valuable bargain of Widhill.[57]

Changes in farm sizes preclude the tracing of rent movements on the Pleydell estates. Rent were static on bargains where the acreage was unchanged, although Pleydell claimed that nearly all rents had increased between 1668 and 1761. Simply to hold rents steady was an achievement from 1730 to 1760, for although the major impact of the 1730–50 depression was felt in the heavy soiled districts, pastoral regions were also affected, especially where convertible husbandry was practised. Pleydell claimed also that he made substantial profits at certain times from surplus rents, amounting to *c.* £3,780 during 1738–42 and nearly £6,000 in the years 1748–53.[58]

Like his neighbours Lord Craven and Viscount Barrington, however, Pleydell was owed substantial arrears of rent by certain tenants. From *c.* 1740 he tried to prevent a build-up of arrears by changing from half-yearly to monthly rent demands, but the accounts do not have any evidence that he was able to enforce this policy. He also threatened to sue and distrain for double the sum owing, as well as voiding the lease, but he could be surprisingly indulgent, especially to Coleshill tenants whom he knew personally.[59] Nevertheless, distraint was taken on several occasions: Moses Herring had all his stock, corn and cattle distrained in 1738, and the perishable goods were sold soon after, while his cheese vessels and farm implements were passed on to another tenant in 1749. Anthony King had his lease called in after distraint in 1755, and Philip Young had to hand over the deeds of his three estates as security in 1750, when Pleydell commented,

'Tis time to be easy after so many yrs *uneasy* and deceiv'd by vain promises. Arrest wd be an injury and clam[our]. Deposit is neither and is the least he can do. To suffer such arr[ear]s is no service to my Ten[an]ts and at the same time a risque and loss to myself.[60]

The real rent could be altered by varying the liability of landlord and tenant for repairs, taxes, and any modus paid in lieu of tithe. It is a well-known feature of the 1730–50 period that landlords stopped trying to shift responsibility for these payments onto their tenants. Like many landlords, Pleydell in his earlier years hoped to make progress in this direction, and a memorandum of 1721 recorded his intention to make his tenants liable for all taxes and chief rents in future leases. One step towards this was achieved by 1724, when Shrivenham tenants agreed to pay the parish taxes for their bargains in return for a fixed allowance of 4½d in the pound.[61] This method, whereby the landlord allowed a discount off the rent in return for the tenant's paying the taxes, was incorporated into the 1735 rules for leases. In practice however, Pleydell undertook to pay the land tax in almost all leases until the 1760s, when he again made tenants liable, with a stated deduction of rent depending on the current rate of tax. This was evidently regarded with suspicion by the tenants, who at about that time began to "harp", as he put it, on "mounds, ditches, fewel, taxes [and] King's bounty money". This enabled Pleydell to extract an agreement from his Coleshill farmers, designed to prevent farm servants and other newcomers from gaining a settlement in the parish and thence a claim on the poor rates.[62]

Liability for repairs fluctuated similarly, with the 1735 rule for leases assigning more responsibility to the tenant than the 1744 rules. Here again, though, the draft leases are a better guide to Sir Mark's policies than the rules, as they often list the specific repairs promised by the landlord. The account books record many payments for leases but they cannot be used to calculate the percentage of income spent on repairs, as the costs of labour and materials are not consistently recorded, nor are repairs to buildings in hand distinguished from those that were leased.

The most expensive repairs, clearly, were for renewing the oak threshing floors of his barns and for replacing thatched barn roofs with stone slates to minimize the fire risk.[63] Therefore the policy followed by Pleydell from the 1740s, at first by encouraging dairy farming and later by forbidding convertible husbandry, reduced his liability for repairs in the long term, although he at first needed to lay out money to improve or supply dairies, cheese lofts, cowhouses and ponds. Further economies were made by throwing farms together, and the problem of cottage repairs was met by charging only a nominal rent while providing no repairs; in each case a social problem was created in order to solve the landlord's economic problem. Pleydell was moving towards the kind of estate owned in 1723 at Beckett, Shrivenham, by Lord Barrington. Here there were no poor because, as a sale particular explained,

The Bargains . . . being all Dairy Bargains Except One . . . there are no outhouses to them Except Small Stables and Cart hovells and Pigg

Stys and Calfs Coops, And there being but 8 farmhouses in the whole Estate, Reparations Come to very Little, besides what the Tennants are bound to [do].[64]

Pleydell's agricultural theories and husbandry covenants

Once the lessor and lessee had agreed on the rent, term and respective liability for repairs and taxes, they would negotiate the husbandry covenants. Sir Mark relied above all on the husbandry covenants for the good management and improvement of his lands, and they constitute the most interesting and innovative aspect of his leasing policy. It is therefore essential to trace the source of his theories before discussing their implementation.

Sir Mark Pleydell's choice of husbandry covenants was based on direct experience and experiment. He never kept a large acreage in hand, nor did he have a home farm in the sense of a model farm, but he showed an interest in agriculture from the time of his marriage in 1719, eight years before he inherited the manor of Coleshill. During these years, to augment his small income, he grew cherries at Shrivenham and hops at Coleshill as cash crops in partnership, and he characteristically experimented with using the hop kilns to dry corn in wet seasons.[65] Although Pleydell gave up farming in partnership when his responsibilities increased, agriculture remained a major, and indeed his only hobby, apart from music and litigation. He never seems to have sought election to Parliament nor, for most of his life, did he hold any county office. He was 62 when he accepted the office of Sheriff and 65 when he became Deputy Lord Lieutenant. His small family did not make the heavy demands on his purse that a number of other Vale landowners experienced as a consequence of their "numerous and healthful issue",[66] and from 1750 onwards, after losing both his wife and his only daughter, he devoted his energies with even greater intensity to the improvement of his estates.

In his early years as squire of Coleshill Pleydell showed an interest in arable farming. Standards of cultivation were high, with particular attention paid to cleansing and fertilizing the soil. Accounts of labour payments on his estate show that corn crops were hand-weeded, beans and peas were "set" in rows rather than sown broadcast, and a drag-plough was used to clear the fallows of couch grass. By the 1730s it was standard practice in the Vale of White Horse to sow clover, rye grass and hop-trefoil, as Pleydell did, but he was among the first to sow turnips and 1739, the year when he recorded hoeing five acres of turnips, is the earliest date found in this region for using turnips as a cleansing crop. Pleydell also showed an interest in lucerne, teasels, liquorice, saffron and rape, although there is no sign that he ever trid to grow any of these cash and fodder crops, while his instructions to the bailiff, compiled in 1728, named a wide variety of dressings for the soil, including rags, coal ashes, malt dust and wood dust as well as animal dung and pigeon dung.[67]

Nevertheless, arable farming by Pleydell's methods was labour intensive in an age when labour costs were rising slightly and prices were falling.

Sir Mark resented what he regarded as the high level of wages, and made petty economies where he could. Professor Mingay remarks on Pleydell's decision, taken in 1728, to supply "only beef and beer" at the harvest home, and "to invite only such as have personally assisted in bringing home the harvest". In the same year he resolved to follow the advice of neighbouring farmers and stop the wages of day labourers who took time off to attend village funerals, even if they claimed to have made up the time by rising earlier to their work; he was soon putting this rule into practice.[68]

The high cost of labour, therefore, when combined with the low price of corn, the relative buoyancy of prices for livestock and hay, and the prevalence of clay soils on much of the enclosed land, made it inevitable that Sir Mark should turn more and more to grassland and stock farming. Here again, he took a personal interest in his livestock, recording the prices paid and showing an awareness of market values. Sheep, including some of the Ryland breed, were bought at Marlborough, Lambourn and Swindon, and horses at fairs in Berkshire and the three adjacent counties. Dairy cattle were bought and sold locally and at Nuneaton, Welsh black cattle at Ross-on-Wye and markets in south and west Wales. In 1743 an agent was made to repay £25 4s after selling sheep below their value and in 1750 another, who had bought six Welsh oxen for 65s each when they were worth only 50s, had to pay the difference out of his wages.[69]

Pleydell's greatest enthusiasm, however, was for the improvement of his grasslands. At first he continued with the established policy of convertible pastures, ploughed for several years and then laid down with grass seeds. By 1754 he had decided on a return to permanent grass, not only because of the high cost of ploughing the clays and the difficulty of establishing sown grass leys, but because he became convinced that the best pastures were those of a natural, undisturbed sward. A "journal of the haining", kept from 1754 to 1767, records the course of his experiments to find the best way of restoring the grasslands. Various methods of management were tried and a number of different dressings, and advice was sought from neighbours, kinsmen and tenants alike. In this project, the geographical spread of his lands across the western cheese region from Berkshire to the Severn valley proved to be an asset. It was at Wootton Bassett, for instance, that he first learned of an earth-burning technique and at Berkeley, near Slimbridge, that in 1764 he first heard about using coal ashes obtained at Bristol as a dressing. He at once obtained some for Coleshill and found by 1766 that these had made "the greatest of all improvem[en]ts". New implements interested him: he used an Essex draining tool and a Norfolk plough, and advocated the Norfolk method of laying pastures flat, eliminating the ridge and furrow.[70]

By 1764 he had identified the "Six Enemies to rich pasture" as ploughs, sheep, stagnating water, furzes, gorse and anthills. It was unusual to bar sheep, which were normally regarded as an essential adjunct to dairy farming, but Pleydell noted from his observations that:

Horses *cut* and eat, but Cows and Sheep only *gath[e]r* into the Cudd and this gathering is tearing up the grass: only Cows, by licking in a great quantity at once, can't tear up the root . . . *Ergo*, Horses more harmless to the root than Sheep, and perhaps as harmless as Cows, but bite closer to the ground th[a]n either.[71]

The optimum method of re-establishing permanent grass, he concluded, was to let the grass sward naturally, feed it with cows only until the sward is as thick as possible, which might take some years, then dung it with all sorts of ashes and feed and mow in rotation. In 1762 Pleydell delightedly recorded that a visitor had said of Dock Close and Thistle Close at Little Brimstone, "I was never so surprizd in my life, I walked over land of a pound an acre."[72]

Pleydell's husbandry covenants changed considerably from 1735 to 1765, rejecting these experiences and experiments. His first attempt at defining husbandry practices for his tenants was made in 1735 in his "Lease Book A", which begins with a list of twenty-eight covenants, about half of which laid down husbandry requirements.[73] Most of these were time-honoured stipulations for safeguarding the fertility and condition of arable land, pastures and timber. Others referred to newer or more advanced techniques, such as the sowing of sainfoin and the use of soot or ashes for dressings, but did not go beyond the accepted practices of the region.[74]

Pleydell's new rules, drawn up in 1744 as an improvement on those of 1735 "which are here contained in a better method", more than doubled the number of covenants and greatly extended their scope.[75] They should not be judged solely by the dozen or so husbandry covenants incorporated in Pleydell's printed lease, which were mainly restrictive in effect and similar to those of 1735. These printed covenants required tenants to spend all manure except wheat straw on the premises; they must not till or dig any lands in grass of any sort, must not mow pasture land, nor feed "sinfoy" between Christmas and Lammas. They must summer-till, with four ploughings or "earths", one-third of the arable each year, and sow no more than one-third with wheat, nor take two wheat crops off the same land successively. They must sow with their last crop any grass seeds provided by the landlord, and give notice of such sowing. The only apparent advance from 1735 in this section of the leases was a reference to turnips, not mentioned in the 1735 list. Professor Mingay therefore, while acknowledging Pleydell's enthusiasm and efficiency in the drawing up of a printed lease, and remarking on some of its unusual provisions regarding residence in the farm house and the selling of ales and spirits, dismisses Pleydell's husbandry covenants as no more than "a number of the accepted covenants governing husbandry".[76]

But the provisions in the printed lease forms were supplemented by forty optional additions which governed the tenants' husbandry in far more detail and certainly went beyond the covenants to be found in other surviving leases of the Vale of White Horse region. By means of the supplementary covenants Pleydell could regulate convertible husbandry, for instance giving instructions as to the years in which each close should be mown, fed, summer-tilled or ploughed, with what corn they should be

sown and in what year laid down with grass seeds. Another clause determined the quantity of acres to be left sown with hop and broad clover,
rye grass, "sinkfoy" or turnips at the end of the lease. The landlord could
order lands to be dressed with lime and potashes or by the "thick water
hatches" of the water meadows. While such covenants were not necessarily
innovative, and may also have been difficult to enforce, they at least show
an attempt to enforce high standards, here as on the Coke estates. Parker
rightly comments that detailed husbandry covenants 'were one of the most
important means by which landlords affected the conduct of their tenants
and advanced good husbandry".[77]

Moreover, Sir Mark Pleydell should be judged not so much by his rules
for leases as by the large number of surviving leasing agreements, printed
and otherwise, which are a better guide to his developing ideas and his
attempts to put them into practice. Turnips, for example, are not mentioned until 1744 in the rules for leases, but as early as 1727 Pleydell
recommended turnips and a summer fallow as a way of bringing some
Shrivenham closes into good order, and by 1732 a tenant at Shrivenham
had agreed to lay down part of his arable with grass seeds, "the whole to
be first cleansed with Summer fallow and Turnips if the Landlord shall
think it needfull".[78]

The leasing agreements also shed light on the extent to which covenants
were observed. Since improvement of the grasslands was Pleydell's prime
concern, standards on permanent arable land were not as closely monitored. Thus at Lyneham Court in 1742 the usual course was said to be
equal parts of wheat, clover, barley and summer fallow, but the tenant
agreed to follow this course only in the last two years of his 21-year lease,
and when negotiating a renewal in 1759 he asked "not to be obliged to
sow Clover the last year". At Duntisbourne, it was reported in 1765 that
the tenant had broken his agreement to use "the Norfolk husbandry".[79]

On dairy farms, and especially at Coleshill, more care was taken to
create and enforce high standards. Like many landlords, Pleydell provided
or improved cowsheds, calf-houses, dairies and cheese rooms where they
were needed. The printed leases also allowed free entry for the landlord
in order to "Hill, Drain, Trench or otherwise to improve the land". This
enabled Pleydell to remove anthills, one of his "six enemies", with his
Norfolk plough, and to use his trenching plough and Essex draining tool
against another "enemy", stagnating water. Leasing agreements show that
he also helped tenants who wished to use the traditional stone "drock"
or gutter to drain their land.[80] As we have seen, the leasing agreements
record that he went beyond the normal provision of long-term capital
improvement in providing capital for his tenants to stock their farms
adequately. In addition, they show that he used husbandry covenants to
ensure that grasslands were managed in the way he considered best,
however eccentric his methods appeared to his tenants.

We can see from the husbandry covenants that for twenty years or more
Pleydell believed in convertible husbandry as a way of restoring worn-out
grasslands, provided it was well regulated. On lighter, stonebrash soils,
such as the enclosed grounds at Shrivenham, arable–grass rotations using

sainfoin and other grasses and legumes were normal, as they had long been on other estates along the Oxford Heights. Conversely, on the heaviest clays at Buscot and Minety the closes were never ploughed. At Coleshill Pleydell experimented with convertible closes on clay, providing grass seeds for the tenants; these included not only clover, supplied from 1729, but sainfoin, although this latter crop was not well-suited to heavy soils and had long been abandoned on the nearby Craven estates in favour of rye-grass.[81] The element of risk was acknowledged by clauses in the leasing agreements, such as that of 1731 when he assured John Pullen that an additional rent would be payable only "in case the said Sinfoy shall prove good and fit to be continued". Similarly, Pleydell offered in 1732 to "alter the husbandry about the sinfoy" on the bargain of Thomas Mildenhall, who in 1729 had agreed to sow some closes with sainfoin, clover and rye grass. It was usual for Pleydell to assure tenants that they would not be the losers if they agreed to co-operate with their landlord.[82]

In the late 1740s, Pleydell was still attempting to lay down closes at Coleshill with sown grasses as part of a convertible system, giving help with his own plough-teams to ensure that a good fine tilth was prepared for the seeds. On Midlease bargain the re-establishment of the sward proved difficult nevertheless, and the tenant wanted to plough the two upper closes, sown in 1742 without success. Pleydell instead proposed an abatement of 5s an acre on these twenty-eight acres, "to see if the herbage w[ou]ld mend", and bargaining continued until 1748, when the tenant accepted compensation of an abatement of £12 out of his arrears of rent and a score of culled ewes, in return for which he agreed not to plough the closes for a further six years.[83]

By the late 1740s it was becoming clear that convertible husbandry was not the best way of managing the Coleshill grounds. Elsewhere in the Vale, other owners were complaining of closes "wrought out" or "worsted" by ploughing, and at the same time the low corn prices and high labour costs of ploughing clays made permanent grass a more attractive choice, especially when cheese could be so easily and cheaply exported by river to London. Pleydell joined other landowners of the region in taking steps to remove the option of ploughing, even in return for a sizeable ploughing rent.[84] The spread of cattle plague, which caused many losses in north Wiltshire, did not deflect him, and the higher prices which came in the wake of the rinderpest probably made dairying even more lucrative. Broad has traced a similar acceleration on suitable soils in the Midlands during the 1740s, and quotes Ellis's 1750 report that many acres in Warwickshire had been laid down in recent years.[85]

The most striking aspect of Pleydell's leasing policy began in the 1750s, when he began to press for the restoration of permanent natural grass pastures, to be dressed with ashes, drained, levelled and alternately mown and fed only with dairy cattle and a minimum number of horses. This was bound to cause difficulties with his tenants, for it was known to Hale and other writers that it might take forty years to restore grassland to top quality; in particular, the exclusion of sheep while swards were forming was incomprehensible to farmers who were used to keeping sheep in conjunction with dairy herds. Indeed, in opposing sheep-keeping Pleydell seems to have differed from his neighbours, and from other improving landowners such as the Verneys, but he had become convinced by his own experience that "A sheep among Cows is both Thief and Cutthroat."[86] Just occasionally, a tenant such as Jonathan Barnes would delight him by his full agreement: Barnes told him at the start of his tenancy that he kept no sheep from choice, "for he had found out their tricks a year or two before", adding that his son-in-law had made 15 cwt more of cheese annually since expelling his sheep.[87]

Sheep were not kept on Pleydell's own grounds after 1754, and he noted that the visible improvement of his grasslands began with this step. From 1754, lease renewals also forbade the keeping of sheep on grass closes, but some of the old-established tenants were difficult to convince, and it seems that such covenants were not easily enforced. William Pullen of Coleshill, for instance, was still keeping sheep in 1755, contrary to his promise, and even in 1764 was putting in sheep on water meadows "after the flood". Pleydell calculated that Pullen would make £10 by the sheep, but would do £100 worth of damage to his meads. Another tenant sowed one of his grounds with natural grasses and then fed it with sheep, with poor results according to Pleydell, who examined it with magnifying glasses in June, 1758:

> The two Headlands had several spots of *red* Trefoil; in all the rest of the Lands noth[in]g but long hairy Couch like Rye grass. On using the Spectacles nothing furth[e]r appeard, nor any prospect of *minute* Trefoil or flat grass too small for the naked Eye. 'Tis rich land *Ergo* the Sheep have rooted up all.[88]

Where a tenant had a 21-year lease, as in the case of Leonard Hawkins of Minety, an elderly landlord like Pleydell had little power of compulsion; Hawkins agreed in 1762 to sell his sheep and buy oxen, but Pleydell observed that in 1763 he spoke in praise of sheep, "*ergo* I imagine he has sold none".[89] In 1765 Pleydell tried giving another tenant a written guarantee that "If the feeding Gerring's barg[ai]n w[i]th nothing but Cow cattle and horses shall hurt Him or his Bargain I will make him sattisfaction: it being my intention to help both and not hurt either".[90] It seems likely, however, that Pleydell died in 1768 leaving many of his older tenants still unconvinced.

There is evidence, nevertheless, that with the newer, incoming tenants it was a different story. These men co-operated with their landlord, provided compensation could be arranged for their loss of income while waiting for the closes to sward over. Pleydell recognized that a full stock of cattle could be introduced only gradually, and was willing to make such recompense as might be agreed by representatives from the two sides. Amos Wilson, one of the first to benefit, received nearly £130 in 1754–5 and £50 more in 1755–6 as a gratuity for his damage "in converting my Farm called Brimstones into a Dairy Bargain".[91] Again, in 1756 Pleydell not only loaned money to William Sayer to stock his farm but also declared:

It is my intention to improve the premises till they are a good bargain at the rent: and in case the allowances already made him by this Lease, to make good the damage he shall suffer till they shall be so improved shall be insufficient, I will from time to time make him further allowances to be settled by two indifferent persons.[92]

A statement of profit and loss on the bargain would be drawn up in these circumstances, and it was usual for about 5s an acre to be allowed during the longhaining process.

More distant tenants were not given financial compensation, but Pleydell went to great trouble to convert them to his views. One of the most refractory was Robert Archer of Duntisbourne, whom he disliked and distrusted. Yet Pleydell went to considerable trouble over Archer, first sending him detailed letters of instruction on how to lay down grassland, and later sending over his most experienced and trusted tenants to explain the method to him on the spot. Finally, in 1765 Pleydell drafted a written assurance that "if ye follow these methods and yet the closes shall not answerin grass, I will alter the husbandry/management of them, and if you succeed in bringing them into good grass I will be your friend in every respect".[93]

The shift from alternate husbandry to permanent pasture on heavy clays between 1650 and 1800 has already been established for the south-east Midlands by John Broad.[94] Pleydell's papers show how a similar change was begun on the estates of one owner in the "dairying track" of the Vale of White Horse. As in Buckinghamshire, Northamptonshire, Warwickshire and Leicestershire, a clearly defined area of permanent grass was to be found in Berkshire by the time of the Board of Agriculture reports. William Mavor, describing the sub-regions of the county in 1809, identified such an area in the north-west, near the borders with Gloucestershire and Wiltshire.[95] Many parishes here were two-thirds in grass, and he singled out Coleshill as consisting of 1,820 acres, only ten of which were arable. Since Coleshill had by no means the greatest expanse of heavy clay, and was not among those parishes enclosed by agreement in the seventeenth century or before, it is highly probable that we can attribute its high proportion of grassland to the leasing policies of Sir Mark Stuart Pleydell more than half a century earlier.

Appendix I

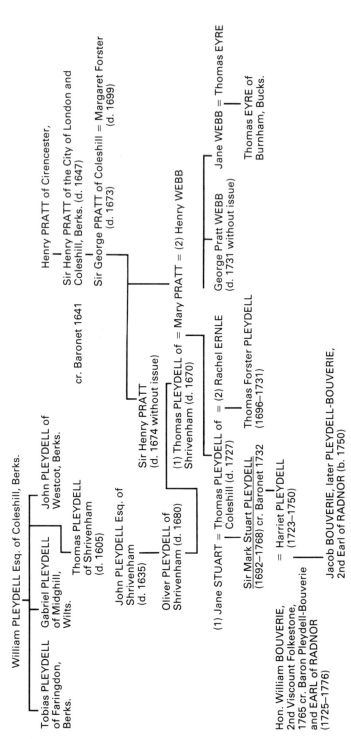

Figure 2.1 Family Tree of SIR MARK STUART PLEYDELL, Bart., of Coleshill, Berks., Sixteenth to Eighteenth Centuries

Sources: WRO Radnor, 490/75

G.E.C. *Complete Baronetage*, II, 113–114: V,73: G.E.C. *Complete Peerage* X,717

J. Burke, *Extinct and Dormant Baronetcies* (1884), pp.415–416.

Appendix II

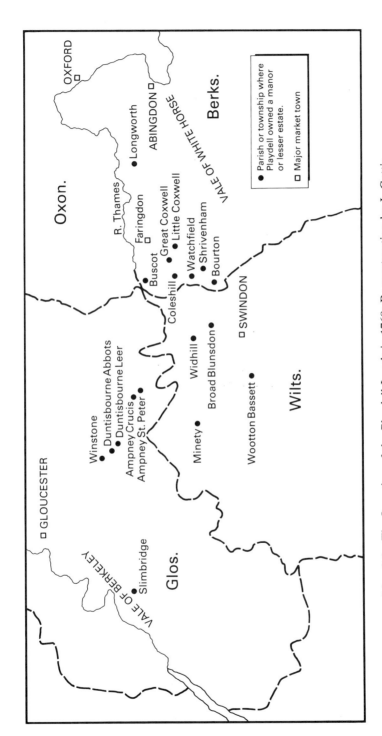

Map 2.1 The Location of the Pleydell Lands in 1768: Reconstruction by J. Cottis

Appendix III

Figure 2.2 COLESHILL HOUSE, c. 1800 from J. Britton, *The Beauties of England and Wales* (London, 1801), Vol. I, p. 132.

Figure 2.3 COLESHILL HOUSE, c. 1920, photograph from *The Victoria County History of Berkshire* Vol. IV (1924), p. 516.

Notes

1 Berkshire County Office holds the main collection, i.e. the Pleydell Bouverie papers, hereafter cited as BRO D/E Pb. The earl of Radnor's papers in Wiltshire County Record Office, hereafter cited as WRO Radnor, have also been used.

2 R. A. C. Parker, *Coke of Norfolk: A Financial and Agricultural Study, 1707–1842* (Oxford, 1975), p. 22; BRO D/E Pb, E5, p. 1: combined valuation of the estates of T. Pleydell, T. F. Pleydell and M. S. Pleydell; D/E Pb, E3, pp. 68–80: leases issued jointly by M. S. Pleydell and T. Eyre.

3 Parker, pp. 19–20. BRO D/E Pb, E5, pp. 17–18 is a partial record of Pleydell's South Sea transactions, but see also E6, p. 18 for a reference to other transactions not entered in the books. Pleydell appears to have lost about £3,600 in 1720–22, about seven times his income at that stage.

4 Parker, p. 23. BRO D/E Pb, E 93–4.

5 Parker, p. 6.

6 C. Clay, "Landlords and estate management in England", in J. Thirsk (ed.), *The Agrarian History of England and Wales*, Vol. 5, *1640–1750*, Pt 2, *Agrarian Change* (Cambridge, 1985), p. 215. J. D. Chambers and G. E. Mingay (eds), *The Agricultural Revolution, 1750–1880* (London, 1966), pp. 46–7.

7 BRO D/E Pb, E5, fols 148v–154. Mary Pratt was the daughter of Sir George Pratt, Bart., Sheriff of Berkshire in 1654–5. Sir George was son of Henry Pratt, created baronet in 1641, who was a member of the Company of Merchant Taylors and Sheriff of London in 1631–2. Henry was the son of a wealthy Cirencester clothier.

8 E. Mercer, "The houses of the gentry", *Past and Present*, vol. 5 (May 1954), pp. 11–32.

9 Clay, in Thirsk (ed.), p. 166.

10 BRO D/E Pb, E1, pp. 103–27.

11 See BRO D/E Pb, E5, p. 1, for lands settled on T. F. Pleydell.

12 BRO D/E Pb, E5, p. 1, for his income in 1713; by the early 1720s he had acquired a wife with a portion of £6,000, but he had also sold lands in order to purchase South Sea stocks.

13 BRO D/E Pb, E8, p. 13.

14 G. E. Mingay, *English Landed Society in the Eighteenth Century* (London, 1963), pp. 22–3.

15 WRO Radnor 490/75; BRO D/E Pb, E7, p. 119.

16 The volume Pleydell called his "purchase book" has not been traced, but the principal transactions are listed in WRO Radnor 490/75 and in BRO D/E Pb, E8, pp. 13, 23; there are also many references in his deed books, lease books, ledgers, receipt books and cash books, i.e. D/E Pb, E 2–13.

17 BRO D/E Pb, E11, p. 197.

18 BRO D/E Pb, E2, pp. 165–76, 179–89; E126; L5, and see also L2. It is interesting to note that Harriet Pleydell married the son of Jacob Bouverie, a London merchant and Kentish landowner who was, like Pleydell, a believer in incorporating specific husbandry covenants in his leases: see G. E. Mingay, "Estate management in eighteenth-century Kent", *Agricultural History Review*, vol. 4, no. 2 (1956), pp. 108–13.

19 BRO D/E Pb, E2, pp. 93–7; E51; L2.

20 BRO D/E Pb, E2, p. 93. Pleydell bought the great tithes of Bourton in 1732, in order to make his own lands at Bourton tithe free: BRO D/E Pb, E51. He then resold some tithes to those who owned the lands on which the tithes were due. This was probably intended from the first, as a way of financing the purchase of the tithes on his own land, and he does not seem to have classed these transactions as true sales.

21 BRO D/E Pb, E3, pp. 108–9, 112.

22 BRO D/E Pb, E3, pp. 9–85; acreage of rack-rented estates estimated from E1–5, *passim*.

23 BRO D/E Pb, E13, part (a), rental preceding cash book, p. 9.

24 E. Laurence, *The Duty and Office of a Land Steward* (Dublin, 1731), pp. 6, 25, 39.

25 J. B. Cottis, "Agrarian change in the Vale of White Horse, 1660–1760" (unpublished Ph.D. thesis, University of Reading, 1984), pp. 94–5, 97–105.

26 BRO D/E Pb, E1, pp. 52–4; E3 pp. 9–25, 108; E4 pp. 2, 98; E11, p. 215. (Note that

E4 is part volume, part scrapbook; some sheets are paginated, some foliated, some numbered in other ways and some not numbered at all.) For other instances see C. Clay, "Life leasehold in the western counties of England, 1650–1750", *Agricultural History Review*, vol. 29, no. 2 (1981), pp. 83–96. Clay points out that the need to shift the burden of repairs and the wartime land tax were additional factors.

27   BRO D/E Pb, E13, fol. 29.
28   BRO D/E Pb, E7, p. 16.
29   BRO D/E Pb, E3, p. 22.
30   BRO D/E Pb, E3, pp. 9–25; E5, fols 141v–142.
31   BRO D/E Pb, E3, pp. 9–25, 85; E22.
32   Cottis, thesis, pp. 187–92, 643; BRO D/E Pb, E5, pp. 13, 37; L5.
33   BRO D/E Pb, E1, pp. 1–52. For the negotiations over enclosure see E5, fol. 144v; E8, p. 20.
34   BRO D/E Pb, M5, p. 130.
35   BRO D/E Pb, E4, p. 216; E22.
36   BRO D/E Pb, E4, pp. 120/H, 205; E5, p. 23, fol. 115v, and see also p. 12 for the commonable area of Nutbene Farm, totalling 372 acres. See also E12, fols 12–13. See also P. J. Bowden, "Agricultural prices, wages, farm profits and rents", in Thirsk (ed.), Vol. V, Pt 2, p. 205, for Bowden's opinion that a projected increase from 2s 6d to 13s 4d per acre for north-east Lincs. after enclosure was improbably large.
37   BRO D/E Pb, E5, p. 37, and see also p. 112 for a 1719 estimate of the land that would be due to him as an equivalent for tithe.
38   Cottis, thesis, pp. 205–9. Of the remaining common-field townships where Pleydell owned land, Ampney was enclosed in 1770, Chiseldon in 1780 and Bourton in 1792. For these awards see W. E. Tate, ed. M. E. Turner, *A Domesday of English Enclosure Acts and Awards* (Reading, 1978), pp. 270–8. Enclosure was being mooted at Ampney during Pleydell's lifetime, however, for in 1762 a tenant proposed that in the event of an enclosure at Ampney he should not be liable for the cost: BRO D/E Pb, E4, fol. 100.
39   Cottis, thesis, pp. 454–7. BRO D/E Pb, E37, p. 105.
40   BRO D/E Pb, E3, pp. 47–83; cf. BRO Elwell papers (D/E EL), E35/17 and D/E Hy, E3.
41   BRO D/E Pb, E1, pp. 1–54; E5, fol. 115v.
42   D. C. Coleman, *The Economy of England, 1450–1750* (Oxford, 1977), pp. 128–9. Mordant, *Complete Steward*, Vol. I, pp. 192–6, cited G. E. Mingay, "The size of farms in the eighteenth century", *Economic History Review*, 2nd ser., vol. 14, no. 3 (1962), pp. 469–88.
43   BRO D/E Pb, E4, *passim*.
44   BRO D/E Pb, E3, pp. 47–83; E4, *passim*.
45   Clay, in Thirsk (ed.), Vol. V, Pt 2, pp. 214–24.
46   BRO D/E Pb, E3 pp. 1–4, 100–7.
47   BRO D/E Pb, E3, p. 5, citing *The Farmer's Maxims*, a quarto treatise on land, fol. 71, entitled "The bad tenant". (This treatise has not been traced.)
48   See BRO D/E Pb, E1 pp. 1–54; E3–4 *passim*; E5, p. 17 for the Hawkins family at Minety, the Crewes at Great Coxwell and the Herrings at Coleshill.
49   BRO D/E Pb, E4, pp. 139/5–6; E8, p. 88.
50   BRO D/E Pb, E33, p. 157.
51   BRO D/E Pb, E33, p. 158; E4, pp. 213–4; E8, p. 125.
52   Regarding Lord Barrington, see BRO D/E EL, E35/17. Professor Mingay notes Pleydell's rule prohibiting the sale of ale and spirits in "The eighteenth century land steward", in E. L. Jones and G. E. Mingay (eds), *Land, Labour and Population in the Industrial Revolution, Essays Presented to J. D. Chambers* (London, 1966), p. 5. For Amos Wilson see BRO D/E Pb, E8 pp. 87, 117.
53   Mingay, *English Landed Society*, p. 177.
54   BRO D/E Pb, E4, p.[130]; E13, p. 63. See also Clay, in Thirsk (ed.), Vol. V, Pt 2, p. 234.
55   BRO D/E Pb, E11, pp. 218–19.
56   BRO D/E Pb, E4, memorandum, 3rd fol. following fol. 193.

57 BRO D/E Pb, E8, p. 125.
58 BRO D/E Pb, E4, p. 8; E7, p. 89; E8, p. 76. Also G. E. Mingay, "The agricultural depression, 1730–1750", *Economic History Review* 2nd ser., vol. 8, no. 3 (1956), pp. 323–8.
59 For Craven and Barrington tenants see BRO Craven papers (D/E C), T85/9; D/E Pb, E8, p. 18. For arrears owing to Pleydell see for example D/E Pb, E8, p. 17.
60 BRO D/E Pb, E8, p. 17, 26; E11, fols 122, 164, 219; E13, fols 63–5.
61 Mingay (1956), pp. 328–30; BRO D/E Pb, E6, pp. 50, 72.
62 BRO D/E Pb, E4, p. 8/3; E7, p. 100; E12, p. 35.
63 BRO D/E Pb, E8, p. 16; E11, p. 14; E12, p. 38; E13, pp. 11, 21, 23. See also E13, p. 115, for the substantial amount of more than £45 paid for a new barn, compared with an estimated £5 for an oxhouse.
64 BRO D/E EL, E35/17.
65 BRO D/E Pb, E6, *passim*, E7, p. 56.
66 For the large families of other Vale gentry at this time see Cottis, thesis, pp, 49, 56, 66.
67 BRO D/E Pb, E6, p. 50; E7, pp. 58, 76; E14, p. 60. Turnips were being hoed on the Massingberd estates in Lincolnshire in the 1750s, but this was said to be fifty years before the practice was standard in the county: B. A. Holderness, "The agricultural activities of the Massingberds of South Ormsby, Lincolnshire, 1638–*c.* 1750", *Midland History*, vol. 1, no. 3 (Spring 1972), pp. 15–25.
68 Mingay, *English Landed Society*, p. 207. BRO D/E Pb, E7, pp. 75–6.
69 BRO D/E Pb, E7, p. 12; E13, pp. 6, 11, 17, 53; E14, pp. 65, 147–53.
70 BRO D/E Pb, E33, pp. 149–63, 196–202.
71 ibid. p. 152.
72 ibid. p. 157.
73 BRO D/E Pb, E3, pp. 1–4.
74 Cottis, thesis, pp. 290–3.
75 BRO D/E Pb, E3, pp. 100–112.
76 Mingay, *Land and Labour*, p. 5.
77 Parker, p. 54.
78 BRO D/E Pb, E3, p. 54; E5, pp. 28–9.
79 BRO D/E Pb, E4, pp. 6–7; E8, p.111.
80 BRO D/E Pb, E4, *passim* E33, pp. 156, 196, 203.
81 BRO D/E Pb, E3–4. Cottis, thesis pp. 291–2.
82 BRO D/E Pb, E4, [pp. 43–4]; E7, p. 87.
83 BRO D/E Pb, E4, fols 24/6, 24/9.
84 Cottis, thesis pp. 390–1.
85 J. Broad, "Alternate husbandry and permanent pasture in the Midlands, 1650–1800", *Agricultural History Review*, vol. 28, no. 2 (1980), pp. 77–89.
86 BRO D/E Pb, E12, p. 105: "Sheep are poison. No Sheep till thick turf. The Akery [sic] by sheep has lost ten years."
87 BRO D/E Pb, E33, p. 158.
88 ibid. p. 155.
89 ibid. p. 198; E8, pp. 28.
90 BRO D/E Pb, E4, follows fol. 176, recto and verso. He adds, "It is also my intention to extend the like sattisfaction to every Tenant of mine who shall enter into the like agreem[en]t."
91 BRO D/E Pb, E11, pp. 252, 264.
92 BRO D/E Pb, E4, endorsement on lease beginning on fol. 193.
93 ibid. fol. 120, J/14–18; E12, pp. 105, 114.
94 Broad, pp. 77–89.
95 W. Mavor, *A General View of the Agriculture of Berkshire* (London, 1809), p. 23.

3 The purchase and management of Guy's Hospital estates, 1726–1806

B. E. S. TRUEMAN

In the early years of the nineteenth century John Duncumb, one of the reporters to the Board of Agriculture, recorded with some dismay the transfer to Guy's Hospital of the Duke of Chandos' private estates in Herefordshire:

> Thus they remain under the mortifying change, that the rents are annually remitted to the metropolis, and the mansions destroyed, or converted to purposes far humbler and less generally useful, than those for which they were designed.[1]

He seemed to be repeating a familiar charge against institutional landlords which Shaw-Lefevre, later in the century, also intimated when he urged such proprietors to consider everyone living on their land and not aim only to make "the utmost net income out of it".[2] The officers of the hospital were certainly aware of the differences between themselves and private landowners, but in reality the management of their estates had much in common with that of private proprietors. Indeed, in some ways it proved superior to it. Operating within a tradition of estate management, the actual nature of the corporation, with its clearly defined central government, made it effective in dealing with the various agents who represented the hospital on the estates, and reasonable with the tenants who sustained it. Although in many instances "charity property may have been handled less efficiently than ordinary land",[3] with the governors of Guy's Hospital it generally proved otherwise. In their case, being answerable to the interests of the charity encouraged efficiency; and it was the careful way in which they actually purchased their property which set the seal on the type of managers they were to become.

In their painstaking search for "a fair & equal bargain and such as will justify their Care in the important Trust they are Engaged in",[4] the governors bought their main agricultural estates during the first thirty years of the charity's history. After this they continued almost annually the process of buying, selling and exchanging small pieces of land, while in the later eighteenth and nineteenth centuries they also made a number of more substantial additions to their property, including the Mynd estate in Herefordshire in 1789, and important urban sites around the hospital itself in Southwark. The last purchase was negotiated during the Second World War when almost 8,000 acres were acquired in Herefordshire; yet it was the property the hospital bought from 1726 to 1756[5] in the three counties of Lincolnshire, Essex and Herefordshire, comprising about 23,000 acres in all, that was to form the main basis of its income for about 150 years. The founder, Thomas Guy, who had died the year before the hospital first opened its gates in 1726, had left specific instructions in his will[6] that the corporation should only buy land, while a later Act of Parliament limited the annual rental to a maximum of £12,000. The rents and profits from this property were to provide for the care of sick paupers as well as for the general maintenance and expenses of the charity itself.

This sort of endowment was not particularly uncommon. Guy's eighteenth-century neighbour and sister hospital, St Thomas's, had for many years derived much of its income from land. What was more unusual was that the governors of Guy's were obliged to purchase substantial holdings, including some complete estates, at a time when the price of land was rising steeply and the market was becoming increasingly dominated by acquisitions of smaller pieces of property.[7] Land prices surged forward from the end of the War of Spanish Succession and, by the 1720s and 1730s, had reached a going rate of between twenty-five and thirty years' purchase.[8] The level of demand has been seen as the main reason for these high prices, a conviction shared by Macpherson, writing of the year 1729, when he said they had risen to twenty-five, twenty-six and twenty-seven years' purchase, considering this as "evident proof that there are more persons able and ready to purchase land than before".[9]

The long period of peace after 1713 and the lack of any noticeable expansion in the National Debt, both associated with Walpole, helped to stimulate this demand and keep up the price of land. Yet although the debt was not actually increasing during this period, it was still sufficiently substantial to involve "a large number of investors and a significant proportion of potential buyers of land".[10] Indeed, the interplay between short-term fluctuations in the funds and the level of demand for property was an important influence on land prices. As prospective buyers usually had to sell stocks to purchase land, they would try and do this when the price of securities was high. This accordingly affected the property market as demonstrated by the spectacular example of the year 1720 when the rocketing price of stock pushed up the cost of some land to as much as forty and fifty years' purchase.[11] The continuing fall in the rate of interest also affected the advancing price of land. Back in the 1690s Abraham de Moivre noticed this connection, saying that "now Interest is abated Land sells for a much higher Value there [areas remote from London] as well as in other places";[12] while in 1729, when writing of the price of land in Herefordshire, the Duke of Chandos observed to the governors of the hospital "that 'tis obvious to every one, how much the low Interest of Mony & other Reasons have made it rise of late Years in its value".[13]

Prospective purchasers certainly did not appear to be faced with any land shortage, and it is difficult to see this as a reason for high prices. Apparent constraints, such as strict settlement, also seem to have had little effect.[14] In fact, the high level of prices actually encouraged an increasing amount of land to come on to the market. With property going at twenty-five to thirty years' purchase, this could be sufficient to impel a number of smaller owners to sell their land, especially if they were then able to stay on as life tenants.[15] Other reasons for selling property included the policy of some landowners to consolidate holdings by selling outlying portions of their estates, while other proprietors were prompted by the more desperate need to discharge heavy debts, including the accumulated portions of youngers sons and marriage settlements on daughters. A number of the hospital's purchases, including some of its major estates such as Great Bardfield in Essex, were of heavily encumbered property.

High prices in the second quarter of the eighteenth century, however, did tend to affect the actual size of land coming on to the market. With prices moving forward so strongly, the rate of return from property would have been less than the yield from the funds. It would therefore not only have been unwise, but also curious, for a landowner to buy a substantial estate when this could well have resulted in a fall in income; and the general tendency was to add smaller pieces of land by piecemeal purchase to already existing estates in order to make them more compact or convenient.[16] In many ways the same also applied to the acquisitions of outsiders such as London merchants who, during the eighteenth century, played a particularly active role in the Lincolnshire land market.[17] This general trend, however, did not mean there were no substantial purchases at all by private owners at this time. Robert Lowther, who became a governor of Barbados, bought a large estate in 1727 for £30,400, while the coal owning Tempest family were purchasing large pieces of property from 1734 onwards.[18] Yet there still seems little to match the sort of land purchases Guy's Hospital made from 1726 to 1756 when almost £200,000 was paid for property yielding, on completion of purchase, the statutory £12,000 per annum. Admittedly this was a special case, as the trustees were compelled by law to buy land. Indeed, as the estates were acquired by a corporation, starting from scratch and governed by committees, its minutes and correspondence illustrate vividly how the trustees actually conducted their negotiations, and the often painstaking care with which they purchased their property. Such records not only give an insight into the way the corporation operated in the early-eighteenth-century land market, they also throw light on its own financial structure during the first thirty years of its existence.

The founder himself accumulated his fortune as a bookseller, financier, and dealer in the funds, the government stock of the day. The South Sea Bubble gave him his most spectacular windfall of £234,000 and, as a result, he was able to leave generous bequests to his relatives as well as a residuary amount "computed to be of the Value of Two hundred thousand Pounds and upwards"[19] for the foundation of the hospital which bears his name. His own property, and thus the original and early assets of the hospital, consisted mainly of personalty; and it was this which provided the corporation with its main source of income while buying its property.

I

At his death, almost £207,000 of Thomas Guy's fortune was held in the form of Bank, East India and South Sea stock and redeemable annuities. Some buying of stock continued immediately after the hospital had first opened its gates, but the will prevented the charity deriving a permanent income from this source. Practically everything had to be converted into land, and so the first thirty years witnessed the gradual transition of the hospital's income from a reliance on interest to a dependence on rent. The funds themselves were only a major source of income during the first five years or so of the hospital's history. Then they were gradually sold either to buy land or to be converted temporarily into mortgage loans; and interest from the latter, in fact, constituted the main income of the charity in those early years (see Appendix I).

For the eighteenth-century landowner the long-term mortgage had become an important means of raising money privately. It had grown in popularity from the early seventeenth century, often as a valuable means of providing family settlements for younger sons and marriage portions of daughters. The development of the capital market and the steady fall in the rate of interest to 5 and 4 per cent in the early eighteenth century had further encouraged its adoption, while the rise in the price of land from the 1710s onward had only helped to give a firmer foundation to this type of loan. It became "more secure, easier to arrange, and cheaper to service".[20] Falling interest rates also encouraged an increase in the actual size of the loan, especially if it were to provide an attractively large marriage portion and, at the same time, help maintain the recipient's income. Property could also bear the weight of a mortgage as security for certain types of arrears, such as tithes. In November 1744 the hospital's treasurer, Benjamin Avery, wrote to the receiver of the Herefordshire estate suggesting that the eldest son of Mrs Seward, who paid the Burghill tithes and who "has a good Estate", should mortgage it to the hospital,

> and so make it a real Security to the Hospl for all arrears due: I will venture to give you orders to take such a mortgage instead of distraining in compassion to the family for whose distress I am very sorry.[21]

The mortgage loan was certainly considered very advantageous to the landowner as borrower. As long as the interest was paid, repayment of the capital sum could be postponed for as long as possible. If lenders wanted the principal returned, it could then be simply assigned to another creditor. This occurred with the Hendon mortgage in the hospital's dealings with the Duke of Chandos, while the charity itself was assigned a mortgage of over £2,500 during its abortive negotiations for the Wyck Rissington estate in Gloucestershire. The mortgage, however, could also create severe problems for the borrower – or at least for his family. As Hazlitt warned: "They will purchase the hollow happiness of the next five minutes by a mortgage on the independence and comfort of years."[22] As the present burdens were eased, so future generations bore the encumbrances on the estate, with interest payments as a permanent annual outgoing. For some families these became so great that a serious financial crisis ensued. Various remedies could be tried, including retrenchment or the creation of a sinking fund to clear the debt.[23] A more drastic solution was to sell some property, and the temptation to do this grew as the eighteenth century progressed because "a debt could be liquidated by the sacrifice of land yielding considerably less than the interest payment which would thereby be saved".[24] For Sir James Lumley in the late 1720s the remedy proved far more desperate in that his whole estate in Essex, including that in entail, had to be sold – with most of it going to the hospital – in order to clear its accumulated debts.

For the creditor, Pressnell has pointed out the greater safety of the mortgage "to the personal security of notes and bonds".[25] It could mean the prospect of a steady income from an interest of 4 per cent or, as in the case of some of the hospital mortgages, as much as 5 per cent. In 1723 Thomas Guy himself had entered the ranks of those who lent money to private landowners when he arranged a loan of £65,000 at 4.5 per cent to Sir William Blackett who held land in Durham and Northumberland. Two years later the governors of the newly created hospital agreed to advance a further £12,000 to Sir William "on the Equity and Redemption of the said Mortgage";[26] and the interest from the enlarged mortgage of £77,000 was being paid to the corporation from November 1727 onwards. Amongst the other mortgages negotiated by the governors were those connected with the Middlesex and Welsh properties of the Duke of Powys and his son. In July 1725 the trustees resolved in committee to provide between £12,000 and £20,000 of the £64,000 the Duke required, although later in the year it was decided to advance as much as £32,000 on his Hendon estate in Middlesex at 5 per cent interest. Bank stock, old annuities and debentures were sold to effect the loan, and the hospital began to receive the interest from 1727. Two years later another smaller loan of £4,000 was agreed on Powys's Welsh estate, and this also yielded 5 per cent interest. This later mortgage, together with £7,000 of the original larger one, was paid off in 1732. The duke, in fact, had threatened to clear the whole debt unless the governors reduced the interest to the more general rate of 4 per cent. As it happened, however, it was soon to be out of the trustees' hands altogether. It was assigned to the Duke of Chandos the same year as part payment for his Herefordshire estate.

Other mortgages were negotiated by the charity, especially during the 1720s and 1730s. Prior to selling his property to the hospital Chandos himself borrowed £25,000 in 1731 at the more usual 4 per cent interest, and this was later transferred to his own account as part of the purchase money for his estate. In fact, together with the Hendon assignment, this £25,000 comprised the main portion of the purchase money, just under £61,000, that the hospital gave for the Herefordshire property. It also appears from what Chandos himself wrote that this practice of borrowing money before the purchase of land was not peculiar to the hospital's negotiations: "I believe it is generally usual to advance, in so large a Purchase, a part of the Purchase Money upon the writings being sent into their Council".[27] A similar type of loan – a mortgage prior to purchase – was made in 1729 to Richard Berney during the abortive negotiations for the Pondhall estate in Suffolk. On this occasion Berney was advanced the sum of £2,000 bearing 5 per cent interest.[28]

A number of smaller loans were effected during these earlier years but, as it has been suggested, what was so significant about them all was that they furnished the charity with an important source of income during the transitional period when it was buying its estates. The loans were gradually eliminated as land was bought; and so until March 1733 interest from stocks and mortgages – the latter from 1728 – constituted the main income of the hospital, while from 1733 to March 1747, when rents were coming in from Essex and part of the Herefordshire estate, the interest from mortgages still played a significant but now smaller role in the composition of the charity's revenue, comprising one-third to half of its total income. It was not until 1747, when the newly acquired property in Lincolnshire began sending its rents to London that interest payments now began to play a very minor role. Three years later, the last mortgage the hospital held – that of Sir William Blackett – was repaid. Stocks such as new and old South Sea annuities were bought with the money as a temporary measure until more suitable land was found. In 1753 the hospital acquired the Leigh's Priory estate in Essex, while the following year the death of the Marchioness of Carnarvon released two-thirds of the hospital's Herefordshire property from the grip of a jointress who had held it for twenty-three years after purchase.[29] The first rents from this jointure estate started to arrive in 1756 and this year, in fact, marked the beginning of the period, lasting well into the second half of the nineteenth century, when the charity depended almost solely on property for its income. It is also ironic that the mortgages on which it had depended during the first thirty years yielded more at 4 and 5 per cent than land which, at the common going-rate at the time of twenty-five and thirty years' purchase, would have brought only 3 to 2.75 per cent net of outgoings.[30]

As the hospital discovered, however, interest payments on mortgages could at times be as erratic as rent returns. On at least three major occasions the charity's largest mortgage, that of Sir William Blackett, gave the hospital a considerable amount of trouble when payments failed to arrive, and arrears subsequently accumulated. Times of economic difficulty could lead as easily to arrears of interest as of rent, and on such occasions the governors could find themselves having to negotiate a smaller percentage on the principal loan. The final crisis came with delays caused by the '45 rebellion – "these public comotions [*sic*]"[31] – and demands by Blackett at the end of the decade for a reduction of the interest to 4 per cent. But by this time the charity was calling in the loan to pay for the estates it acquired in the late 1740s and 1750s. These purchases marked the end of the first phase of its history, and thereby finally satisfied the conditions of the endowment.

II

The trustees purchased their first piece of property soon after the founder's death. It comprised some leasehold houses and "a small piece of Ground in the Maes [Maze Pond Road in Southwark] near the South side of this Hospital".[32] The governors already held a lease of some land and a wharf at Blackfriars which had been left by Guy himself, and they continued to show an interest in acquiring urban property, usually in the vicinity of the hospital, throughout the charity's history. One reason was the physical expansion of the hospital itself, and another the need to control the area around the building to ensure, for instance, adequate light and a good circulation of air. Therefore the prospective sale of any property near the hospital usually created interest, and during the early years special sub-committees were established to consider the purchase of houses and a wharf in St Thomas and Gracechurch streets. But the trustees did not make any really substantial purchases of urban sites until 1789 when they bought the Snowsfield estate. After this, during the following century they purchased a succession of urban sites near the hospital. The Snowsfield estate cost £4,200, for which the governors had to borrow the money, while in 1806 they bought the Maze Pond property for £10,200 from the sale of detached parts of Herefordshire and Essex.

These urban "estates" consisted of parcels of land covered with housing, warehouses and inns; and one way the hospital used some of these acquisitions is indicated in the minutes for November 1799 when it reported that a number of houses had been demolished to build the charity's new wing and a lunatic house. In controlling the area around the hospital the governors could also prevent patients "frequenting Publick-Houses or Brandy Shops"[33] and in 1802 one of the neighbouring inns was rented for £50 per annum in order to remove "the nuisance which has been so long complained of".[34] One part was then let to a tenant-at-will while the other was used to house the hospital beadle "whose apartments will now be required for the new arrangement which is necessary to make for the Surgery".[35] The hospital later continued the policy of employing its urban property either for its direct use, to accommodate servants, or for leasing to private tenants. In the mid nineteenth century it also rebuilt some decaying warehouses in order to regulate their height and control their distance from the hospital. Yet although purchases of urban sites were significant during the nineteenth century, in the charity's early years reports of such property for sale were still rare compared with those for agricultural land; and it was on this that the governors concentrated their attentions first of all. But if their criteria for buying urban land were generally straightforward, those for purchasing agricultural estates were far more varied.

From the long negotiations the governors undertook it is not only evident that price was a primary concern, but that they were determined to get as good a bargain as possible. They usually tried for land below the going price of twenty-five to thirty years' purchase, although they would give this for an estate which promised few management problems and had the prospect of good rent improvements. One reason for their interest in Essex was probably evidence of rents increasing in the county.[36] When they were negotiating for land in Beaumont-cum-Moze the governors were clearly willing to pay twenty-five years' purchase. Despite the drawback of having to maintain at least a mile of sea walling, there was a definite possibility of rent improvements on property "of a good kindly nature" with "a very good burthen of grass".[37] Rents on this estate in fact did increase by 39 per cent during the first fourteen years of the hospital's possession. Similarly, the prospect of rent improvements on property at Leigh's Priory, described as "the most compleat and Compact Estate in this County",[38] persuaded the governors to agree to as much as twenty-eight years' purchase. Conversely, one of the sticking points in the Herefordshire negotiations were "the Raised Rents on the Joynture Estate"[39] which made any rent increase unlikely in the foreseeable future.

The character and condition of an estate were other criteria determining price and purchase. Both Herefordshire and parts of the hospital's Essex property contained extensive woodlands which could bring valuable contingent profits. The type of lease – the most favoured being that which specified a number of years – as well as the condition of the farms and state of repairs were also taken into consideration. But in their pursuit of a bargain the governors often had to balance immediate disadvantages with an estate's future prospects. Indeed, much of the property they bought had evident drawbacks, such as the huge jointure estate in Herefordshire which delayed the hospital's possession, and the more permanent problem of clay farms in the northern sector of that estate. The enormous cost of maintaining the banks and sluices of Lincolnshire, which were always at the mercy of fierce spring tides, had to be weighed against the benefits of property which was likely to increase substantially in size with the enclosure of salt marshes, and for which the governors only gave just over fourteen years' purchase. This meant that the usual net yield of the estate in its earlier years was around 4 per cent.

Location was another important criterion. The convenience to London of Essex, and even of south Lincolnshire, goes some way to explain the governors' interest in property there; and most of the reports they received concerned land lying in this eastern region. Essex in particular had close economic links with the capital whose markets relied heavily on the county's agricultural produce, and from the seventeenth century onwards it had become increasingly popular with individuals and corporations seeking land convenient to London in which to invest their funds.[40] Guy's itself was further encouraged to look towards Essex because its sister hospital, St Thomas's, also held land there. A number of trustees were governors of both institutions, and so a visit to view the property of one could take in the lands of the other.

In January 1727 Guy's Hospital received a particularly favourable account of an Essex estate at Great Bardfield in the north of the county. This was the property of Sir James Lumley. It contained a number of good farms, none of which was let for three lives, and many of the tenants were warmly commended. The timber was also "computed to be worth at least £2,000"[41] and some recently opened chalk and lime pits promised to yield "exceeding good Manure . . . and may be of considerable yearly value to Sell to mend the Neighbouring Lands".[42] Above all, there was a good chance of a bargain as the property had to be sold in a hurry to settle heavy debts.

III

From the late seventeenth century onwards, the history of the Lumley estate was one of mounting encumbrances through three generations, with a personal tragedy, the madness of Sir James, striking the final blow. His own father, Sir Martin Lumley, had left "mortgages on many parts of his Estate to a great Value",[43] with debts and legacies totalling about £20,000. The legacies included a substantial one of £5,000 for his daughter as a portion payable either on her twenty-first birthday or her marriage, while a jointure estate was provided for his wife. Sir Martin also attempted to secure the landed future of his son by leaving part of the estate in entail, and then protecting the rights of any future heirs by the device of establishing a trust "to preserve contingent remainders".[44] In his will he had arranged to pay some of his debts by leaving a few farms in the hands of trustees, although this hardly eased the situation, especially as Sir James himself was soon accumulating debts of his own. He proceeded to mortgage "some of ye Estate yt had not been mortgaged by Sir Martin" and "contracted many debts by judgmt & many more by simple contract".[45]

A number of familiar solutions to this problem of mounting debt were sought. After Sir James had failed in his attempt to marry "a Wife with a large Fortune that wod have enabled him to have cleared [a] great part of the debts and Incumbrances on his Estate",[46] the main portion of his property was transferred to two trustees for a limited period of ten years. During this time part of the annual yield from rents and profits was to go to the creditors. Sir James himself was to receive an annual allowance of £400, while the more distant parts of the estate were to be sold. But then came the *coup de grâce*. In June 1725 a commission acting on a Chancery writ declared Sir James a lunatic and placed him in custody. By this time the debts of both father and son amounted to almost £40,500. Out of this about £35,000 consisted of mortgages and other encumbrances carrying an interest of 5 per cent which in itself amounted to almost £1,800, and it was declared that

> without the sale of the sd Estate or the great part thereof . . . the debts and Legacies . . . Cod not be paid as in Justice they ought to be by reason whereof he [Sir James] wod be more and more involved in expensive Suits wch together with the sd debts wod probably swallow up his whole Est[ate] and leave him destitute of a reasonable support.[47]

It was therefore decided to sell all the estate not in entail. Certain complications, such as the lunacy of the proprietor and the trust set up to pay the creditors, meant that an Act of Parliament was required to put the property in the hands of yet more trustees for the specific purpose of sale. The original intention was to divide the estate and sell it in its three natural parts, the largest portion being just over 1,000 acres in the parish of Great Bardfield, while the others were the 400-acre jointure estate of Sir James's mother and three farms near Billericay in south Essex. Before the hospital appeared on the scene other negotiators had been declared best buyers of all three parts with twenty-two and a half years' purchase for Great Bardfield itself, and twenty-seven and a half for the southern farms nearest London. Only six and a half years' purchase had been offered for Lady Lumley's jointure, reflecting the unpopularity of land when possession so often depended on the death of the occupant.

By January 1727 the governors had made it clear that they were prepared to give another £1,000 for the main estate and southern farms, with ten years' purchase for the jointure, and they were subsequently declared best buyers at £28,000. This meant they had to pay as much as twenty-seven years' purchase for two sections of the estate; but with Lady Lumley's jointure, which they were fortunately able to possess immediately, they managed to secure the whole property for just over twenty-three years' purchase. A jotting on the cover of one of the Essex papers indicates they were in fact thinking along these lines.[48]

If the negotiations for the estate had been involved, paying for it proved even more complicated. In July 1727 a special sub-committee reported that the encumbrances on the property "did exceed the purchase money [by] about £5,000";[49] but it was still ordered to pay off the Lumley creditors by selling stock, and the final instalment of £5,211 was paid in January 1731. By this time it was clear that in settling all the debts, the charity had given about £9,000 more than the agreed purchase price. The only land left for the pathetic Sir James was his entailed property, and to sell this another Act of Parliament was required. Such a move was censured as unfeeling by one of the hospital's correspondents, but in reply the clerk defended the action. He stressed that the Act would raise a fund for Sir James's support, and therefore the hospital had in fact preserved the poor lunatic "from a distress otherwise unavoidable" and it was "in . . . Compassion to him that the Gov^rs of the hospital concern themselves in this mre [matter]".[50] The remainder of the Lumley property was eventually sold for £16,000 to a local landowner. The charity itself had considered buying it but refused to go higher than £15,500, its target price of twenty-three years' purchase.[51]

IV

Altogether the hospital was to hold about one-third of its property in Essex. Its largest estate lay in Herefordshire; and if the reasons for buying land in Essex are generally understandable, those for acquiring it in such a distant county are less obvious. It is true the area had much to commend it, "where every Farm hath such a vast quantity of proper Ground belonging to it" as one surveyor optimistically reported.[52] The climate was mild, the farming notably diverse, and the woods and hedgerows contained an impressive amount of timber. Like Essex, Herefordshire was also a heavily enclosed county and, although remote, it was not particularly isolated. It was an important source of agricultural produce, especially wheat, for the Severn Vale area and a number of its landed families had close ties with London.[53] The property in which the hospital was interested, that of the Duke of Chandos, was also on the market as a complete estate, and this usually had the advantage of being more convenient and cheaper to buy than negotiating for a number of smaller units. Its very distance offered the prospect of a reasonable price, unlike estates near London where "27 & 28 [years] is the lowest any is to be purchast at".[54] There was also the chance of another bargain as the Duke of Chandos seemed desperate for money.

Described as a notable figure among the second-rank men of his time[55] Chandos possessed considerable wealth and extensive property; but he was extravagant to a fault and "a bubble to every project and a dupe to men that nobody else would almost keep company with".[56] His numerous ventures proved costly, and he also suffered considerable losses in both the John Law and South Sea schemes. He was certainly not ruined by his extravagant behaviour and foolhardy enterprises, but by the end of the 1720s he was at least experiencing financial embarrassment. Although the immediate reason for selling the Herefordshire estate was to make a settlement for his sons, in 1730 he did complain to a correspondent of the "many & various calls I have upon me . . . & more than I am able, without great Expense, to struggle thro".[57]

For the governors the possibility of a bargain was enhanced by a particularly heavy burden on the property itself in the form of a huge jointure comprising about two-thirds of the whole estate. This was held as a settlement by the Marchioness of Carnarvon, wife of the duke's eldest son, and even the ever-optimistic Chandos thought the governors might pull out of the deal when they discovered its size. He therefore thought of offering his Radnor lands instead. However, the trustees not only continued to show interest in Herefordshire, but also expected definite concessions because of the encumbrance and remoteness of the estate. They certainly jibbed at Chandos's initial demand of twenty-five years' purchase, although they did agree to view the property on this basis. But the eventual report was so unfavourable that their inspection in the autumn of 1729 marked the beginning of two years' protracted negotiations by which the hospital painfully sought to squeeze a growing number of concessions out of a reluctant and increasingly desperate duke.

In their report, the governors complained about the number of buildings, the state of repairs, the over-valuation of much of the land as "a direct Misrepresentation of the Surveyor"[58] and that although the property was being sold as a complete estate, it was not a particularly compact one. They suspected that its management, which required a person of "good Credited Substance to look after it",[59] would greatly exceed the £100 per annum indicated by the duke, although their greatest complaint was that they saw little prospect of any rent improvements. This especially applied to the jointure estate, which mostly comprised newly purchased land, and consequently the rents had already been increased fairly considerably.

Not surprisingly, the duke was both irritated and dismayed by this report. He protested about

> how these Gentlemen have treated me, by keeping me in hand a year & an half & going down to view the Estate in so publick a manner, & afterwards raising Objections that I believe were never made before in the Purchase of any Estate.[60]

Even worse, when he supplied detailed answers to the governors' objections, in their reply they merely reiterated at greater length all their former complaints. This encouraged Chandos to try and find other purchasers who would take enough land to make his financial position "perfectly Easy",[61] and he even toyed with the idea of selling his estate piecemeal. But he never found a real alternative. The hospital was the only prospective buyer prepared to consider taking the whole estate, and in fact the duke continued negotiating with the governors all the time he was seeking other buyers. He also tied himself even closer to the corporation by borrowing money from it. The previous August he had explained to a correspondent that he thought it usual to do this before purchase, and "if I could be accommodated with this money from these Gentlemen, my affairs would be easy to me till such time as the whole Bargain can be completed."[62] In April 1730 the Duke's "particular necessity"[63] of £6,000 to pay off a mortgage was sanctioned and South Sea annuities were sold to raise the amount.

In early 1730 provisional agreement was reached. Although twenty-five years' purchase was still the acknowledged price, the duke made so many substantial concessions, such as £4,000 for the quantity and condition of the buildings, that it was effectively reduced, according to Chandos himself, to "under Three & Twenty".[64] The hospital would not go that far. It later calculated the price at twenty-four years' purchase with half this for the jointure estate. Then, after a further dispute over the value of the timber, the final arrangements were made much sooner than Chandos had apparently expected. He wrote that "the Gentlemen of the Trust are disposed to make everything as easy as they now can to Me, & to finish with it as expeditiously as may be".[65] It seemed that a report on "the Dowager Lady Carnarvon's health may have contributed a great deal towards this change in their behaviour".[66] If this meant the jointress's health was failing, and if she had died before any agreement had been concluded, then the jointure would have cost the full twenty-four years' purchase with the rest of the estate. But if she had obligingly perished soon after the hospital had paid the £30,690 it gave for the jointure, it would indeed have been a splendid bargain. Unfortunately for the governors their gamble did not pay off. The marchioness apparently made a striking recovery and lived another twenty-two years. For the hospital this meant a loss, at 4 per cent compound interest, of about £14,300,[67] although the governors still got the estate for a reasonable sum.

Altogether they gave £60,000 for the property. Most of this purchase money consisted of loans, over £30,000, the hospital had made to the duke prior to purchase, together with the transfer to him of the £25,000 mortgage on the Duke of Powys's Hendon estate. When the governors received their first rents from Herefordshire in 1733 these were only from the estate in possession – the one-third of the property outside the marchioness's control. After Lady Carnarvon's death in 1754, when the hospital eventually took over the complete estate of 10,000 acres, the governors valued the property a few years later at the rather modest sum of £94,436.[68] Therefore, even with their calculated loss as a result of the marchioness's longevity, the estate had still only cost the charity just over £75,000.

V

The trustees took another risk with their next major purchase – that of the south Lincolnshire estate of Sutton Marsh, later known as Sutton Bridge. This was "a large Tract . . . of between 4 and 5000 acres lying altogether"[69] in flat marshland of "innumerable dreyns and dykes of water"[70] Its advantages included proximity to some thriving towns and ports, while the area had strong connections with London in that it was "almost entirely employed in breeding and fatting [*sic*] of Cattle particularly a large sort of Sheep designed for the Smithfield market".[71] It also lay a convenient distance from the hospital's property in Essex which was later to supply some of the wood for its gates and fences. The land of Sutton Marsh consisted of "a very rich soil"[72] chiefly used for pasture which usually yielded more rent per acre than arable. There was also "no reasonable fear for want of Tenants",[73] and the "very few & inconsiderate buildings"[74] would help keep down the cost of repairs. Another attraction was the prospect of rent improvements which were linked to the likely enlargement of the estate through the enclosure of its salt marshes. In the mid-1740s there were already eighty acres ready for embankment, although the governors' major reservation relating to the estate was the considerable cost of defending these enclosures from the ravages of the sea.

The hospital had previously shown an interest in Sutton Marsh in 1728 and again in 1737, but the reports on the cost of maintenance were so discouraging that they were undoubtedly an important reason for the governors' hesitation in negotiating for the property. In one of their own reports in 1745 they pointed out as much as nine miles of banking to keep in repair, and seven miles of this had been very poorly built. Spring tides were the main hazard. The governors warned that parts of the embankment were not very firm, and "were liable to receive a great deal of Injury by the bulging and dashing of the Waves".[75] These defences, in fact, needed almost £1,000 to put into immediate repair, although the governors estimated the annual cost of maintenance after that at the much lower and somewhat optimistic figure of £200.[76] There were also a number of other heavy outgoings, such as the upkeep of miles of fencing; yet in the event the governors still decided to purchase the estate, especially as by 1746 there was every possibility of getting it for a very reasonable price. When they had first shown interest, the owner had demanded as much as twenty-three years' purchase. Almost twenty years later the hospital was to give just over fourteen years' purchase for the property.

There was, however, another important reason for the trustees' earlier uncertainty. In 1731, when it was decided to proceed no further for the time being with the negotiations, it had been noted that the estate was "under several Incumbrances and Suits in Law & Equity".[77] Indeed, before the hospital eventually bought the property the woeful history of Sutton Marsh was one of disputed title, intricate law suits, speculation, the burdens of heavy mortgages, and bankruptcy.

The estate was first mortgaged in 1691 and 1692, and it was to clear these debts that the land was sold in 1718 for £31,800 to a certain Augustus Wollaston. He mortgaged the land again for £28,000 the day after the conveyance was made over to him. Then, in 1720, he decided to cash in on the South Sea mania in order to raise more money, and consequently made his estate "a Bubble".[78] It formed part of a speculative scheme based on a patent Wollaston had obtained for extracting oil from radish seed. This project attracted as much as £20,000, but it was soon involved in numerous disputes among the creditors. In order to settle "a continued chain of schemes & projects"[79] the creditors introduced a bill in 1731 to have the estate sold to settle their debts, although it took another six years before the property went to William Newland for £35,167.

He then did exactly the same as the previous owner. In order to pay for the estate he immediately mortgaged it by arranging two loans. One was for £25,167, while the remaining £10,000 was borrowed from Lascelles Metcalf from whom the hospital eventually bought the property. Newland also borrowed a further £9,300 from Metcalf to enclose 1,800 acres of marshland, but failed to pay the interest on the largest mortgage and so was eventually declared bankrupt. As Metcalf held both a mortgage on the estate and also shared its profits, he was allowed to bring in a bill for its sale. This was when the hospital appeared on the scene again.

The governors offered £37,000 or about thirteen and a half years' purchase, giving the high cost of maintenance as the principal reason for proposing such a low price. They asserted that the purchase money "wod have been a great deal more In Case this estate had not been subject to great outgoings monthly on account of yᵉ imbanking from yᵉ Sea".[80] As the mortgagees of the first and larger loan of £25,167 began pressing for payment, in January 1746 Metcalf tried to persuade the governors to proceed with the purchase as quickly as possible. But as they feared there might be old claims on the estate as a result of its complex history, they insisted that an Act of Parliament should settle the title on the newly embanked land. In return, they agreed to pay the principal and interest on the largest mortgage, but insisted that the rest of the purchase money should remain on deposit until the Act had been secured. This was passed in 1747.

In the meantime the hospital had taken possession of the estate to carry out essential repairs on the banks, although Metcalf was soon to demand more for his own contribution to the cost of a new drain and sluice gate. Another complicated dispute followed which was only settled in Chancery in 1752. As a result, the hospital gave Metcalf an extra £2,000 which raised the price of Sutton Marsh to just over fourteen years' purchase.

VI

The amount the governors gave for Sutton Marsh was well below the going rate for land in the 1740s of between twenty-four and thirty years' purchase, and it was even under the lowest price for property in Lincolnshire itself which Holderness puts at seventeen years' purchase for the period 1741–60.[81] They certainly took a considerable risk in buying an estate with such large outgoings, with the real danger that spring tides could break through the embankments and thereby destroy all chance of any return at all for at least a year.[82] But if this was a risk, it was a calculated one. Sutton Marsh was agriculturally rich, and had every prospect of rent improvements by its growth in size through enclosure. In normal times the annual net return in the earliest years was about 4 per cent which was the largest the hospital received from any of its lands. From Herefordshire and Essex the net return was more in the region of 3 per cent but the hospital did pay more for these estates. The yield from land, anyway, could rarely match that from the mortgages on which the hospital relied when acquiring its estates. It is true that the charity's experience demonstrated that payment of interest could be as irregular as that of rent, and it certainly did not occasion "virtually no bother to the lender".[83] But land was still notorious for its low returns, and as late as 1949, in a review of policy relating to its Herefordshire property, Guy's estate committee explained that it was only generally expected to yield a net return of 2 per cent.[84]

The governors, of course, had no option but to buy land. A will and an Act of Parliament dictated the terms of their trusteeship; but they did at least try to hunt for as many bargains as possible. They bought a number of their estates and smaller pieces of land below contemporary market prices, although this often involved an element of chance. Their gamble on the Herefordshire property, depending as it did on the life of Lady Carnarvon, did not apparently satisfy their hopes at the time as the marchioness lived longer than expected. But even with their estimated loss, the governors still got the estate at a very reasonable price. They calculated the cost of the smaller estate in possession, which they were able to enter immediately in the 1730s, at twenty-four years' purchase. When they eventually took over the whole estate on the marchioness's death in the mid-1750s, at its lowest the price was only nineteen years' purchase. If based on the hospital's own calculation of the value of the complete estate in 1760, it was certainly no more than twenty-one and a half years' purchase.[85]

The governors had already driven for a bargain in their first major purchase at Great Bardfield – an estate under siege from its creditors. For this they had given twenty-three years' purchase which was below the going rate of the time, but this was only because the property also included jointure land at ten years' purchase. In this case the governors had been fortunate in being able to enter possession immediately. For the other parts of the property they willingly gave as much as twenty-seven years' purchase, and in fact if an estate did receive a particularly favourable report, as in the case of Leigh's Priory and Beaumont, the price could fall well within the higher range of twenty-five to thirty years' purchase.

In general the governors displayed a consistent thoroughness in the buying of land. Once they had purchased a major estate, a logical pattern developed in that soon afterwards they began arranging exchanges or buying smaller holdings around the main estates to make them more compact and manageable. As with the larger purchases, the governors usually tried to buy these smaller pieces of land for a price below the going rates for the time, generally veering towards twenty-four years' purchase. There were a few exceptions. They paid twenty-six years' purchase for the 240-acre Panfield Hall farm near Great Bardfield, and unsuccessfully offered more than thirty years for some farms intermixed with their Herefordshire holdings. The governors also tidied up their property by buying some of the charges on the estates, such as various manorial payments, and tithes. In 1737 they thought it worth paying as much as twenty-eight years' purchase for the Great Bardfield tithes, and spent a long time haggling with the Duke of Chandos for four-fifths of those of Llangarron in Herefordshire. They then continued for a further eight years treating with a local landowner for the remaining fraction.

The painstaking and often tedious wrangling accompanying so many of the governors' dealings could well indicate an admirable dedication to their trust, but it also reflected the corporate character of the negotiators. They were controlled by committees and governed by standing orders. Special working parties were established by the court of committees, the main administrative body of the hospital, to report on notices for the sale of land in the areas of special interest. Almost sixty of these were received during the first thirty years, and each prospective purchase was preceded by a report of a surveyor or group of governors. As with Sutton Marsh, in some cases more than one report was submitted over a number of years. When the deliberations had reached an advanced stage, some of the governors inspected the estate usually accompanied by the clerk and a local expert or neighbouring landowner. On the Sutton Marsh inspection of 1744, for example, they were accompanied by a Mr Lens,

who resides at Langley in Norfolk and there served Mr Proctor . . . in the capacity of Steward. He was recommended to us as an honest intelligent man Skilfull in the nature and value of Lands and of some considerable Experience in Banks raised for the security of Lands exposed to inundations.[86]

Before going to the Herefordshire estate the governors also had to agree to view it with a certain price in mind; while soon after land had been bought they then made another inspection, although in the case of the Herefordshire jointure this was impossible until the death of the marchioness.

In their negotiations particular attention was given to the state of the timber, both in woodland and hedgerow, as this could provide valuable casual profits. The burden of taxes and demands from manorial payments and tithes were also considered in detail. Haggling over apparent trifles often continued for months, although some of the traditional charges on estates could be quite substantial. One instance was the annual Crown rent of £300 on Sutton Marsh, which dated back to a grant made by Charles I. Some purchases, including the major ones in all three counties, involved recourse to Acts of Parliament to clear the estate of such encumbrances as previous trusts or future jointure arrangements. In the case of Sutton Marsh a judgement in Chancery was also required.

Payment for an estate could also be protracted and complex. The arrangements for settling the Herefordshire transaction, for instance, stretched over a year. Stocks were sometimes sold to pay for land, and in some instances, such as the purchase of Great Bardfield, the money had to go directly to creditors. When the corporation bought Panfield Hall farm in 1736 the reason for the sale was to discharge a mortgage debt, and out of the purchase money of £3,515 only £753 went to the owner himself. The assignment of mortgages was also used to pay for land. The Hendon loan was passed to the Duke of Chandos as part payment of the Herefordshire property, while the governors took over an old mortgage prior to their intended purchase of Wyck Rissington in Gloucestershire. The negotiations certainly demonstrated the flexibility of the mortgage. The hospital organized such loans to some landowners before the purchase of their estates had been completed. The Duke of Chandos benefited from this arrangement, as did Richard Berney during the abortive negotiations for Pondhall in Suffolk. In general, the hospital's transactions also indicate that, although mortgages could in many ways secure a family's possession of its property, the accumulation of such debts, and the eventual need to settle them, led to an increasing amount of land being put on the market; and it was a trend which became particularly noticeable in times of agricultural difficulty.[87]

In his negotiations with the hospital, the Duke of Chandos voiced his growing impatience with the governors' slow and searching methods of inquiry. "There is so little likelyhood", he wrote, "after so much time spent, of coming to an Agreem^t with the Gentlemen of the Trust."[88] "If the Gentl. I am in treaty with are so unreasonable . . . I intend to break off any further treaty with them."[89] "I have met with so many delays & unaccountable objections, I wish I had never had anything to do with them."[90] The governors certainly became involved in some complicated tangles, but in all their negotiations they carefully balanced the benefits of an estate with its liabilities, and they squeezed as many concessions as they could out of reluctant landowners in order to acquire property at reasonable prices. In many respects the hospital represented a special case in having to buy substantial pieces of land in a high-priced market dominated by smaller purchases. Their achievement, however, can be measured not only in the way they negotiated for their property in a difficult market, but also how they then administered it. Their later management, in fact, underlines the careful approach they displayed in the buying of land.

VII

An essential consideration for the governors was always the charitable trust they served. They never showed interest in purchasing anything merely for "the sake of encreasing their property".[91] They had no concern for any status possession of land brought nor in the ostentation it could display. Neither were they distinguished as promoters of new agricultural techniques. During the eighteenth century they were known to encourage for a time the growing of turnips in Herefordshire, and their building policy in the same county drew praise from one of the writers for the Board of Agriculture.[92] But their strength as proprietors lay far more in the efficient way they used the apparatus of eighteenth-century estate management to benefit both their property and their trust. For them the holding of land was a practical, businesslike arrangement to provide a regular income for the hospital, and yet they were also clearly aware of the dangers of becoming heartless rack-renters. The charity could only prosper if its tenants did; and if an early treasurer might declare "the Hospitall is not for buying anything but what will produce a Profit",[93] another insisted that the governors were only anxious to know when "an Estate may be raised without oppressing the Tenant".[94]

The efficiency of the hospital's management can be measured in a number of ways: in its own organization centred on Southwark it can be seen in contrast to the estates it bought, in its relationship with the tenants, and by considering its expenditure on the estates and general rental policy. From the earliest years the hospital established a firm basis for the future conduct of its property. In many respects this was within a familiar framework of eighteenth-century management. Its methods of book-keeping, extensive use of agents and semi-permanent officials, preference for leases for years, and a repair policy in which the landlords committed themselves to most major undertakings – all this became part and parcel of the apparatus of efficient estate management. But the corporate nature of the institution, with its various committees and sub-committees, also promoted the establishment of a tightly controlled central organization. Although initiative by the stewards was encouraged, and the hospital often deferred to their opinion, they were always expected to work through the administration in Southwark. As the clerk informed the Ross agent in 1784, all legal contracts "cannot be determined but by a Court of Committees",[95] while some years earlier he had reminded the Essex agent:

As you act for a Corporat[n] I see not what previous instruct[ns] you can have but this Genl one That if Lady Yonge's Steward will make any proposal or suggest any terms to you wch you think worthy the Govrs attention you will communicate 'em to me to be laid before a Court of Commees. As from yourself you may suggest or propose anything to them but it must not be binding on the Govrs till you have reported some scheme of accommodatn mutually approved by you two as Agents, provided it is acceptable to your principals.[96]

The governors also ordered periodic surveys of their land, while their representatives made a number of personal visits to inspect the estates, especially the condition of the expensive sea banks in Lincolnshire. Such well-regulated administration was certainly in stark contrast to the wretched state of some of the property the hospital purchased.

Great Bardfield had long been crippled by heavy debts, while the hospital's early reports on Chandos's Herefordshire estate revealed neglected buildings, racked rents, and an impoverished tenantry. Soon after the governors entered possession of the jointure estate in 1754, they were so mortified by the wasteful behaviour of the late marchioness and her steward that a writ in Chancery was filed for the counterparts of leases and other deeds they had apparently lost, and for almost £6,000 to be paid for neglected repairs. The marchioness's leasing policy was also severely criticized. She had not only preferred to let for lives, thus profiting from windfall fines, but these leases had often fallen into the hands of absentee tenants who then "let them on a rack rent and live on the advanced rent".[97] All the real tenant wanted was to make as much as possible out of the holding, "and for this purpose he is often induced to connive at his undertenant neglecting repairs, using the land ill and purloining the Timber".[98] Similarly in Lincolnshire, before the hospital had bought Sutton Marsh the estate had so frequently changed owners and stewards that

> during these Changes the Tenants have, as it were, acted as Lords of the Land and done as they please with little or no control and were not so easily to be brought under the Regulations which are usual between other Landlords and Tenants.[99]

The charity discovered many tenants exploiting the land to such an extent that they "have ploughed without a Fallow for Seven, Eight or Ten years successively under a Pretence that the Land is strong enough to bear it".[100] Under its own administration the hospital restricted their ploughing to only two years together without a fallow, and thereafter kept a watchful eye on the behaviour of all its tenants.

In common with private proprietors the trustees were most anxious to see they paid their rents regularly and kept to the terms of their leases. In the charity's earliest years from the late 1730s to the early 1750s extensive building operations in Southwark coincided with a period of agricultural distress on the estates. The governors showed particular concern about tenants falling heavily into arrear when "our Expenses are great and return every month".[101] Stern reprimands were sent to dilatory tenants with the treasurer exhorting the agent "to be very Sharp with Peeters and Smith and all others that are in Arrear for their Rent".[102] Threats to distrain mounted during the 1740s, while a similar situation occurred in Herefordshire at the end of the period in 1801 when

> at these most extravagant dear times, it now appears that the Tenants never intend to reduce their Arrears therefore the Treasurer and Governors by an Order at the next Court of Commees will give all the Tenants notice to quit their Farms unless their arrears are immediately paid up to Michas or Lamas last according to their leases.[103]

Yet although various treasurers and clerks often sent severe warnings to what they recognized, from distant Southwark, as negligent tenants or careless agents – and, armed with clear regulations they certainly believed they had "the right on our Side: we will defend that Right to the Utmost"[104] – they usually adopted a generally pragmatic approach to their daily problems. Threats were as much sharp reminders as preludes to action. When they did distrain a slack tenant, they usually knew of another in waiting – the governors having an even greater fear of farms being left untenanted. They adopted a similarly practical approach to their leasing arrangements. As with many private landowners, the governors considered the lease a flexible type of contract. It was useful as the ultimate legal weapon against the most recalcitrant tenants,[105] although its main purpose was the avoidance of waste and ensuring good husbandry, especially in the final years of the agreement. On taking possession of the main part of the Herefordshire estate in 1754, standing rules were soon drawn up for the administration of the property. These, however, became as much guidelines as rigid policy, and local practice was often taken into consideration. For instance, the governors soon altered the clause preventing tenants ploughing any arable land in succession without a fallow, which they had intended to include in every lease, to a fallow after every two years, or even three for Ross tenants, as this "appeared to be the Custom of the Country".[106] On the advice of their agents, the governors would make special arrangements with some tenants to suit particular circumstances. In 1787, for example, a major Lincolnshire tenant was granted a licence "to plow up the three pieces of New Marsh Land . . . which have been overflowed with Salt water [.He] is to plow them two years and lay them down the third year properly".[107] Yet although the hospital might be flexible it was never lax. It usually aimed to ensure the tenants kept to their covenants and the standing rules as much as possible.

The type of lease the governors preferred was the one for a period of years, as they considered this encouraged the most improvement. They disliked both the lease for lives and tenancies at will, believing they gave the tenant too much of an upper hand. Leases for years, on the other hand, were not only considered safer for the landowner, but they could also give the tenants sufficient security to encourage investment in their farms. During the later eighteenth century, when annual agreements were

becoming increasingly popular in Lincolnshire, the hospital made considerable efforts to persuade tenants to hold longer contracts; and a list of 1788
indicates their success in making a number of leasing arrangements from
seven to twenty-one years, with eleven being the most popular.[108]

The terms of the leases usually showed the trustees content to follow
well-tried practices. Later in the century, for example, the use of rye grass
and clover was frequently mentioned in covenants,[109] but by this time they
had become part of sound, though normal, farming management. The
hospital's more direct involvement was in large undertakings such as building operations and major repairs, the consolidation of intermixed farms,
the maintenance of sea banks in Lincolnshire, and some enclosure of salt
marshes in the 1760s and from the late 1790s onwards. In fact, the charity's
expenditure on its estates was rarely insubstantial and, in some areas, very
extensive.

From 1762 to 1806 its total outgoings on all its property, including taxes
and agents' salaries, amounted to about one-third of its income. Where
the agricultural estates alone were concerned, the hospital paid an average
of 19 per cent of its gross rents and 16 per cent of its total annual produce[110]
for repairs, work on sea and river banks, fencing and allowances for
tenants. In Herefordshire and Essex this expenditure, which was mainly
on buildings, amounted to 14 and 11 per cent of its gross rents respectively.
In 1775 Nathaniel Kent estimated that after his property had been put
into good repair, a landlord should spend on average about 7 per cent of
his rental on large farms, and up to 11 per cent on the smaller.[111] In
considering repairs on buildings alone, it was the hospital's Herefordshire
estate that proved the most costly with an average of 12 per cent from
1762 to 1806. For the same period, Essex reached Nathaniel Kent's higher
percentage of 11 per cent. Admittedly, none of this ever matched the
considerable expenditure on buildings by the progressive Holkham estate
in the late eighteenth century – an average of almost 14 per cent during
1786–95 and as much as 19 per cent during 1796–1805.[112] But it compared
extremely favourably with the amount spent by some other private landowners. The Duke of Kingston, for example, could only manage 1–5 per
cent on his Nottinghamshire estates for most of the century, while on
some of the Leveson-Gower's Staffordshire property the proportion from
the 1720s to the 1780s was "always less than 10 per cent of the rentals
and usually less than 5 per cent".[113]

In Lincolnshire the hospital's expenditure on buildings and repairs was
much lower than on its other estates. For the period 1762–1806 it spent
an average of about 6 per cent of its gross rents, although some years
recorded no outlay on this item at all. Indeed, one of the property's
attractions for the governors had been its small number of buildings,
although one of their nineteenth-century agents evidently thought that
they had gone too far in their neglect, having only "six convenient Farmhouses with a small Barn and Stable for Cart horses, but scarcely any
other buildings". He also considered that "the drainage was in a wretched
state",[114] but this becomes all the more understandable when seen against
the hospital's outgoings on its sea defences. From the beginning the gover-

nors had realized that these would be a costly item. The very low price they had paid for the estate reflected this knowledge and yet, after initial repairs, they still expected the banks to be maintained for about £200 per annum. In fact, it was frequently over £1,000. From 1762 to 1806 the average cost in each decade only fell below that figure during the 1760s (£924) and 1780s (£873), and in no decade did it fall below 29 per cent of the property's gross rental. It certainly appears that the governors did saddle the charity with a more difficult estate than they had anticipated – and the rent increases in Sutton Marsh did not match this kind of expenditure. From 1763 to 1793 they rose only 23 per cent; and although they moved forward more strongly during the French war period – 36.5 per cent from 1793 to 1806 – this increase also reflected the enclosure of salt marshes from the later 1790s onwards. On the other hand, the governors' efforts in securing the long sea defences did bring high praise from a surveyor in 1788. He saw it as "a mere private work and such as our Law of Sewers take no Notice of", and called it "a kind of second security to the County".[115] The hospital's outlay on its property could certainly not be described as moderate, and in some areas it was almost enlightened.

But another test of its management was its policy relating to agricultural rents on which it so depended for the major source of its income. While it clearly realized that it was unwise to "screw everything up as far as it will bear"[116] this did not mean the governors "who loved to know the value of their Estates"[117] were not anxious to see their farms reflecting their true worth. In 1796 the clerk wrote that rents "ought to be raised in proportion to the encreased Expences of the Hospital which is at least 20 PC^t more than of a few years since".[118] Four years previously he had reported that the governors now preferred not to let their Lincolnshire farms for more than seven years in future "as they consider all their lands much increased and still increasing in value".[119] Yet in comparison with those of some private landowners during the later eighteenth century, the hospital rent increases were generally modest. While the Duke of Kingston's rose 48 per cent from 1750 to 1790, and those of Lord Monson went up an extra 44.5 per cent over a similar period, the hospital rents from their three estates increased only about 30 per cent from 1762 to 1793. They rose to just over 50 per cent in the period 1762–1806, but this was partly during the French wars when rents of other estates pushed forward even more vigorously. Arthur Young estimated that in the twenty-five years from 1780 "the rise in rent has amounted to 105 per cent",[120] although the hospital's increase during the same period was just over 27 per cent. The estates themselves, however, would certainly benefit from such moderate rises as the tenants thereby had the means to invest in their farms which the hospital's preference for leases for years also encouraged. Nor did the charity itself noticeably suffer from the trustees' policy. Admittedly, it did experience the occasional financial crisis, but this was more the result of its physical expansion in Southwark than the way it managed its estates.

For much of the eighteenth century the hospital carried out a vigorous building programme on its own premises, often in conjunction with import-

ant developments on the medical side. Teaching started at Guy's during
the 1760s, and in 1769 the union with St Thomas's began for training
medical students. The following year the governors built the hospital's
first lecture theatre, and this coincided with the appointment of Dr Saun-
ders who lectured three times a week on chemistry and medicine. In 1805
the governors proposed to build some detached fever wards and proper
accommodation for convalescent patients "and for various cases of such
complicated missery [*sic*] to whom under present regulations no public
charity can afford relief".[121] During the 1780s the condition of the hospital
drew praise from the influential reformer, John Howard. He admired the
"clean and fresh" new wards, the unadulterated drugs, and the "excellent
baths, in clean neat rooms". He also commended the governors' determination to provide patients with a free circulation of air in "a very close
part of the town and surrounded with buildings".[122]

VIII

In both their administration of the charity and the management of the
estates the governors had to steer a course between consideration for the
hospital and fairness to their property. Aspects of their policy relating to
both can certainly be criticized. Despite Howard's praise of the new
additions, the condition of some of the older wards was condemned by
him and other contemporaries, while there was also no increase in the
number of resident patients during this period. In their search for bargains
the governors also saddled the hospital with some difficult property – from
the clay lands in Herefordshire's northern division to the defence of part
of the Lincolnshire coastline. The suspicion remains, especially in the
purchase of Sutton Marsh, that immediate benefits had prevailed too much
over the clear indications of future problems. The actual nature of the
corporation itself also gave it more than a physical remoteness from its
property. There was little personal rapport with the tenants, while the
claim that "we are never forward to raise our rents"[123] was as much the
result of administrative rigidity as any generosity of spirit. As treasurer
Benjamin Avery pointed out, public bodies could not "give their orders,
review, alter, and amend them with so much ease, and in so little time as
particular persons can do".[124]

Yet in other respects its very structure, based on a well defined administration, brought the hospital, as a later report declared, "in line with the
best managed institutions of the day".[125] It enabled it to pursue a policy
of management which never abused the charity and yet generally benefited
its agricultural estates. While continuing to develop the hospital in Southwark, it kept a watchful eye on its tenants and always preserved close
contacts with the agents. Its heavy outgoings ensured the proper upkeep
of the estates, while its rental policy and leasing covenants gave tenants
both security of tenure and incentive to invest in their holdings. The
governors had been obliged to search for property in a difficult market
dominated by small purchases. This provides one explanation of the type

of land they bought, especially as they were initially determined to purchase complete estates if possible. This at least enabled them to acquire land with some tradition of management on which they could build and work effectively within a familiar administrative framework. In their quest for property, and in the management of the estates they eventually bought, the patient persistence of the governors, whose only privilege in the hospital they served was the doubtful one of recommending in turn a lunatic for admission, displayed a heartening devotion to a trust founded by a man who had happened "to fall into that delirious ambition of erecting a palace for beggars"[126] and who left firm instructions that the income of his urban charity should closely depend on the fortunes of agriculture.

Appendix I   Income of Guy's Hospital, 1726–57

Date (NS) (ending March)	Rents and profits	Interest on stocks, etc.	Interest on mortgages	Legacies	Others	Total	Loss: Amount spent beyond income
			expressed as % of income				
1726		£8,466 (64.6%)	£4,641 (35.4%)			£13,107	
1727	£198 (2.3%)	£6,886 (79.4%)	£1,576* (18.2%)		£14 (0.1%)	£8,673	
		*only ½ year's interest on Blackett mortgage received					
1728	£170 (1.4%)	£5,630 (45.6%)	£6,541* (53.0%)			£12,341	
		*½ years' interest on Blackett mortgage received					
1729	£367* (3.5%)	£4,731 (45.9%)	£5,215 (50.6%)			£10,313	
		*1st rent (1 year) from Elizabeth Lumley's jointure estate					
1730	£170 (2.2%)	£2,000 (26.0%)	£5,513 (71.8%)			£7,683	
1731	£1,983* (20.3%)	£2,360 (24.1%)	£5,385 (55.1%)	£50 (0.5%)		£9,778	
		*1st rent (three years) from Beaumont estate received					
1732	£786* (8.4%)	£1,296 (13.8%)	£7,288 (77.8%)			£9,370	
		*1st rent from Thaxted received					
1733	£749 (11.5%)	£866 (13.3%)	£4,788 (73.4%)		£120 (1.8%)	£6,523	£1,095 (16.8%)
1734	£7,136* (61.7%)	£869 (7.5%)	£3,465 (29.9%)	£100 (0.9%)		£11,570	
	*1st rent from Hereford estate in possession (1 year) and from Llangarren tithes 1st rent from Lumley's Great Bardfield estate (4½ years) received						
1735	£4,799 (58.0%)	£3 (0.1%)	£3,468 (41.9%)			£8,270	£918 (11.1%)
1736	£2,923 (45.7%)		£3,470 (54.3%)			£6,393	£397 (6.2%)
1737	£4,284* (41.2%)	£2,439 (23.5%)	£3,470 (33.4%)		£200 (1.9%)	£10,393	
		*Panfield Hall (Essex) purchased (February 1737)					
1738	£5,015 (46.0%)	£773 (7.1%)	£3,618 (33.2%)	£1,500 (13.7%)		£10,906	

Appendix I   (Continued)

Date (NS) (ending March)	Rents and profits	Interest on stocks etc.	Interest on mortgages	Legacies	Others	Total	Loss: Amount spent beyond income
			expressed as % of income				
1739	£4,470 (59.3%)	£682 (9.0%)	£2,327* (31.7%)			£7,479	£6,562 (87.0%)
			*only ½ year's interest of Blackett mortgage received				
1740	£4,151 (42.4%)	£642 (6.5%)	£5,006* (51.1%)			£9,799	£1,524 (15.5%)
			*1½ years' interest of Blackett mortgage received				
1741	£4,325 (54.5%)	£522 (6.6%)	£3,088 (38.9%)			£7,935	£3,584 (45.2%)
1742	£4,378 (69.7%)	£360 (5.7%)	£1,548* (24.6%)			£6,286	£3,672 (58.4%)
			*½ year's interest of Blackett mortgage received				
1743	£4,463 (57.2%)	£260 (3.3%)	£3,082* (39.5%)			£7,805	£759 (9.7%)
			*1½ year's interest of Blackett mortgage (no extra ½ year)				
1744	£4,279 (56.2%)	£240 (3.2%)	£3,092 (40.6%)			£7,611	£265 (3.5%)
1745	£4,088 (55.3%)	£220 (3.0%)	£3,080 (41.7%)			£7,388	
1746	£4,328 (51.7%)	£958 (11.5%)	£3,080 (36.8%)			£8,366	
1747	£4,024 (56.6%)		£3,080 (43.4%)			£7,104	£632 (8.9%)
1748	£7,219* (83.0%)		£1,480 (17.0%)			£8,699	£568 (6.5%)
*1st rent (1 year) from Lincolnshire received							
1749	£7,007 (78.0%)		£1,973 (22.0%)			£8,980	£423 (4.7%)
1750	£6,932 (64.2%)	£598 (5.6%)	£2,993 (27.7%)	£268 (2.5%)		£10,791	
1751	£7,415 (81.3%)	£1,710 (18.7%)	– *			£9,125	
			*Blackett mortgage repaid				
1752	£6,729 (79.2%)	£1,666 (19.6%)		£100 (1.2%)		£8,495	
1753	£7,686 (86.0%)	£1,251 (14.0%)				£8,937	£291 (3.2%)
1754	£8,688* (85.6%)	£1,440 (14.2%)		£25 (0.2%)		£10,153	
		*1st rent (6 months) received from Leigh's Priory, Essex					
1755	£8,905 (99.7%)			£25 (0.3%)		£8,930	
1756	£12,630* (99.8%)	£21 (0.2%)				£12,651	
*Received rent (1 year and 16 days) from *all* the Herefordshire estate, including Lady Caernarvon's jointure							
1757	£15,528 (99.4%)	£95 (0.6%)				£15,623	

Source: Guy's Hospital records, Greater London Record Office: H9/GY/D1/1 Ledger A, 1724–1738/9; H9/GY/D1/2/1 Ledger B, 1738/9–1759.

Notes

1   J. Duncumb, *A General View of the Agriculture of the County of Hereford* (London, 1805), p. 23.
2   G. Shaw-Lefevre, *Agrarian Tenures* (London, 1893), pp. 276–7.
3   D. Owen, *English Philanthropy, 1660–1960* (Cambridge Mass., 1964), p. 73.
4   Guy's Hospital records (hereafter cited as GH), Greater London Record Office (RO), H9/GY/E26/4. Copy of Thomas Matthews's Letter to the Duke of Chandos [1729]. I should like to thank the governors of Guy's Hospital for permission to use their archive material.
5   For this survey 1756 has been taken as the final date for the first period of the hospital purchases. In this year the charity began receiving rents from the Herefordshire jointure estate.
6   Dated 24 September 1724.
7   C. Clay, "Landlords and estate management in England", in J. Thirsk (ed.), *The Agrarian History of England and Wales*, Vol. 5, Pt 2 (Cambridge, 1985), pp. 182–4, 198.
8   C. Clay, "The price of freehold land in the later seventeenth and eighteenth centuries", *Economic History Review*, 2nd ser. (1974), pp. 182–5. One year's purchase was the annual rack rent value of the land.
9   D. Macpherson, *Annals of Commerce*, vol. 3 (London, 1805), p. 147.
10   Clay, "Freehold land", p. 186.
11   ibid., pp. 186–7.
12   [A. de Moivre] *The Value of Church and College Leases Considered* (London, 1731 edn), p. 67.
13   GH, Greater London RO, H9/GY/E26/1–5. *The Duke of Chandos' Answers* (1729).
14   C. Clay, "Property settlements, financial provision for the family, and sale of land by the greater landowners", *Journal of British Studies*, 21 (1981), p. 22–3.
15   Clay, "Landlords and estate management", p. 173.
16   At this time even a number of the greatest landowners could not necessarily afford large holdings out of their agricultural incomes alone. When they did buy large pieces of property, the transaction was often balanced by the simultaneous sale of more distant parts of their estates. This was usually for purposes of consolidation. See Clay, "Landlords and estate management", p. 187 and 196–8.
17   B. A. Holderness, "The English land market in the eighteenth century: the case of Lincolnshire", *Economic History Review*, 2nd ser., vol. 27 (1974), pp. 559, 569.
18   Clay, "Landlords and estate management", pp. 190, 192.
19   Guy's Hospital, 11 Geo. I, c. 12, The Act of Incorporation, 1725, preamble (1944 edn), p. 4. A number of copies of the will and Act

of Incorporation are also in GH, Greater London RO, H9/GY/ A48/1 to A50/2.

20 G. E. Mingay, *English Landed Society in the Eighteenth Century* (London, 1964), p. 37.

21 GH, Greater London RO, H9/GY/A102/1. Avery to Fortune, 17 Nov. 1744, *Treasurers' Letter Books* (hereafter cited as *TLB*), 1737/ 8–73, p. 168.

22 W. Hazlitt, *Table Talk* (London, 1903 World's Classics edn), p. 339.

23 Clay, "Property settlements", p. 30. For other possible remedies see p. 34.

24 ibid., p. 34.

25 L. S. Pressnell, "The rate of interest in the eighteenth century", in L. S. Pressnell (ed.), *Studies in the Industrial Revolution* (London, 1960), p. 187.

26 GH, Greater London RO, H9/GY/A3/1/1. 5 May 1725, *Minutes of the Court of Committees* (hereafter cited as *MCC*), *1725–33*, p. 9.

27 Stowe Coll., ST57. Chandos to Watts, 2 Aug. 1729, *Chandos Letter Books* (hereafter cited as *CL*), Vol. 33, p. 217. All references to ST57 are reproduced by permission of the Huntington Library, San Marino, California.

28 GH, Greater London RO, H9/GY/A3/1/1, 14 Feb.–6 Dec. 1729, *MCC* 1725–33, pp. 173 and 189.

29 GH, Greater London RO, H9/GY/D1/1 *Ledger A*, 1724–38, and H9/GY/D1/2/1 *Ledger B*, 1738/9–59 for information on Guy's Hospital's income 1726–1757.

30 Clay, "Landlords and estate management", p. 183.

31 GH, Greater London RO, H9/GY/A102/1. Avery to Richmond, [?] Nov. 1745, *TLB* 1737/8–73, p. 185.

32 GH, Greater London RO, H9/GY/A3/1/1, 21 July 1726, *MCC* 1725–33, p. 30.

33 Quoted H. C. Cameron *Mr Guy's Hospital 1726–1948* (London, 1954), p. 76.

34 GH, Greater London RO, H9/GY/A3/5/1. 7 May 1802, *MCC* 1797–1821, p. 43.

35 ibid.

36 K. H. Burley, "The economic development of Essex in the later seventeenth and early eighteenth centuries" (unpublished PhD thesis, University of London, 1957) p. 75.

37 GH, Greater London RO, H9/GY/E30/1–2: *Report . . . of the Journey of Mr Joshua Gee and the Clerk to the Beaumont Estate* (1728).

38 Essex RO, D/DGh//14: *A Particular & Valuation of an Estate called Leeze Priory* (1753).

39 GH, Greater London RO, H9/GY/E26/4: *Copy of Thomas Matthews' Letter to the Duke of Chandos*.

40 Burley, "Economic development of Essex", p. 69.

41 Essex RO, D/DGh/L3: *A Particular of the Several Estates of Sir James Lumley* (1732).

42 Essex RO, D/DGh/E2. Report of Matthew and Neville, *A Particular of the Estate of Sir James Lumley.*

43 Essex RO, D/DGh/E2: untitled and incomplete MSS listing the Lumley debts. See also C. Fell Smith, "Bardfield Lodge and the Lumleys", *Essex Review*, vol. 33, no. 9 (1906), p. 17.

44 L. Bonfield, *Marriage Settlements, 1601–1740* (Cambridge, 1983), pp. 55–6.

45 Essex RO, D/DGh/E2: no title; begins "9th Nov. 1709 Sr Martin Lumley by Will Devised".

46 Essex RO, D/DGh/E3: *Abstract Title of Blagdon Farm* (1729), p. 3.

47 ibid., p. 3.

48 Essex RO, D/DGh/E2: *Computation of the Value of Sir James Lumley's Estate.*

49 GH, Greater London RO, H9/GY/A3/1/1. 21 July 1727, *MCC* 1725–33, p. 109.

50 Essex RO, D/DGh/E2: unnamed correspondent to Thomas Matthews, 21 March 1729.

51 GH, Greater London RO, H9/GY/A3/1/1. 23 Dec. 1730, *MCC* 1725–33, p. 209.

52 Stowe Coll., ST57: Chandos to Halsey, 10 June 1729, *CL* Vol. 33, p. 138.

53 J. Thirsk, "The south-west Midlands", in J. Thirsk (ed.), *The Agrarian History of England and Wales*, Vol. 5, *1640–1750*, Pt 2 (Cambridge, 1984), pp. 176–7.

54 Stowe Coll., ST57; Chandos to Halsey, op. cit.

55 C. H. Collins Baker and M. I. Baker, *The Life and Circumstances of James Brydges, First Duke of Chandos* (1949), p. xi.

56 ibid., p. 337.

57 Stowe Coll., ST57; Chandos to Montgomery, 9 Jan 1729/30, *CL* Vol. 34, p. 119.

58 GH, Greater London RO, H9/GY/E26/4: *Thomas Matthews . . . further observations.*

59 GH, Greater London RO, H9/GY/E26/2: *Copy of Thomas Matthews' Letter*, 8 Dec. 1729 [fourth observation].

60 Stowe Coll., ST57. Chandos to Davies, 1 Jan. 1730, *CL*, Vol. 34, p. 101.

61 ibid., p. 102.

62 Stowe Coll., ST57. Chandos to Watts, 2 Aug. 1729, *CL*, Vol. 33, p. 217.

63 GH, Greater London RO, H9/GY/A3/1/1. 30 April 1730, *MCC* 1725–33, p. 194.

64 Stowe Coll., ST57. Chandos to Gibson, 17 March 1730, *CL*, Vol. 34, p. 221.

65 Stowe Coll., ST57. Chandos to Watts, 4 June 1730, *CL*, Vol. 35, p. 47.

66 ibid.

67 GH, Greater London RO, H9/GY/D5/2: *Journal, 1753–63*, p. 85.

68   GH, Greater London RO, H9/GY/D18/1/1: *Abstract of Accounts, 1760–1870*. The year 1760 is being referred to here.
69   GH, Greater London RO, H9/GY/A8/1: *Report of the Sub-committee appointed to view Sutton Marsh Estate*, p. 8.
70   D. Defoe, *A Tour through the Whole Island of Great Britain*, first published 1724–6 (1928 edn), Vol. 1, p. 74.
71   GH, Greater London RO, H9/GY/A8/1: *Report of Subcommitee . . . Sutton Marsh*, p. 10.
72   ibid.
73   ibid.
74   ibid.
75   ibid., p. 5.
76   GH, Greater London RO, H9/GY/D18/1/1: *Abstract of Accounts, 1760–1870*. See below p. 72.
77   GH, Greater London RO, H9/GY/A3/1/1. 30 July 1731, *MCC 1725–33*, p. 222.
78   GH, Lincolnshire RO, Bundle 280: *A Short History of Sutton Marsh Estate collected from ye Title Deeds*. The Guy's Hospital records in the Lincolnshire RO are still in the process of being catalogued and therefore, at present, the old bundle numbers are still in use.
79   ibid.
80   GH, Lincolnshire RO, Bundle 335: *Copy of Mr Metcalf's Case with ye Atty Genls. Opinion*.
81   Holderness, "The English land market", p. 576.
82   Spring tides were to cause considerable damage in the years 1809, 1860 and 1883.
83   F. M. L. Thompson, "Landownership and economic growth in the eighteenth century", in E. L. Jones and S. J. Woolf (eds), *Agrarian Change and Economic Development* (London, 1969), p. 55.
84   Guy's Hospital. April 1949: *Minutes of the Estates Committee, 1948–1952*, p. 26.
85   GH, Greater London RO, H9/GY/D5/2: *Journal, 1753–63*, p. 85, and H9/GY/D18/1/1: Abstract of Accounts.
86   GH, Greater London RO, H9/GY/A8/1. *Report of the Sub-committee . . . Sutton Marsh*, p. 1.
87   Clay, "Landlords and estate management", p. 171.
88   Stowe Coll., ST57. Chandos to Jones, 4 July 1729, *CL*, Vol. 33, p. 175.
89   Stowe Coll., ST57. Chandos to Watkins, 8 Jan 1730, *CL*, Vol. 34, p. 118.
90   Stowe Coll., ST57. Chandos to Davies, 21 July 1730, *CL*, Vol. 35, p. 139.
91   GH, Greater London RO, H9/GY/A105/2/1: Harrison to Woodhouse, 21 June 1781, *Letter Book of the Clerk (LBC)*, 1778–1807, p. 53.
92   J. Clark, *General View of the Agriculture of the County of Hereford* (London, 1794), pp. 58–9n.

93   GH, Greater London RO, H9/GY/A102/1. Hollister to Fortune, 11 April 1738, *TLB* 1737/8–73, p. 13.
94   GH, Greater London RO, H9/GY/A102/1. Avery to Yeldham, 13 Nov. 1756, *TLB* 1737/8–73, p. 345.
95   GH, Greater London RO, H9/GY/A105/2/1. Harrison to Keyse, 6 Jan. 1784, *LBC* 1778–1807, p.108.
96   GH, Greater London RO, H9/GY/A105/1/1. Neale to Yeldham, 24 Sept. 1762, *LBC* 1761–78, p. 37.
97   Hereford RO, C99/III/235. *Sub-committee Report of the View of Herefordshire Estates* [1754] p. 4.
98   ibid.
99   GH, Greater London RO, H9/GY/A4/1. 22 Oct. 1754, *MCC* (duplicate) 1725–63, p. 443.
100 ibid., p. 444.
101 GH, Greater London RO, H9/GY/A102/1. Avery to Scribo, 17 May 1750, *TLB* 1737/8–73, p. 255.
102 GH, Greater London RO, H9/GY/A102/1. Hollister to Yeldham, 9 Sept. 1738, *TLB* 1737/8–73, p. 27.
103 GH, Greater London RO, H9/GY/A105/2/1. Richardson to Woodhouse, 27 Jan. 1801, *LBC* 1778–1807, p. 257.
104 GH, Greater London RO, H9/GY/A102/1. Hollister to Yeldham, 14 July 1739, *TLB* 1737/8–73, p. 50.
105 Clay, "Landords and estate management", p. 228.
106 GH, Greater London RO, H9/GY/A4/1. 24 Oct. 1755, *MCC* (duplicate) 1725–63, pp. 465–6.
107 GH, Greater London RO, H9/GY/A105/2/1. Harrison to Russell, 28 March 1787, *LBC* 1778–1807, p. 158.
108 GH, Lincolnshire RO, Bundle 293: *Abstract of Leases of Sutton Marsh Estate*, 1788.
109 Essex RO, D/DGh/E15/3 [Abstract of Leases].
110 "Annual produce" includes the proceeds of timber sales which were considerable on the Herefordshire estate during the 1780s and war years.
111 Clay, "Landlords and estate management", p. 247.
112 R. A. C. Parker, *Coke of Norfolk* (1975), p. 94.
113 J. R. Wordie, *Estate Management in Eighteenth Century England* (1982), p. 85. Also, G. E. Mingay, *English Landed Society in the Eighteenth Century* (1963), p. 178 [for Kingston].
114 GH, Lincolnshire RO, Bundle 284: [William Skelton] *A Report of the condition and management of the several Farms in the County of Lincoln, the property of the President and Governors of Guy's Hospital* (1873), p. 27.
115 GH, Lincolnshire RO, Bundle 335: *The Report and Opinion of James Creasey on the Plan now proposed for inclosing the common marsh* [etc.] 12 April 1788.
116 GH, Greater London RO, H9/GY/A102/1. Avery to Yeldham, 13 Nov. 1756, *TLB* 1737/8–73, p. 345.
117 ibid.

118   GH, Greater London RO, H9/GY/A105/2/1. Richardson to Wood-house, 10 Oct. 1796, *LBC* 1778–1807, p. 231.
119   GH, Greater London RO, H9/GY/A105/2/1. Harrison to Russell, 23 April 1792, *LBC* 1778–1807, p. 209.
120   A Young, "An enquiry into the progressive value of money in England", *Annals of Agriculture*, vol. 46, no. 270 (London, 1812), p. 104.
121   GH, Greater London RO, H9/GY/A3/5/1. 6 March 1805, *MCC* 1797–1821, p. 64.
122   J. Howard, *An Account of the Principal Lazarettos in Europe* [etc.] (London, 1791), pp. 135–6.
123   GH, Greater London RO, H9/GY/A102/1. Avery to Yeldham, 13 Nov. 1756, *TLB* 1737/8–73, p. 345.
124   GH, Greater London RO, H9/GY/A102/1. Avery to Fortune, 18 Nov. 1755, *TLB* 1737/8–73, p. 320.
125   Guy's Hospital: Annual Report for 1929, p. 23 in *Annual Reports, 1927–30*.
126   House of Commons, *Report from the Select Committee on Mortmain* (24 July 1844) p. 16. Also G. Jones, *History of the Law of Charity, 1532–1827* (Cambridge, 1969), p. 109n.

4 A progressive landlord: the third Earl Spencer, 1782–1845

E. A. WASSON

During the late eighteenth and early nineteenth centuries, the role of landowners in the economic, social and political life of the nation was pre-eminent, and the landed elite enjoyed a great era of aristocratic dominion. A number of excellent monographs have appeared in recent years dealing with the management of landed estates at this time, but these studies have tended to focus upon the estates themselves, and on the agents entrusted with their administration. The landlords who owned and managed them do not usually receive such a comparatively thorough examination. This chapter is, therefore, devoted to the personal study of just one individual member of that landowning class, the third Earl Spencer, born in 1782.

John Charles Spencer has been numbered among that lordly generation which consciously attempted to project aristocratic leadership at the national level into an increasingly hostile and uncongenial environment.[1] He was unquestionably one of a small group of Whig magnates whose political leadership did much to determine the direction of reform in many areas of the society of his time. He also stood second only to Coke of Norfolk as the most important aristocratic proponent of agricultural progress during the first half of the nineteenth century, and was hailed by his contemporaries as "the great patron of English agriculture".[2] He headed the two most prominent farming organizations of his time, the Smithfield Club and the Royal Agricultural Society.

It is not, however, as an architect of the Great Reform Act or the new Poor Law, nor as the prominent advocate of agricultural innovation, that this study introduces Lord Spencer. Rather, it deals with the man said by contemporaries of diverse social and political standing to epitomize the English country gentleman of his era. Indeed, on occasion, he claimed to speak for this group during his years in the House of Commons. Historians have called him the most typical representative of the Whig aristocracy, and cited him as a notable example of an agricultural improver on his own estates.[3]

Like his ancestors, Spencer held sway in the rural world surrounding his own lands. Unlike his predecessors, however, he was prepared to pay a high price to maintain that supremacy. The standards of his class were changing to meet the challenges of an increasingly industrial and more politically sophisticated society. Duty, religion and progressive political and social attitudes made him work harder and longer at the business of being a landed magnate than previous Spencers would have considered seemly or necessary. He was not quite a professional at any of the jobs he undertook, but he came close to being one in several different fields at once, unlike most of his middle-class contemporaries. How numerous men such as Spencer were it is hard to say, but they were numerous enough to keep power in the localities and at the centre for the better part of the nineteenth century.

I

The Spencers have been a prominent family in the Midlands for half a millennium. First recorded as landowners in 1330, they had established themselves as sheep farmers in Warwickshire and Northamptonshire by the end of the fifteenth century. The extraordinary entrepreneurial prowess of the family gained them great wealth under the Tudors. They were perhaps the only dynasty among the English nobility to rise solely through agricultural enterprise.[4] Knighthoods, a barony, and an earldom followed, earned by shrewd management and careful saving. A dukedom (Marlborough) was acquired by marriage, creating sufficient resources to establish two lines: the senior branch at Blenheim and the junior remaining at Althorp Park. The latter family was subsequently raised to an earldom in its own right. A number of Spencers achieved eminence as politicians over the succeeding centuries, most notably Sir Winston of the senior line. Now the Crown itself has become the family heirloom of the Althorp branch.

The Spencers of Althorp, though overshadowed until recently by the grandeur of their cousins' palace and ducal coronet, nevertheless enjoyed a great inheritance and held intact the carefully assembled sheepwalks of their forebears that lay in huge concentrated blocks near their principal seat. Only a few dozen families owned a significantly larger acreage in England, and fewer still possessed land better positioned in terms of fertility and proximity to markets.[5] The Spencers were not among the supernovas of wealth such as the Russells and Percys. However, their rich property in the Midland shires compared favourably to the English acreage of even the leviathans such as the Leveson-Gowers, Cavendishes or Fitzwilliams.

The third Earl Spencer took little direct part in the management of the estate until his father's death in 1834, when the son was 52. However, he had come into possession of a substantial property in Nottinghamshire upon his marriage in 1814 to an heiress, Esther Acklom of Wiseton. He took personal control of the home farm immediately, and also became the tenant of a farm belonging to his father at Chapel Brampton near Althorp. The latter holding was quite a large one, with an annual rental of over £2,000 in 1834. It was managed by a bailiff, John Elliot, under the general supervision of Spencer's agent, John Beasley, who lived in the farm house there. Beasley was one of the best known agents of his day and a notable breeder of shorthorns and Leicester sheep. His reputation attracted students who came to learn the business of estate management from him, and he was author of a book on the subject. Chapel Brampton consistently produced good profits and won praise from experts for advanced management.[6] There is insufficient evidence available, however, to tell how closely the Earl was involved in the farm's management. Although he visited it on a regular basis and because the Northampton-shire Agricultural Society held its annual show there from 1819 onwards, we know that Spencer must have been proud of its condition, but he was more personally associated with the Wiseton farm.

The latter estate was worth about £4,000 a year in rentals. At first Spencer was preoccupied with restoring the manor house and estate build-ings, which had been much neglected during a long period of absenteeism. New gardens, barns, cottages and stables were built. Within a decade he had raised the rental by nearly 25 per cent.[7] John Hall, originally a footman of the household, was continued as bailiff from the previous administration. He acted as agent for the whole estate and also assisted Spencer in the management of the home farm. An expert in animal husbandry, he proved a useful and able subordinate.

From the start, however, Spencer was in personal charge of the Wiseton operations, although he did not begin to study agriculture scientifically until after his wife's death in 1818. This shock altered the direction of his whole life. He gave up foxhunting, until then his passion, as a penance, and turned to farming as his principal occupation away from the House of Commons. His interest in breeding had been whetted by experiments with foxhounds made while he was Master of the Pytchley Hunt. He found that improving stock was the only project that aroused him from profound mourning and allowed him to "build castles in the air". He was fortunate in turning his attention to cattle breeding at a moment when the most important early herd of shorthorns developed by the Colling brothers was put up for sale. Spencer "bid very dashingly" at the auction and later purchased several more of the Collings' animals.[8] He soon made the acquaintance of the two leading breeders of his generation, John Booth and Thomas Bates, and picked their brains for technical information and advice.

Spencer has been called a noble minor star beside men like Bakewell and the Collings in the development of modern cattle breeds. Undoubtedly his role as a popularizer and propagandist was more important than the work he did at Wiseton, but his operations there were of considerable significance. The careful comparisons he conducted between the qualities of various breeds were well known. His work with shorthorns was highly successful, and half a century after his death farmers were still going to Wiseton bloodstock to start new strains. One breeder wrote: "Of all the herds of shorthorns that have been bred with care, none ever did more good in the improvement of cattle for farmers' use than the Wiseton herd."[9]

Whenever Spencer was away, weekly reports were sent to him about the progress of the herd with special bulletins about Sparkles, Spot and other favourite bulls, whose pedigrees he worked out to the nth degree.

He kept the herd book himself, decided which breeders would have use of his bulls and set the fees.[10] His sales became extremely popular, and he was sought after as a judge both of large shows and private competitions. He was not the sort of man who confined himself to the committee room and speaker's platform, only occasionally staggering around the barns on a wet day. His expertise was practical and renowned, and the breeding and feeding of animals seemed to dominate many of his waking hours. "I am afraid that my head is much fuller of shorthorned cattle, sheep, and turnips than Ireland just now", was a typical apology to a political correspondent. That he was "up to his ears in shorthorned cattle, monsters of sheep, and wallowing hogs" was the plaintive refrain in family letters.[11] In spite of Spencer's Evangelical piety, it was necessary for a clerical brother to admonish him for riding around his farm on the Sabbath. His obsessive interest in every detail of stock management was the despair of Cabinet colleagues like Lord John Russell who found being dragged out to the sheds to see fattening oxen, "which are not to me very instructive or entertaining", a crashing bore, while his friends who were agents or farmers like John Grey of Dilston were delighted to rise after dinner for "just another look" at more sheep.[12]

Although Spencer was no more than an amateur scientist, he had a strong interest in agricultural chemistry and developed a close personal friendship with a leading academic in the field. He conducted breeding experiments using rabbits in the old kennels at Althorp Park, used an innovative drainage engine at Wiseton to convert boggy acres to grazing meadows, routinely made decisions on the medical treatment of his cattle, and published the results of a variety of experiments he conducted on nutrition and other topics in leading agricultural journals.[13]

It has been argued that model farms run by aristocrats were "expensive, trivial, and ultimately ephemeral".[14] According to this view they were often sponsored out of a sense of duty to set an example for tenants or simply served as a fashionable amusement to occupy idle hours. It is said that farmers regarded them as useless because they were not profitable and the economic structure underpinning a model farm differed greatly from the realities of everyday farming. This was certainly the case, for example, with the Woburn Abbey home farm, even though the seventh Duke of Bedford was seriously interested in agricultural improvement. It has also been shown that the Holkham home farm was an uneconomic and extravagant showpiece.[15]

Wiseton was never a consistently profitable enterprise. Indeed, there were frequent losses, which had to be absorbed by estate income. Spencer did not represent his operation as a typical farm, however, or run it in the same manner as Chapel Brampton. He once actually called Wiseton "an expensive amusement", but this was characteristic of his self-deprecating nature.[16] In fact he was running an agricultural research station, funded out of a private endowment. Moreover, had he chosen to operate in Northamptonshire, where he once confessed he had no bad land, instead of in Nottinghamshire where he had no rich pastures, his profits would have been greater. At Wiseton he had to purchase most of the fodder for the animals in order to keep his herd in good condition. Loyalty to his wife's memory which made him decide to live in her old home made it necessary to breed cattle in adverse conditions. He did all he could to encourage an efficient and cost-conscious administration, paying two-thirds of all profits as well as a salary to his bailiff for example, and there were some good years. As a long-term investment, Wiseton yielded richly. The already reduced herd sold after his death for over 10,000 guineas,[17] and against considerable odds Spencer achieved national fame as a breeder and earned the respect of his fellow farmers, who treated him in professional matters as an equal. Spencer's interest in his farm was not so much in setting an example as in the challenge of breeding useful and profitable animals. Furthermore, like other progressive aristocrats of his era, Spencer was willing to master even the most detailed aspects of his business operations.[18]

II

Spencer's devotion to the classic triad of landlord occupations – sport, local philanthropy and politics – was also almost professional in its intensity. The passion for foxhunting, for example, was deeply planted in his family. Spencer went out with the Pytchley, of which his father was master, while still little more than an infant. He took control of the hunt, one of the two most prominent packs in England, at the age of 26. His field, which included great magnates, foreign princes, statesmen twice his age, and local farmers who settled arguments with horsewhips, was no easy group to satisfy, and the management of it, he later recalled, "taught him more of human nature than he had learnt in any other way".[19]

The mastership of such a pack was a position of enormous prestige both in the rural community and on a national level. Lord Willoughby de Broke placed himself as MFH the next most important figure in the county after the Lord Lieutenant.[20] The sport brought virtually the entire countryside above the station of labourer together in a surprisingly homogenous manner and was a prime position for the display of aristocratic leadership. The days in the field and the other sporting and social occasions associated with hunting helped to forge cohesiveness within the rural community.

Spencer's position was further enhanced by the brilliance of his leadership in the field. "No one", confessed a keen sportsman but inveterate political opponent, "knew more of hunting than he did ". He brought the Pytchley, which during the later years of his mastership was known simply as "Lord Althorp's Hounds", to "the zenith of its glory". Aspirant masters came to learn the management of hounds under his tuition. It was during these years that he began his work as a breeder, striving to evolve lighter-boned, quicker animals for the chase.[21]

Two aspects of Spencer's sporting career are worth special notice. First was the intense professionalism he brought to the job. During the years immediately after he took over the mastership, he devoted himself to virtually nothing else. Many enthusiastic aristocratic hunters would have balked at living in a simple cottage in the remote countryside for months on end, missing the London Season, to accustom themselves to a pack and train it to perfection.[22] Everything about Spencer's management smacked of his businesslike efficiency. Secondly, he broke with tradition by demanding subscriptions from hunt members. The costs of great aristocratic hunts were at this time still regularly borne by the magnates alone, and such patronage was considered one of the best ways to win popularity and political influence. Spencer, however, was prepared to make those who enjoyed the benefits of his leadership bear a portion of the costs. At first the response to this innovation was extremely negative. The Duke of Bedford, whose son paid the entire cost of the Russell pack, shuddered at the "abuse which is so unsparingly bestowed on Lord Althorp [Spencer's courtesy title] in the estimation of the world" for charging fees.[23] The quality of the sport was so high, however, that soon few protests were heard, although Althorp had abandoned an important source of political and social prestige.

Service to local institutions was a duty to which most landowners paid at least nodding acknowledgement. Those seriously interested in political power usually became quite active in the management of local affairs. Spencer certainly devoted much labour to community service, but, as we shall see, he had ambivalent feelings about his efforts.

He was commissioned as a cornet in the Northamptonshire Yeomanry, of which his father was colonel, in 1802. Since he was more assiduous in carrying out duties than many of his peers, he often found himself conducting drills and exercises as the only officer present. He headed the meetings of virtually every institution and society in Northamptonshire during the first half of the nineteenth century, became chairman of the general infirmary while still in his twenties and continued to serve on the board until his death forty years later. He also looked after the lunatic asylum. He put in obligatory appearances at the Northampton race meetings and the productions of the Music Society. He chaired meetings of the Northampton Bible Society and supported other school and church activities. He was active in the foundation of the Northamptonshire Agricultural Society and put up substantial sums for its prizes. It was sometimes referred to simply as "Lord Althorp's Agricultural Meeting".[24]

As a young man Spencer was quickly groomed to replace his father as chairman of the county Quarter Sessions. Much of the responsibility for local government thus fell into his hands. Through his leadership on the Bench, he became the chairman of the commission governing the navigation of the Nene River, and hence involved in the licensing of canals, responsible for the appointment of the Chief Constable and the county Surveyor of Bridges, a supervisor of the local prisons, and closely involved with the work of the county finance committee.[25] As MP for the county from 1806 to 1834, he stood at the head of the Whig Party in Northamptonshire and was responsible for much of the county business that required attention in Westminster. He attended all the county meetings of the period and was usually a decisive force in the shaping of petitions and resolutions.

Of his myriad of responsibilities Spencer relished only the chairmanship of Quarter Sessions. Many of his activities brought him nothing but discomfort and even agony. Presiding at Bible Society meetings, he noted, involved sitting through "four hours of Methodist preaching, not unmixed with blasphemy". The election of a matron at the infirmary produced "disgraceful scenes", he wrote feelingly, which "disgusted me most completely". On another occasion after a particularly nasty wrangle for some local place he lamented: "My own advice to any friend of mine would be that he had better put a pistol to his head than take any public office at Northampton." His aversion to parliamentary service is well known. During the Reform Bill crisis he removed a set of pistols from his bedroom for fear of the temptation to shoot himself to gain relief. "I bitterly repent ever having had anything to do with politics" was a frequent refrain in his private correspondence.[26]

This intense dislike for political strife has led some historians to see Spencer's premature retirement from Westminster as a signal of aristocratic retreat.[27] Others argue that the octopus-like grip he had on county offices should be taken as a sign of aristocratic resurgence.[28] Certainly even a progressive landlord like the earl had a traditional element in his makeup. His mother noticed that especially in small matters he was "bigotted to ancient habits and ways". He loved beefsteak and old England. Not only did he hunt and shoot, he even occasionally fished. His aversion to public speaking and sense of personal inadequacy while holding Cabinet office were genuine, but, as Emily Eden once observed, there was no state of inertness "from which an Englishman may not be roused by the stimulus of politics".[29] Spencer was a political animal, and even after his retirement he continued to interfere in national affairs until he died. His interest in Northamptonshire also clearly had a traditionalist flavour. For example, when he was offered the Lord Lieutenancy of Nottinghamshire, he turned it down despite his preference for Wiseton as his place of residence, because he thought it right to wait for the vacancy in his native county where most of his property lay. He refused to seek easy and inexpensive selection as MP for radical urban constituencies which were offered to him when Tory attacks mounted to a crescendo in Northamptonshire during the early 1830s, because he felt to retreat would be to run away from his natural position. His Northamptonshire Agricultural Society openly proclaimed its aim to encourage "the general good conduct of farming labourers". Spencer could not have been ignorant of the fact that leadership in hospital work, education, foxhunting and local government garnered prestige and influence. He once denied that the yeomanry was a means to acquire political power, but he praised it as a mechanism to enhance rural stability.[30]

Habit, tradition and common sense were all likely to contribute to a landlord's participation in private and public administration. However, in Spencer's case four other factors contributed to and modified these activities. These elements – Evangelical morality, advanced Whiggism, a spirit of efficiency or professionalism, and an enthusiasm for scientific and other forms of progress – need to be examined in turn.

The Evangelical spirit increasingly penetrated aristocratic circles during the course of the nineteenth century. Professor Spring and others have written extensively on this topic and it need not detain us here. Even those who did not embrace the movement formally were likely to be more conscious of the need for philanthropic activity. To Spencer it was insufficient to be good; one had to do good to achieve God's grace. God's judgement was likely to be uppermost in his mind as he made major decisions about the allocation of his time and resources.[31]

Spencer's political ideology was also a powerful force in shaping his sense of duty. He once said he was more attached to the Radicals than any other party, although he never went as far in this enthusiasm as the Earl of Radnor, for example, and remained publicly associated with the Whigs. He electrified the House of Commons, speaking as the leader of his party and a minister of the Crown, by delivering a panegyric on the July Revolution in France and the tricoloured flag. Tories called him a Jacobin.[32] He left office in part to escape being made Prime Minister, a post for which he felt totally incompetent, partly to devote time to a private financial disaster, and also because he had been moved by his father's death to the House of Lords, which he regarded as a "Hospital for Incurables".[33] It had been his plan for many years to withdraw from the national scene when he was translated into what he considered to be a backwater.

Spencer's political opinions actually weakened his position in Northamptonshire, yet he refused to conceal them. For example, he outraged a meeting of the local chapter of the National Society for Educating the Children of the Poor in the Principles of the Established Church by telling them he thought schools with students of mixed religious backgrounds would be preferable to their efforts. His public declaration in favour of repeal of the corn laws led him to resign hastily from the Northamptonshire Agricultural Society in order to save it from dissolving in chaotic outrage. His violent criticism of Lord Liverpool's administration during the aftermath of the Peterloo massacre led to a sustained and nearly successful attempt to eject him from the chair of the Quarter Sessions. In 1832 he did resign under a withering wave of abuse against his leadership of the parliamentary reform movement. "Anything I propose", he admitted, "would be infallibly rejected merely because I proposed it." Yet, his response to those who criticized his frankness was stout loyalty to liberalism: "If people do not like [to hear my opinions] I cannot help it."[34]

Spencer's lack of interest in political control can best be seen in his attitude towards the franchise. Prevailing scholarly opinion suggests that landowners expected deference and wanted to continue exercising the political prerequisites of this system. Men like the second Marquess of Bute even considered members of his militia units who voted against his wishes mutineers.[35]

Spencer, however, showed considerable willingness to abandon political influence. He made this clear both by such minor acts as his unhesitating disposal of the deer herd in his park, a traditional source of political presents, and the extraordinary decision he made to allow the Boundary

Commissioners of the Reform Act, whom he supervised, to draw the line bisecting Northamptonshire into two constituencies through the heart of the Spencer estates. They even left Althorp Park in the southern division, which was the area least likely to be sympathetic to his candidacy.[36]

The earl's instructions to his agent about voting were clear:

> I would certainly like that my tenants should know that if they like to vote according to my wishes I should wish them to vote [for the Whig candidate] . . . But that if they feel any objection to this I consider that I have no right to interfere with their votes which belong to them and not to me.[37]

He gradually came to support universal manhood suffrage and was early concerned about "the tyranny of Great Men". When his relative, the Marquess of Exeter, turned out tenants who voted against the landlord's instructions and got into difficulties, Spencer had little sympathy for him. "It really appears as if Grandees never could learn anything", he wrote. "I am sorry for Lord Exeter, but he deserves what will happen to him in the abuse he will meet with."[38]

Spencer's grandfather had fought titanic battles to impose his will on the voters of Northampton borough. The third earl, on the other hand, declared that he was glad his family's influence in borough politics was over and nothing would induce him to engage in them again. Recent research has shown that progressive landlords increasingly attempted to avoid heavy-handedness in the exercise of political influence, what Spencer caled "an undue interference".[39] He undoubtedly expected the electorate to turn to men like himself for leadership, but he wanted the decision to be freely made.

Spencer was by no means conducting a retreat. His vigorous activity in national and local affairs belies any such notion. Moreover, anything he turned his hand to was tended with painstaking efficiency. His attitude toward foxhunting has already been mentioned in this regard, but one sees it too in his administration of the Treasury, in his management of the Smithfield Show, drilling the yeomanry, or presiding over the Society for the Diffusion of Useful Knowledge where he corrected proofs, solicited authors, and raised money. Even when a Cabinet minister, if the House rose late he would ride through the night to Northampton in order to attend a meeting where he felt it his duty to appear. He once spent a night in the bedroom assigned to the Assize judge to ascertain whether that worthy's demands for refurbishment were a justifiable expense to the county's exchequer.[40] Spencer abhorred laziness and inefficiency. He held to businesslike virtues both in his private affairs and public conduct.

This sense of professionalism derived in part from Spencer's enthusism for science. He attended lectures in chemistry even before going up to Cambridge, where he did particularly well in mathematics and logic. Later he began a systematic study of agricultural research, straying into economics, geology and biology. After becoming a widower, he set up a laboratory in his rooms at Albany.[41] Although the amateur scientist was by no means unknown among the English nobility, Spencer represented a new wave in a broader sense. Coke of Norfolk opposed the foundation of the Royal Agricultural Society because he felt support for further research was unnecessary and that faith in the utility of chemistry to agriculture was fallacious. The sixth Duke of Bedford, the other leading agriculturalist of Coke's generation, abandoned the Smithfield Club and his sheepshearings because he thought advances in breeding techniques had already reached their peak. Spencer became the president of both these institutions because he was convinced the benefits of further research were incalculable. It was he who gave the Royal Agricultural Society its motto in the speech in which he called for "the application of *Science to practice*".[42] We can see this faith reflected in other areas of his life as well. For example, Spencer's support for the Northampton Infirmary was based more on interest in the advanced medical prowess of its surgeons than in attempting to maintain aristocratic control. He overcame strong reservations, caused by the absence of a theology department, to the foundation of London University and became a fervent supporter, "for it undoubtedly will be a great benefit to the country", he told his father, "to put scientific instruction within the reach of so many more people".[43] It was not for nothing that Henry Brougham dedicated his edition of Paley's *Natural Theology* (1835) to Spencer.

The progressive landlord responded enthusiastically, if often naively, to the march of the intellect and spirit of his times. Spencer changed kennels for committee rooms and hunting books for volumes by Lyell and Ricardo. He advocated efficient management both in public and private affairs. The new Poor Law, the unpopularity of which made him fear assassination, was typical of this thinking on the national level, and he was anxious to apply it to his estates as well, even though this too might undermine aristocratic authority. There was the lesson before him of the Duke of Sutherland, who lost his political influence when his Staffordshire estates were overhauled for the sake of economic efficiency.[44] However, when Spencer at last gained control over his inheritance in 1834, he found he had no time or resources to make dramatic innovations in estate management. He spent most of the rest of his life in a desperate struggle just to keep the estate solvent.

III

The Spencer estate was divided into three units of administration with the addition of a number of auxiliary properties not in themselves income-producing. The latter category included a dower house in Hertfordshire, a marine villa on the Isle of Wight, and the heir's seat near Northampton. There were also two large dwellings to support the family's periodic descents on the capital: Wimbledon Park was a suburban retreat kept to escape the smoke and bustle of London during intervals in the Season while Spencer House, facing onto Green Park, today one of the last surviving palaces of Whig society, was the magnificent backdrop for lavish entertainment and political intrigue.

The three main blocks of property, each administered separately under the general supervision of an auditor in London, were North Creake, a shooting and agricultural estate in Norfolk near Holkham, the south bank of the Thames running from Battersea to Putney, still then mainly open fields, and the estate heartland in Warwickshire and Northamptonshire surrounding Althorp. There were a few outlying farms in Leicestershire and Bedfordshire, and the third earl's marriage brought Wiseton into the family.

With the exception of a few houses next to Spencer House in St James's Place and a bit of commercial property on the Thames opposite Chelsea, the Spencer estates were exclusively agricultural. Mixed farming was practised in Norfolk and the Midlands. In the 1790s the gross rental stood between £30,000 and £35,000 p.a.[45] In 1834 this had risen to £47,000 which reflected, in addition to some increase in rents, the income from Wiseton and from a large estate in Northamptonshire purchased by the second earl. Few families in the kingdom enjoyed such bounty. However, there was also a debt of just under half a million pounds attached to the inheritance. Interest in addition to annuities and customary payments totalled £30,000 p.a., and the fixed expenses of the estate such as taxes, repairs, charities, etc. stood at over £15,000 p.a.[46] Thus, Spencer was left with virtually no discretionary income at all.

The debt had accumulated over three generations. The first earl had spent prodigally. His grandson thought he had been "spoiled by having been placed at too early a period of his life, in possession of what appeared to him inexhaustible wealth".[47] Building projects and elections during his fortunately brief tenure mounted up quickly, and the second earl had a similar taste for extravagance: he was a builder on a heroic scale, and his wife was a lavish hostess. Above all he was the slave to a collecting mania, aiming to create the finest private library in Britain, if not Europe. At his death Althorp and Spencer Houses were crammed with well over 100,000 volumes, including a large number of incunabula and fifty-five Caxtons. He also purchased the estate previously referred to for £133,000 without compensatory sales of outlying property.[48] The third earl had added his own contribution to the accumulating pile. He borrowed heavily in 1814 to stock his farms at Chapel Brampton and Wiseton. Redecoration of his new house cost more. He leased a town residence in Pall Mall and a hunting lodge in the country. At one point he was so hard pressed for cash that he seriously considered paying extortionary interest of 10 per cent on £12,000 just to get over an immediate crisis. By 1833 he had accumulated debts of £60,000, although much of this had been invested in productive agriculture.[49]

Spencer must also bear some of the blame for the great size of the debt because he did little to curb his parents' spending. It would appear that when the estates came out of settlement upon his attaining his majority they were resettled under the joint management of father and son. The second earl seems to have been virtually unlimited in his power to raise mortgages. Spencer had written him shortly before his marriage: "I am not much afraid at my future prospects being at your mercy".

Spencer seemed to care even less how much his father spent. "Do as you please," he told the old man in 1832.[50] Henry Brougham, who knew the family well, recollected that when a survey of the indebtedness was made, probably in the 1820s, and the estate was found very much embarrassed, Spencer insisted that his parents change nothing in their style of living. He would shoulder the burden and restore prosperity on his accession. However, judging by his surprise and dismay in 1834, he did not grasp the full extent of the danger. There were signs that the second earl was trying to rectify the situation in his last years. He offered to sell North Creake to Coke in 1827, and he did lease Wimbledon to the Duke of Somerset.[51] But these were mere fingers in the dike.

"Debt was a constant feature of life for the early modern aristocracy", one authority has noted recently. J. E. Denison guessed that two-thirds of English land was encumbered at this time. Some families had acquired debts even larger than that which faced Spencer. The Duke of Devonshire's obligations stood at £1,000,000 in 1844. Earl Fitzwilliam owed £800,000 at around the same time, and the Marquess of Londonderry £600,000 a few years later. Others stood at a figure similar to Spencer's debt, including those of the Dukes of Portland and Bedford and the Marquesses of Bute and Donegal.[52]

In most cases, however, large indebtedness was connected with even larger incomes. The crucial factor was what proportion of income was consumed by interest. Among the leviathans such as Devonshire, Fitzwilliam, Bute and Bedford, this percentage never seems to have been much more than a quarter of their gross income. The Duke of Sutherland could spend like a drunken and demented sailor, and still not seriously endanger himself. However, when the Marquess of Ailesbury found he was paying £20,000 interest out of an income of £54,000, his advisers grew seriously alarmed. Other magnates, who allowed the proportion to rise a good deal higher, crashed, as the bankruptcies of the Duke of Buckingham and Marquess of Donegal showed. In 1835 interest alone was consuming three-quarters of Spencer's income. The estate was gravely crippled with no prospect of increased industrial or mineral income, which was the salvation of a number of other heavily indebted families.[53]

Clearly something drastic had to be done. David Cannadine has argued that aristocratic debts were usually not paid off, but rather that old debts were sustained and new debts incurred. However, progressive landlords were likely to be uncomfortable about debt. Sir James Graham wrote: "Debt is an intollerable and degrading Burthen, and the payment of it is a paramount duty." Spencer, too, disliked debt on principle, and when he was forced to accumulate obligations of his own, favoured "getting quite clear at once". His auditor, John Shaw Lefevre, agreed: "I believe that the best of all investments", he told the earl, "is the investment in paying off debts and charges."[54] Of course, the Spencer case in 1834 was extreme, but paying off debts, closing ledgers and clearing decks appealed to the ethical and business spirit of the progressive landlord.

As a widower without children and as a man of simple tastes, Spencer assumed that he would be in a good position to live frugally and gradually unburden the estate. But his inheritance was like a supertanker, extremely hard to slow down and even more difficult to turn around. Great houses were expensive to operate even without undue pomp and extravagance. Woburn Abbey in full panoply cost the sixth Duke of Bedford more than the entire net income of the Spencers, and the cheeseparing seventh duke was only able to bring this down to £25,000 a year in 1840.[55]

Spencer let the park to a market gardener, although it was painful to dismiss the fifty outdoor servants. In the past he had been praised by the local newspaper as an exemplary employer. Now he fired most of the forty indoor ones as well and ceased to entertain. However, basic services had to be maintained to keep out the damp and preserve the paintings and books. A librarian's salary continued to be paid, and there were charitable projects that had to be kept going. Spencer tried to consolidate mortgages at lower rates of interest, but he was determined to keep the family charges at a full 5 per cent. Even during the worst period of indebtedness he refused his brother's offer to take £1,000 off his allowance, and he continued to pay out smaller annuities and pensions, keeping up for example his father's payments to the rustic Northamptonshire poet, John Clare.[56]

He planned to pare the maintenance of Althorp down to £1,000 p.a. and live on a squire's income of a few thousands a year at Wiseton. Yet in the first full year of his administration expenditure exceeded income by £6,575. "I do not", he told Shaw Lefevre, "see how it is possible for me to go on."[57]

Inevitably, Spencer had to consider the sale of property. Even great magnates such as the Duke of Devonshire were reluctant to contemplate disposal of land, fearing it "might lower the position of my family". David Cannadine therefore argues that an unencumbered but reduced landowner was a "lesser person" than an indebted one with broad acres. Furthermore, F. M. L. Thompson has stated that even heavy indebtedness in early Victorian England was unlikely to cause extensive sales of lands. However, neither of these judgements are confirmed by Spencer's experience or for that matter by that of a number of his contemporaries. Devonshire ended up selling over £1 million worth of land between 1813 and 1844. Coke of Norfolk, the Dukes of Portland and Sutherland, and the Marquess of Downshire all turned to sales.[58] It would be difficult to prove in any of these cases that there was a significant loss of caste.

Of course, none of these families sold significant portions of the estate core. Most sellers put only peripheral possessions on the block. Also, in Spencer's case, as in others, sales of outlying property could be justified on the grounds of compensatory purchases which increased efficiency of management and perhaps even increased influence. Alienation of other bits and pieces such as leases of London houses, Battersea Bridge shares, and parcels of land for railway construction was also accomplished without fuss. He contemplated letting Spencer House go and even put together an entrepreneurial package of palace, paintings (especially those with figures "in a state of nakedness without even figleaves") and the Marlborough diamonds, all for £60,000, but found no buyers.[59] None of these transactions made a serious dent in the debt. Massive sales were necessary, and Spencer turned to the one large block of land outside Northamptonshire, the south London estate.

He sold at a time when prices were low, and, as we know now, had the family held on to this property as the metropolis expanded there would have been a fabulous return.[60] Even in those days before massive urban growth, the sales produced extraordinary prices: £324,660 at a loss of only £8,964 p.a. rental. Spencer toyed with the idea of building and leasing villas in Wimbledon but ultimately sold the park to a developer for £80,000. The house was finally sold to the Duke of Somerset. The debt was successfully liquidated and a still stupendous inheritance was passed on to his successors. Spencer was so pleased with the result that he advised fellow magnates who were in debt to sell land as he had done.[61]

The management of the debt and the associated sales that stretched over seven years left Spencer little time for farming. Moreover, funds for innovative practices were hard to come by. As late as 1841, he confessed, "I don't have one farthing that I can dispose of as I wish". It was not until June 1845, a few months before his death, that Althorp Park was fully reopened and a major house party entertained.[62]

Spencer insisted on treating his tenants justly and generously throughout the indebtedness crisis. He refused to allow any reduction in the percentage of income spent on building repairs, drainage, carpentry, plantations and fences. His emphasis on mixed farming and improved livestock ultimately proved a wise policy. Estates managed on this system were not to suffer so heavily in the agricultural depression of the later part of the century. A few years after his death, a noted agricultural writer called the Spencer estates among the best run and most progressive in Northamptonshire. Originally, Spencer had favoured the long leases of which Coke had been such a vigorous advocate, but the earl found that his own tenants preferred yearly ones and that he could control cropping quite as effectively with this system as the squire of Holkham. Some families had held farms on the Spencer estates since the reign of Henry VII and he valued their trust and goodwill. However, Spencer knew there were bad landlords and supported efforts to draft legislation to protect tenants at will,[63] who had no lease but were subject to one year's or six months' notice to quit.

IV

Recently, David Cannadine has argued, citing H. J. Habakkuk, that we have overemphasized the landed elite's concern with developing their estates and promoting political influence. According to this view owners saw their land first and foremost as a plaything to enjoy. R. J. Olney suggests that landowners selected by their peers to serve in the House of Commons regarded themselves as unfortunate, as if they had received the short straw or lost at musical chairs. M. L. Bush sees them as almost totally unconnected with the agricultural process. On the other hand, David Roberts has suggested that there was a resurgence of paternalistic activity during the early nineteenth century. This more aggressive claim on local leadership reflected anxiety on the part of landowners to reassert their basic social philosophy in answer to growing criticisms of their special privileges and failings. The challenge of radicalism, non-conformism and middle-class success was met by strengthening aristocratic control over society. Heather Clemenson cites evidence that political influence was the primary interest in aristocratic circles late into the century. Harold Perkin argues that "the one overriding pursuit of landed gentlemen was government".[64]

What motivated the progressive landlord? As we have seen the Evangelical spirit was often a factor: in Spencer's case a strong force. It was, he told his most intimate friend and co-religionist, the fifth Earl Fitzwilliam, their duty "to produce as much happiness and to alleviate as much misery as is in our power". Their earthly lives were but "a stepping stone to the next". The suggestion of Cannadine that land was held principally to provide for personal enjoyment would have disgusted men such as these or the seventh Duke of Devonshire, the seventh Duke of Bedford, the fourth Earl of Dartmouth, the second Earl Fortescue, the seventh Earl of Shaftesbury, and many other magnates and country gentlemen. Spencer saw himself as only a "nominal" owner of his estate, holding it in trust both for his successors and for the purpose of benefiting those who lived on it. To be sure the earl was aware of the leadership expected from a man of his "rank and station in society". It was easy to see that many of his pursuits as a landlord brought him prestige, popularity and power. But again, his religion taught him that these prizes were ephemeral and would be of no value on Judgement Day.[65] His willingness to antagonize local political opinion, offend rural orthodoxies, and advocate universal manhood suffrage and the secret ballot does not suggest a man intent on increasing paternalistic power.

The progressive landlord's interest in agricultural improvement could derive from a desire to be in fashion or, out of a hope to compete with rising bourgeois incomes, an attempt to stay richer than the new rich. Some became creative and innovative entrepreneurs on a large scale in their own right.[66] However, progressive agriculture was not likely to bring returns as high as even simple investment in the funds, let alone venturesome commercial enterprise. Many historians argue that the willingness to accept a smaller dividend was motivated by a desire to maintain deference.[67] Perhaps equally important, however, in Spencer's case was his enthusiasm for science which led him to favour heavy investment in innovative methods and new technology. He was a new and different kind of landowner. He conformed in many respects to G. M. Young's portrait of the typical heir of a late eighteenth-century aristocrat:

His son will be a county member too, but he will, in speech and attire, conform to the standards of his more refined age, and will debate the Corn Laws on the principles of Ricardo, or lecture to his tenants on

Liebig's Agricultural Chemistry . . . The country gentleman of the nineteenth century is an administrative and scientific man.[68]

Young says that the standards of the class had changed, and the evidence presented here suggests that his description of a progressive landlord in the first half of the nineteenth century was an accurate one. While not every aristocrat conformed to this stereotype, Spencer and most of his friends did: Tory and Whig, magnate and squire. What preserved their power and their acres was not a revival of paternalism, but an adjustment to the spirit of the new age.

Notes

1   David Spring, *The English Landed Estate in the Nineteenth Century: Its Administration* (Baltimore, 1963), pp. 20 and 51.
2   *Farmer's Magazine*, vol. 7 (Oct. 1843), p. 295.
3   B. R. Haydon, *Diary*, ed. W. B. Pope (Cambridge, Mass., 1963), Vol. 4, p. 46. John Gore (ed.), *Creevey's Life and Times* (London, 1934), p. 363; Charles Greville, *Memoirs 1814–60*, ed. Lytton Strachey and Roger Fulford (London, 1938), Vol. 2, p. 203, 24 Sept. 1831; *Hansard's Parliamentary Debates* (hereafter cited *Parl. Deb.*), X, 647, 2 Mar. 1824; Elie Halévy, *The Liberal Awakening 1815–1830* (London, 1961), p. 259; E. W. Bovill, *English Country Life 1780–1830* (Oxford, 1962), p. 65; Russell M. Garnier, *History of the English Landed Interest* (London, 1893), Vol. 2, p. 358. For his activities as an agricultural organizer see E. A. Wasson, "The third Earl Spencer and agriculture 1818–1845", *Agricultural History Review*, Vol. 26, Pt II (1978), pp. 89–99.
4   Mary E. Finch, *The Wealth of Five Northamptonshire Families 1540–1640* (Oxford, 1956), 38–65; Georgina Battiscombe, *The Spencers of Althorp* (London, 1984), pp. 11–22.
5   They held 27,185 acres in the 1870s. This figure was probably about the same in 1845. In 1830 it would have been over 30,000 acres.
6   Althorp MSS (hereafter cited as AP), third Earl's papers. Used by kind permission of the Earl Spencer while still uncatalogued and at Althorp Park. See also Spencer Trust papers in the Shaw Lefevre MSS (hereafter cited as SLP) kept at the House of Lords Record Office. G. E. Mingay, *Rural Life in Victorian England* (London, 1977), p. 139. A good picture of Beasley is provided by James Caird, *English Agriculture in 1850–51* (New York, 2nd edn 1967), pp. 421–32. See also John Beasley, *The Duties and Privileges of the Landowners, Occupiers and Cultivators of the Soil* (London, 1860).
7   AP box 18, 1812 rental £3,924, and box 13, and Spencer to Shaw Lefevre 23 Nov. 1834.
8   Sir Denis Le Marchant, *Memoir of John Charles Viscount Althorp* (London, 1876), p. 169; AP 3rd Earl Spencer to 2nd Earl 29 June and 3 Oct. 1818; Fitzwilliam MSS (hereafter cited as FP) kept at the Northamptonshire Record Office X1606 Spencer to 5th Earl Fitzwilliam 3 Oct. 1818.
9   R. Trow-Smith, *A History of British Livestock Husbandry 1700–1900* (London, 1959), pp. 233–9; Wasson, "Spencer", p. 92; George T. Burrows, *History of Dairy Shorthorn Cattle* (London, 1950), p. 42; E. Clarke and Sir Harry Verney, "The third Earl Spencer", *Journal of the Royal Agricultural Society of England* (1890), pp. 144–5.
10   The Druid (H. H. Dixon), *Saddle and Sirloin* (London, 1895), p. 124; AP 4th Earl's recollection; Ossington MSS kept at Nottingham University Library C123 Spencer to J. E. Denison 10 Jan. 1838.
11   AP Spencer to R. N. Bennett 22 Aug. 1824; Lady Sarah Lyttelton, *Correspondence, 1787–1870*, ed. Mrs Hugh Wyndham (London, 1912), pp. 246 and 239.
12   Father Ignatius MSS kept at St Anne's Retreat, Sutton, St Helen's, Lancashire; George Spencer's diary 26 Jan. 1829; British Library (hereafter cited as BL) Add. MSS 51680 fol. 175: Lord John Russell to Lady Holland 21 Dec. 1843; Josephine Butler, *Memoir of John Grey of Dilston* (London, 1874), p. 153.

13 Wasson, "Spencer", pp. 90–3.

14 Stuart Macdonald, "Model farms", in G. E. Mingay (ed.), *The Victorian Countryside* (London, 1981), Vol. 1, pp. 224, 214, 216.

15 R. A. C. Parker, *Coke of Norfolk* (Oxford, 1975), p. 170. Spencer thought this at the time – Druid, *Saddle and Sirloin*, p. 125.

16 FP Spencer to Fitzwilliam 5 Jan. 1832.

17 ibid. AP – it cleared £300 in 1825 and £1,125 in 1832; BL Add. MSS 35155 fol. 91. Clarke and Verney, "Spencer", pp. 145–6.

18 E.g., Graham Mee, *Aristocratic Enterprise: The Fitzwilliam Industrial Undertakings, 1795–1857* (Glasgow, 1975), pp. 78–93.

19 George Ticknor, *Life, Letters, and Journals* (London, 1876), Vol. 1, p. 443.

20 David Cannadine, "The theory and practice of the English leisure classes", *Historical Journal* Vol. 21, (1978) No. 2, p. 466. David Itzkowitz suggests this may be a bit of an exaggeration – *Peculiar Privilege: A Social History of English Foxhunting 1753–1885* (Brighton, 1977), p. 84. It would depend on the hunt and the county.

21 Le Marchant, *Althorp*, pp. 143–5; Guy Paget, *A History of the Althorp and Pytchley Hunt 1634–1920* (London, 1937), pp. 114–16; George F. Underhill, *A Century of English Foxhunting* (London, 1900), pp. 126–9 – which gives incorrect dates for his mastership (should be 1808–18); Earl Bathurst, *The Earl Spencer's and Mr John Warde's Hounds, 1739–1825* (Cirencester, 1932).

22 Paget, *Pytchley*, p. 111.

23 R. J. Olney, "The politics of land", in Mingay (ed.), *Victorian Countryside*, Vol. 1, pp. 62–3, and *Lincolnshire Politics 1832–1885* (Oxford, 1973), pp. 44–5. Whitbread MSS kept at the Bedfordshire Record Office W1/Z462: Bedford to Samuel Whitbread 4 April 1809.

24 *Northampton Mercury*, 14 Sept. 1822.

25 ibid., 23 Dec. 1809. Goodwood MSS kept at the West Sussex Record Office 1616/1425: Spencer to the Duke of Richmond 1 Feb. 1840; AP 3rd Earl to 2nd Earl Spencer 21 July 1813, 14 Mar. 1812, and 21 Oct. 1815; FP CQ 3 Spencer to Fitzwilliam 29 Dec. 1842.

26 AP 3rd Earl to 2nd Earl April 1812 Weds; FP EX Spencer to Fitzwilliam 23 Jan. 1845, CU 30 Mar. 1845; BL Add. MSS 56556 f. 71 12 Feb. 1832; Ellice MSS kept at the National Library of Scotland: Spencer to Ellice 5 Nov. 1834 and 30 Dec. 1832; AP 3rd Earl to 2nd Earl 21 Dec. 1831 and Spencer to Henry Brougham 14 Dec. 1824.

27 Peter Mandler, "Liberalism and paternalism: the Whig aristocracy and the condition of England, 1830–1852" (unpublished PhD thesis, Harvard University, 1984), pp. 121–50.

28 See note 64.

29 AP Lavinia, Countess Spencer to 2nd Earl 20 Feb. 1820; Emily Eden, *The Semi-Attached Couple* (New York, 1982), p. 209.

30 Melbourne MSS kept in the Royal Library and used by kind permission of Her Majesty the Queen: RA MP 52/76 Spencer to Melbourne 30 April 1839; Public Record Office, London (hereafter cited as PRO) 30/22/3C f. 241: Spencer to Lord John Russell 1 May 1839; E. A. Wasson, "The spirit of reform, 1832 and 1867", *Albion* Vol. 12, No. 2 (1980), p. 169; AP box 2; *Parl. Deb.* Vol. 14, 1110, 3 Mar. 1826.

31 David Spring, "Aristocracy, social structure, and religion in the early Victorian period", *Victorian Studies* Vol. VI, No. 3 (1963), pp. 263–80; E. A. Wasson, "The Young Whigs: Lords Althorp, Milton, and Tavistock and the Whig Party 1809–1830" (unpublished PhD thesis, University of Cambridge, 1975), pp. 20–30; AP Spencer to Brougham 5 and 8 April 1835 and Spencer to Sir Francis Baring 21 Jan. 1835.

32 BL Add. MSS 56556 fol. 71 12 Feb. 1832 and fol. 72 10 Dec. 1830; A. Aspinall (ed.), *Three Early Nineteenth Century Diaries* (London, 1952), p. 33. Charles Arbuthnot, *Correspondence*, ed. A. Aspinall (London, 1941), p. 135.

33 Lord Broughton, *Recollections of a Long Life*, ed. Lady Dorchester (London, 1909), Vol. 4, p. 64.

34 *Northampton Mercury* 4 April 1812; BL Add. MSS 35155 fol. 90: FP CQ Spencer to Fitzwilliam 12 Jan. 1844 and Y 5 Jan. 1832; Wasson, "The Young Whigs", pp. 143–5; Gotch MSS kept at the Northamptonshire Record Office: GK 1219 Spencer to J. C. Gotch 13 Oct. 1832; Ellice MSS Spencer to Ellice 30 Dec. 1832.

35 John Davies, "Aristocratic town-makers", in David Cannadine (ed.), *Patricians, Power, and Politics in Nineteenth-Century Towns* (Leicester, 1982), p. 37.
36 AP 3rd Earl to 2nd Earl 9 June 1834 and Spencer to Brougham 2 Sept. 1832; Royal Library, Queen Victoria's journal 22 Oct. 1838.
37 SLP Spencer to Shaw Lefevre 2 Feb. 1841.
38 Gotch MSS GK 1219 Spencer to Gotch 13 Oct. 1832; AP 3rd Earl to Lavinia, Cts. Spencer 12 Oct. 1830.
39 AP Spencer to unknown correspondent re Banbury election 18 June 1832 and 3rd Earl to 2nd Earl 7 Dec. 1817 and 17 Mar. 1808; Olney, *Lincolnshire Politics*, pp. 12, 18, 33–9 and 42–5.
40 For his activity with SDUK see Spencer correspondence with Thomas Coates, SDUK MSS kept at University College Library, London; *British Farmer's Magazine*, vol. 5 (Nov. 1831), p. 466; AP Spencer to Charles Markham 18 July 1845.
41 AP Spencer to Georgiana, Countess Spencer 8 Dec. 1799; 3rd Earl to 2nd Earl 9 Oct. 1814; Brougham correspondence 1830s and 1840s.
42 Parker, *Coke*, p. 161; *Northampton Mercury*, 29 Dec. 1821; J. A. Scott Watson, *The History of the Royal Agricultural Society of England 1839–1939* (London, 1939), p. 13; Lord Ernle, *English Farming, Past and Present*, 6th edn (1961), p. 362; AP 3rd Earl to 2nd Earl 5 May 1820.
43 FP EX Spencer to Fitzwilliam 23 Jan. 1845; AP 3rd Earl to 2nd Earl 5 Sept. 1825.
44 Eric Richards, "The social and electoral influence of the Trentham interest, 1800–1860", *Midland History* Vol. III, No. 2, (1975), pp. 120–37; J. R. Wordie, *Estate Management in Eighteenth-Century England: The Building of the Leveson-Gower Fortune* (London, 1982), pp. 260–1.
45 Northampton Record Office YZ 9688 gives £27,572, but does not include Surrey or Norfolk property.
46 AP 3rd Earl's papers. This was about 30 per cent of gross income, in the middle range for such estates. F. M. L. Thompson, "The end of a great estate", *Economic History Review* Vol. VIII, No. 1, (1955), p. 39. Indebted or extravagant landlords often cut operating expenses to meet their needs. Thompson, "English landownership: the Ailesbury Trust 1832–56", *Economic History Review* Vol. XI, No. 1 (1958), p. 121–32; Susanna W. Martins, *A Great Estate at Work: The Holkham Estate and Its Inhabitants in the Nineteenth Century* (Cambridge, 1980), pp. 94–5.
47 Le Marchant, *Althorp*, p. xix.
48 AP 2nd Earl to 3rd Earl 23 Aug. 1829.
49 Chatsworth MSS used by kind permission of the Duke of Devonshire: Spencer to 6th Duke 7 June 1825; AP 3rd Earl to 2nd Earl 21 June 1826, 12 Aug., 19 Sept., 2, 9 and 16 Oct. 1814; Spencer to Viscountess Althorp 23 June 1814; J. Hall to Spencer 17 Mar. 1816 and 9 Mar. 1818.
50 AP 3rd Earl to 2nd Earl 27 Oct. 1813; SLP Spencer to Shaw Lefevre 17 June 1832.
51 AP Brougham recollection and 3rd Earl to 2nd Earl 20 Sept. 1833; Parker, *Coke*, pp. 156 and 195.
52 David Cannadine, "Aristocratic indebtedness in the nineteenth century: the case reopened", *Economic History Review* Vol. XXX, No. 4 (1977), pp. 627 and 630–2; David Spring, "The English landed estate in the age of coal and iron: 1830–1880", *Journal of Economic History* Vol. I, No. 1 (1951), p. 15; D. Cannadine, "The landowner as millionaire: the finances of the Dukes of Devonshire, *c*. 1800–*c*.1926", *Agricultural History Review* Vol. 25, Pt II (1977), p. 82; D. Spring, *English Landed Estate*, p. 35; Davies, "Aristocratic town-makers", pp. 34–44; W. A. Maguire, *Living Like a Lord: The Second Marquess of Donegal 1769–1844* (Belfast, 1984), p. 83.
53 Cannadine, "Aristocratic indebtedness", p. 631; Spring, *English Landed Estate*, p. 36, and "English landownership in the nineteenth century: a critical note", *Economic History Review* Vol. IX, No. 3 (1957), p. 480; D. and Eileen Spring, "The fall of the Grenvilles, 1844–48", *Huntington Library Quarterly*, Vol. XIX, No. 2 (1956), pp. 165–90; Maguire, *Living Like a Lord*; D. Spring, "English landowners and nineteenth-century industrialism", in J. T. Ward and R. G. Wilson (eds), *Land and Industry: The Landed Estate and the Industrial Revolution* (Newton Abbott, 1971) pp. 51, 62n and

172. An unsuccessful search for coal was carried out on the Norfolk estate: Spring, *English Landed Estate*, p. 129.

54 Cannadine, "Aristocratic indebtedness", pp. 628 and 638; David Spring, "A great agricultural estate: Netherby under Sir James Graham, 1820–1845", *Agricultural History*, Vol. 29, No. 2 (1955), p. 81; AP 3rd Earl to 2nd Earl 9 Oct. 1814; SLP Shaw Lefevre to Spencer 19 Feb. 1843.

55 Spring, *English Landed Estate*, p. 32.

56 SLP 3rd Earl's papers; Spring, *English Landed Estate*, pp. 25–30, 35 and 36. The Spencer family charges only amounted to £82,762 as compared, for example, to the Russells' £283,910. AP 3rd Earl's papers and 3rd Earl to 4th Earl 6 July 1836; BL Egerton MSS 2249 fols. 269 and 354.

57 SLP Spencer to Shaw Lefevre 22 Nov. 1835 and 11 Jan. 1835; AP box 20.

58 Spring, "Age of coal and iron", pp. 19 and 17; Cannadine, "Aristocratic indebtedness", p. 638; Thompson, "End of a great estate", p. 52; Parker, *Coke*, pp. 129–30; D. Cannadine, *Lords and Landlords: The aristocracy and the Towns 1774–1967* (Leicester, 1980), p. 287.

59 SLP account of progress 2 Jan. 1835; Spencer to Shaw Lefevre 3 Feb. 1836, 26 Mar. 1835, and 30 April 1836; Shaw Lefevre to Spencer 6 Feb. 1835.

60 F. M. L. Thompson, "The land market in the nineteenth century", in Walter Minchinton (ed.), *Essays in Agrarian History*, Vol. 2 (Newton Abbott, 1968), p. 39.

61 AP Blue ledger; SLP Spencer to Shaw Lefevre 25 May 1836 and 30 April 1845; Seymour of Berry Pomeroy MSS kept at the Devon Record Office 1392 M/38/3 and 43/9; Lord William Russell, *Letters from Various Writers 1817–1845*, privately printed (1915–17), Vol. 1, p. 312.

62 PRO 30/22/4B fol. 9 Spencer to Bedford 4 July 1841; Brougham MSS kept at University College Library, London, Spencer to Brougham 24 June 1845.

63 Caird, *English Agriculture*, pp. 432–3; modern historians doubt the usefulness of long leases in any case: B. A. Holderness, "The Victorian farmer", in Mingay (ed.), *Victorian Countryside*, Vol. 1, p. 234; J. A. Perkins, "Tenure, tenant right, and agricultural progress in Lindsey, 1780–1850", *Agricultural History Review*, Vol. 23, Pt. I (1975), p. 22; PRO 30/22/4C f: 31 Spencer to Lord John Russell 27 Oct. 1842; Ossington MSS C128 Spencer to Denison 2 Sept. 1844; *Parl. Deb.*, Vol. II, p. 662, 11 May 1824.

64 Cannadine, "English leisure classes", pp. 461–62; Olney, *Lincolnshire Politics*, p. 232; M. L. Bush, *The English Aristocracy: A Comparative Synthesis* (Manchester, 1984), p. 186; David Roberts, *Paternalism in Early Victorian England* (New Brunswick, 1979), pp. 130–2; Heather A. Clemenson, *English Country Houses and Landed Estates* (New York, 1982), p. 96; Harold Perkin, *The Origins of Modern British Society 1780–1880* (London, 1969), p. 56.

65 FP Spencer to Fitzwilliam 4 Nov. 1818; AP Spencer to Sir Francis Baring 21 Jan. 1835; Gotch MSS GK 488 Spencer to Gotch 26 Nov. 1835; AP 3rd Earl to 4th Earl 12 Jan. 1833.

66 John Marshall, "Great landowners, leadership, and industrial development in Cumberland and Furness in the nineteenth century", in M. D. G. Wanklyn (ed.), *Landownership and Power in the Regions* (Wolverhampton, 1978), p. 60; Maguire, *Living Like a Lord*, p. 159; Spring, *English Landed Estate*, p. 40; W. D. Rubinstein, *Men of Property: The Very Wealthy in Britain since the Industrial Revolution* (London, 1981), pp. 205ff.

67 Cannadine, "Aristocratic indebtedness", pp. 643, 641 and 638; Thompson, *English Landed Society*, p. 290; Parker, *Coke*, p. 201, Spring, "Netherby", pp. 80–1; W. A. Maguire, *The Downshire Estates in Ireland 1801–1845* (Oxford, 1972), pp. 21–2; Eric Richards, *The Leviathan of Wealth* (London, 1973), pp. xvii and 285; Martins, *Holkham*, pp. 98–9; Mingay, *Victorian Countryside*, Vol. 1, p. 14.

68 G. M. Young, *Last Essays* (London, 1950), pp. 149 and 151.

5 Estate development in Bristol, Birmingham and Liverpool, 1660–1720

C. W. CHALKLIN

Introduction

Little is known about urban estate development in seventeenth-century England, beyond the bounds of London. As a preliminary study, this essay investigates the role of the landowners who supplied building land in three rapidly growing provincial towns. It describes the location and size of the building areas and deals with the layout of the building plots and the terms on which they were leased or sold. In some instances, the landlords were eager to prescribe the style of the houses that the builders were to erect.

While the population of England and Wales increased only slowly between 1650 and 1750, rising from about 5 to 6 million, and nearly all the urban centres developed slowly, about twelve provincial towns grew very rapidly. Several economic changes accounted for this development: they included the rapid emergence of trade with North America and the West Indies, the expansion of manufacturing in parts of northern England and the Midlands, and the general growth of domestic trade which was the result not only of the increase in industrial production but also of the improvement of agriculture, the development of inland waterways and a rise in the standard of living for most of the population. In the nineteenth century these towns became England's leading provincial cities.

Of the three towns in this study, Liverpool grew most quickly, with a population of about 1,500 in 1673, over 5,000 in 1700 and about 22,000 in 1750. In the mid seventeenth century the town was still a relatively insignificant port, with a little coastal, Irish and French trade. By 1700 it had emerged as one of England's leading ports, based particularly on the import of tobacco from North America and of sugar from the West Indies, but also on the growth of coastal and Irish commerce, the consequence of the rising living standards in north-west England and parts of Ireland, of Liverpool's favourable location, and of the increasing range of goods with which it dealt, especially imported sugar and tobacco and Cheshire salt.[1]

Birmingham's population grew from about 3,500 in 1671 to about 6,000 in 1700 and 11,500 about 1720. This increase was based both on its industrial transformation and its development as a commercial centre for industrial south Staffordshire. From the later sixteenth century the town had increasingly concentrated on the manufacture of nails, saddlers' iron-mongery and edge tools: by the 1690s Birmingham was a centre of gun manufacture and the making of buckles, buttons and steel toys (brooches and other ornaments). It was also developing as a centre for merchants supplying raw materials to the hardware manufacturers of much of the rest of the Black Country, and selling and despatching its finished products to London, other parts of England and overseas.[2]

Bristol's population grew from 12,000 to 20,000 during the seventeenth century, and increased substantially in the early eighteenth century. It differed from Liverpool and Birmingham in already being one of England's largest towns in the sixteenth and early seventeenth centuries. After London, it was England's leading port. Like Liverpool, in the later seventeenth century it benefited from the rapidly growing North American and West Indian commerce, which was added to its existing trade with Ireland and southern Europe. The volume of shipping entering the port from the West Indies rose from 1,900 tons in 1670 to 5,200 tons in 1700, and the number of ships from Virginia doubled between 1660 and the end of the century. Its position at the focal point of two systems of water communications, that of the Bristol Channel and the River Severn, enabled it to distribute not only imported sugar and tobacco, but Black Country metal goods, West Country cloth, Welsh coal and wool, and Cornish tin, as the output and prosperity of the west Midlands, south-west England, and south Wales steadily grew.[3]

In all three towns in the later seventeenth century the landowners or developers (who acquired land for housing schemes) were laying out building plots and new streets and builders were erecting homes for the growing population. Compared with London in the same century (where the population rose by several hundred thousand) and with these towns at a later period, the number of houses erected was small. Bristol probably added about 1,500 dwellings to its housing stock over the whole century, 1600–1700, and some of its 2,000–2,500 dwellings inherited from an earlier period were rebuilt or altered. If half the existing stock was rebuilt, an average of only about 25 or 27 homes was built each year. In fact Bristol was almost certainly growing faster after the 1650s than in the early seventeenth century, so that probably an average of between 30 and 40 dwellings was erected each year in the later seventeenth century. Birmingham probably added about 500 houses to its stock between 1670 and 1700: making an allowance for rebuilding (say 200 houses), an average of about 24 dwellings was erected each year. The numbers probably accelerated in the 1680s and 1690s. In the 1700s, when building reached an unprecedented level, the normal figure was at least 50, declining sharply for several years after about 1715. In Liverpool the normal average number of homes erected (allowing for some rebuilding) between 1660 and 1700 was probably between about 27 and 35.[4]

Only 10 or 20 per cent of these dwellings in all these towns were substantial houses of, say, eight or ten rooms. Writing in 1858 of Liverpool as it existed in the first quarter of the eighteenth century, when many old houses still survived, the historian J. A. Picton said four streets had the most respectable houses, but elsewhere they were mostly cottages, with two rooms on the ground floor and one or two storeys above, the upper storey being partly in the roof.[5] A substantial minority of the population (if not more) lived in only two or three rooms. In Birmingham in 1671 almost half the houses had only one hearth, suggesting dwellings of one, two or three rooms.[6] The average number of houses being built was approximately similar to that in many small but growing market towns in Victorian England, although the amount of accommodation (in terms of number of rooms) being provided was probably slightly bigger (on average) in the Victorian towns.

Building was still important in several ways in the three seventeenth-century towns. Most obviously it provided accommodation for the growing population. Work was available for local building craftsmen, particularly carpenters, masons and bricklayers, and timber merchants, brickmakers and suppliers of building stone. These were numerous in the working population: in Bristol in 1671 the masons, bricklayers and paviours petitioned to form a city company or guild of their own. Out of forty-six immigrants into Birmingham named in a register of settlement certificates drawn up between 1686 and 1726, whose occupations are stated, nine were in the building trades.[7]

Housing and mortgages on housing were an important investment for the savings and spare capital of many of the more prosperous townspeople, at a time when people did not look beyond the locality for outlets for their money. From another point of view, nearly all these dwellings were to be rebuilt in the next 100 or 200 years as a central business district emerged in a town many times its size, but the street pattern which the contemporary landowners and developers created still remains.

The Bristol Corporation Estate

Bristol in the later seventeenth century covered about 300 acres on both banks of the River Avon. Much of the building land was provided by private landowners, but probably about a quarter or a third was Corporation property. The Corporation was aware of the financial advantages of letting building land in terms of a higher rent per acre than if let for farming purposes, and sought to make it as profitable as possible. Before the Castle lands began to be let in 1656 the Corporation decided to buy out the interest of a chamberlain in a house on a property, as, if he took possession, "the City cannot so well improve to their best profit and benefit the rest of the buildings and ground".[8] The Corporation bargain books summarized agreements to lease by the surveyors of the city lands for building and rebuilding, and most though not all contracts appear to have been recorded. They reveal the Corporation owning land suitable for development as well as house property in many parts of the city. Building was undertaken in various locations in the early as well as the later seventeenth century.

A study of the bargain books between 1660 and the 1700s show that the grant of building sites was very spasmodic. Thus there were Corporation developments in several parts of the city in the 1660s and 1670s but none in the 1680s and 1690s. In the Marsh area adjoining the River Avon an exceptional number of leases were made in 1664, and a few in 1673, and a grand scheme (Queen Square) began in 1699. Bursts in the growth of the wealth and population of Bristol no doubt affected the demand for building sites, and may to some extent explain the exact timing of Corporation grants, although no precise evidence of this has been traced. The reversion to the Corporation of a close or large piece of property at the end of a lease permitted it to make several grants of building land at the same time; on the other hand it was possible for the Corporation to buy out a tenant whose interest blocked building development. The availability of land in favourable locations on private estates on the edge of the city may partly explain the absence of Corporation grants of new sites in some periods, although little is known at present about the history of these estates. Probably the Corporation did not have any more land suitable for building on the edge of the town (apart from the Marsh) in the 1680s and 1690s.

There were two major Corporation building developments proceeding in the 1660s. One was in the area of the Old Castle, in the eastern part of the town, and the other in King Street on the edge of the Marsh on the south-west edge of the town. The Corporation had bought the Castle and its possessions in Bristol (as well as those in Gloucestershire) in 1630. The Castle was demolished in 1656 and the "letting and setting" of the land was handled by a committee, using a "platform", or topographical plan. Leasing began in 1656, and the whole area of between seven or eight and ten acres was built up by the early 1670s.[9] It lay within the eastern city wall, beyond which houses stretched for several hundred yards to Lawford's Gate and the London Road; the building plots were thus well within the built-up area of the city. In addition to at least thirty-four leases granted between 1656 and 1660, twenty-eight building leases were registered between June 1661 and March 1669, half of them in the first three years. The plots were mostly in Castle Street, which was about 250 yards long, with several in the roughly parallel Castle Green (Street) and the short Tower Street which linked them. As was usual, they were oblong, with the narrow end fronting the street. They varied in frontage length between about 20 and 80 feet, and frequently had a depth of 70 or 80 feet. The leases required tenants to build a façade aligned to those of the other buildings in the street (written as "uniform to the rest of the Castle buildings") and sometimes the bargain-book entry adds "three storeys high besides the roof". They are recorded as being for 41 years or four lives, or for one of these terms. These were intended as building lease terms: 41 years was longer than the normal 21-year lease, and four lives than the usual three lives. In 1657 several lessees complained about the hardness of their bargain, and in 1661 another complaint was dismissed for the time being and the surveyors told not to let for more than 41 years or four lives. Most of the sites were let at a rent of between 1*s* and 1*s* 6*d* per foot frontage. Tenants were allowed between two and five years to erect houses and most of them did so: some of the plots with a frontage of only 20 feet were intended for one house; on the rest two, three or four houses were erected.[10]

The King Street development consisted of one broad street about 250 yards long. It lay on the edge of the Marsh, a flat area used partly for recreation and partly for grazing. In 1663 it was decided to build a new street of uniform houses, with the surveyors of the city lands letting and setting the ground. Eighteen leases were registered early in 1664.[11] There were no existing buildings on any of the plots: they had a frontage of between 20 and 83 feet and a uniform depth of 80 feet, and were intended for one, two or three front houses. They were required to be three storeys high and in some cases the entry includes a reference to them being uniform with the rest of the buildings. Probably on account of the complaints about the terms on the Castle estate, the builders were given the longer term of 99 years determined on five lives, and the rent was 1s 6d per foot frontage. The street had the advantage of being within a few hundred yards of the High Street and very close to the Keys, and was attractive to (and probably partly designed for) merchants and well-to-do mariners. The length of the leases and the insistence on three-storey buildings suggest that it was intended for substantial houses.

There was also a small amount of building in one or two other locations on the Corporation Estate in the 1660s, particularly Rosemary Lane which lay beyond the city wall on the eastern edge of the town. Four sites were leased in 1667 in Rosemary Lane. The city was probably not concerned in this case in getting large houses built, for there were no building covenants and the leases were only for three lives, the same as a non-building lease. The tenants were expected to pitch the street in front of the site. The site was not salubrious and had to be made fit for housing: "by reason of the ditch running through the midst of it a very noysome place to the neighbourhood thereabouts and dangerous to children". A man was leased some empty ground at the upper end of the lane, having "been at considerable charges for building up a wall for the passage of water and making of houses of office". Small tenements were built on this land.[12]

In 1669 the Common Council considered a proposal to build further on the Marsh, and resolved that

> upon consideration of the Cities engagements and the better discharging of debts; and considerable sums owing, it is this day ordered and agreed that it shall be referred to the Mayor and Surveyor of the Citty lands to view the void ground round about the Marsh and to consider what number of feate may be conveniently allowed, and to lease the same out for the uniform building of houses there and make a good key. . . .

Thus the scheme combined facilities for shipping with housing. The leases were to be for 99 years "if five lives live soe long" and the project was again intended to be for substantial houses. In fact only four leases are recorded, in February 1673. In addition to the covenants to build uniform three-storey houses, the lessees were expected to build in oak, a reflection of the fact that timber building was still normal in Bristol until near the end of the seventeenth century.[13]

In 1676 the Castle orchard, six acres to the south of the Castle Street, having reverted to the possession of the Corporation, was leased for building. A bridge was made over the Castle ditch, and a new road 20 feet broad (Queen Street) laid out through the property. The ten leases granted during the year required the builders to erect houses three storeys high within three years. They were given the choice of the normal building lease term or 50 years absolute, and chose the latter.[14]

The following year the site of some house property on the south side of Bristol bridge near St Thomas Street was redeveloped for housing. This was in the heart of the built-up area and the leases were exceptional in several ways. The Corporation was especially careful about the façades of the new houses and charged a very high ground rent. The fronts were to be "uniform and beautiful to the street(s)", the first storey 10 feet, the second 9½ feet and the third 8½ feet. As an example of the high prices charged, a site 56 by 38 feet was let at £37 per annum during the 50-year term. The houses had to be erected in the unusually short space of nine months.[15]

The bargain book for the 1680s and 1690s reveals no major estate development by the Corporation until 1699. Instead it is concentrating on rebuilding improvements and alterations, to various property on which new leases were needed, in different parts of the City. It was common to insist on the expenditure of a certain sum on building. Thus on property in Redcross Street leased in 1652 as a messuage, garden and workhouse which was now out of repair a new lease was granted on 17 August 1689 for a fine of £35 and a condition that £200 was spent on building and repair within three years.[16]

At the end of the 1690s the Corporation launched an outstandingly ambitious scheme, involving the construction of a large square, Queen Square, surrounded by blocks of houses divided by the roads entering the square. The project is described in some detail by Mr Ison, particularly from the architectural aspect. He thought that Lincoln's Inn Fields in London probably provided the model. At a meeting of Council on 23 October 1699, "Mr Mayor acquainted the house that Dr Reede [Vicar of St Nicholas] has made a Proposell to build an house on the Marsh and he heares severall other Cittizens are willinge to build on the Marsh. Question was put whether tenures and estates should be granted to persons to build houses on the Marsh". A committee was appointed to treat and make contracts. As a lease of a site in the Square was granted on 20 November it is clear that the general scheme was already prepared.

The square was about 550 by 550 feet. The lessees of the plots were required to erect the houses with a court in front, to make brick façades with stone quoins, with the height specified. A typical lease was that granted to the mariner Woods Rogers on 8 December 1702 for a term of

52 years. Behind the court 10 feet deep the house front was "to be made with brick the quoins with ffreestone"; with at the top a carved wooden eaves-cornice. The other walls were to be stone: timber and ironwork were to be substantial: the roof windows were to be lucarnes. The first storey was to be 11 feet in height, the second 10 feet and the third 9 feet. Nevertheless, there was a limit to the uniformity of the houses as, in Ison's words, "No particular effort appears to have been made to ensure symmetry by deciding beforehand the positions of the single- and double-fronted houses, or by parcelling the ground into regular units." Clearly the Bristol builders preferred a fixed-year term, and this was accepted by the Corporation.[17]

Most of the sites were leased and built on between 1700 and 1718, and the last leases were granted in 1725. Prominent local merchants and mariners were among the lessees as well as the usual building craftsmen. A sign of the exclusive character of the development was the prohibition of noisome trades, which naturally excluded some working craftsmen as tenants. Thus in Reade's lease "no tenement to be lett out to any sort of Tenants particularly no smiths shopp brewhouse not to any tallow-chandler or to any other tradesmen who by noyse danger of ffire or ill smells shall disturbe or annoy any of the inhabitants who shall build near it".

While the development of Queen Square was fundamentally a response to the ever-growing prosperity of the merchant community of Bristol the precise timing of its start late in 1699 may have been the consequence of the years of good trade between 1698 and 1701 which followed the end of the French Wars of 1689–97. There was a boom in building elsewhere in England in the last years of the century. It is not known how much other house building there was in Bristol in these years, but the public building is one sign of the local prosperity at this time. Several almshouses were built in about 1700; the Council House was rebuilt in 1703 and 1704, and Colston's great school was erected after 1709.[18] The link with trade is shown by the erection of a Customs House in the Square on the site by the Corporation in 1710–11. It was forty years since the erection of King Street and Bristol had become much larger and more prosperous; the time had clearly come for another and greater building project for houses for merchants and other wealthy citizens.

Building Estates in Birmingham

In Birmingham the surviving documentary evidence, consisting mainly of deeds and abstracts of title, shows that in the last quarter of the seventeenth century and the beginning of the eighteenth century the building land lay in many closes, typically of several acres, owned by at least a dozen people. Some of the owners were gentry who did not live in Birmingham, such as William Colmore of Warwick. The governors of the Grammar School held parcels of land as well as house property. Some of the owners laid out fields or parcels of several acres for building, preparing at least one street and marking out and selling or leasing the building plots. Others sold or leased the land to one person, or two acting jointly, who then acted as developer, preparing the streets and building plots.

In the 1670s houses were concentrated round the main Bull Ring market and along a short high street leading out to the north, beside a main street for about half a mile leading south-eastwards from the Bull Ring through the low-lying districts of Digbeth and Deritend (the road for Stratford, Coventry and Warwick), and for 150–200 yards along five main lines of communication in the opposite direction to market towns and industrial centres in Staffordshire and Worcestershire.

There is little documentary evidence about building in the 1650s and 1660s, but by the 1680s physical growth is apparent. Between 1670 and about 1700 the pattern of building expansion took several forms. The growing value of a location adjoining the market place led to the more intensive use of existing sites by the erection of tenements in back yards. At the same time housing adjoining main roads out of the town to the north, west and east increased, the land naturally being supplied by several owners. This presumably reflected the town's growing commercial and industrial ties with neighbouring towns.[19]

More important was the layout of at least five short new streets about 100–200 yards long on small crofts owned by several people comprising about twelve acres in a rough square bounded on three sides by the Bull Ring and the High Street and existing houses in Edgbaston Street and New Street. This development may have reflected the growing value of sites within a short distance of the market-place. Activity was most intensive between 1687 and 1692. A Birmingham short cutler, Robert Mansell, bought at least one croft before 1689 and both built houses and sold plots to other builders. Thus in August 1690 Robert Bridgens, carpenter, purchased a site for £17 with a frontage of 4 yards 1 foot adjoining a new street on which he was to build a house.[20] In the same year Colmore leased the school croft to three building craftsmen on a 99-year lease which was intended for houses and a new street 9 yards wide.[21] In 1692 another Warwickshire gentleman, Robert Phillips, was leasing plots in Ashford croft adjoining Phillips Street, which he probably laid out himself; in May 1692 he leased John Jennens, mason, a site with a 10-yard frontage to the street, for 99 years at 13*s* 4*d* per year, and a similar site at the same rent to Richard Pinley, bricklayer, on which he built two houses.[22]

Building was widespread in the 1700s. Birmingham building craftsmen, manufacturers and tradesmen were preparing land either as original owners or (probably more typically) on property acquired for development. In 1702 Pinley and a carpenter (Thomas Lane) leased Barn croft, on the west side of the town, from a local charity estate for 99 years at £3 10*s*. In July 1707 they rented Betteridge croft nearby for 99 years at £7 10*s* from another developer, Samuel Vaughton, a Birmingham gunsmith, who had himself on 25 March rented several fields (perhaps about 12 acres) from an absentee owner, Richard Smallbrook, a Fellow of Magdalen College, Oxford, who had inherited the estate. On Betteridge croft Pinley and Lane were sub-leasing small plots in 1708. The Vaughton family were still leasing plots in the 1720s.[23]

On the opposite side of the town there were two more considerable building schemes. Stephen Newton, baker, bought three closes and staked out two new streets, Lichfield Street and Newton Street, each 10 yards wide. A surviving abstract of title states that in June 1709 he sold William Stevens, bricklayer, a plot 15 by 35 yards for £15, having already sold several building plots.[24] In about 1702 on adjoining land called the Priory (about ten or twelve acres) John Pemberton, a wealthy Birmingham iron-monger, laid out a small square of about 60 yards, with a street leading out of the middle of each side to link (in three cases) with existing thoroughfares. He sold building plots around the square and in the streets. Both the dedication of land for a square and the forbidding of certain offensive trades on the estate show that Pemberton intended to form a small select quarter. The substantial size and value of the houses round the square and the occupations of early residents – several merchants like Pemberton and professional men – point to the success of the project.[25] Its dating suggests that Queen Square in Bristol was the inspiration for this much smaller scheme.

There was a lull in the opening of new housing estates in the 1710s, although some building continued. Together with the construction of Birmingham's second parish church under an act of 1708, the development of the square in the 1700s symbolizes the first great burst of building on the outskirts in the history of the town. It was on a scale vastly greater than that in the years about 1690.

The Bristol Corporation developments suggest that in at least some parts of Bristol there was an attempt to ensure the building of houses of substantial, uniform type in streets by the use of building covenants. The Birmingham building leases and sales of plots suggest that in most cases the landowners and developers did not try to control the type and style of the houses. The deeds of about 1690 relating to Phillips Street and neighbouring roads do not include building covenants. After about 1700 it became more common to require lessees to erect one or more houses within a stated period, sometimes specifying a minimum sum to be spent, or just a substantial house. In a few instances the number of storeys to be built is stated. In some streets the absence of covenants probably means that landowners did not intend substantial houses to be built. But in others the matter seems to have been left to the builders. In one known case, Bell Street in 1700, the builders agreed among themselves to erect houses with an exact elevation specified, "to the intent that the same common streete or way and the building thereof on both sides the same way be uniforme handsome and comodious and therefore the more gratifull and pleasant to such persons as shall inhabit therein". In two streets grants of a plot some years after other nearby sites were conveyed to builders in-cluded covenants to ensure that houses were built similar to those already erected; this may have been at the request of the existing houseowners or tenants to maintain the general quality of the street's environment, but whether landlords or tenants had tried to regulate the earlier house-building is not known. Thus in some of Birmingham's streets, as at

Bristol, streets of substantial houses were built uniformly, but the land-owners appear to have been only partly responsible.[16]

The Moore Estate in Liverpool

A principal source for estate development in later-seventeenth-century Liverpool is the Moore rental. The Moores were one of the two principal urban landowning families of the time, holding property on all of the seven original streets of the town, which formed a double cross on land above the River Mersey and in the neighbouring fields (Map 6.1, p. 119).[27] The family had been landowners in Liverpool for 450 years when the document was drawn up by Edward Moore in the years 1667 and 1668. Described by the editor Thomas Heywood in 1847 as, "a species of rent roll raisonne", it consists of comments on the property held by each of his tenants, street by street, written for the use of his son. This document is of such great interest that it deserves a section on its own.

Edward's father, Colonel Moore, had died leaving a debt of £10,000, and Old Hall at Liverpool had to be leased by his son. This may have made Edward tighter in his dealings with his tenants than many landowners, and particularly interested in the future development of the estate.[28] He was at once quick to condemn men whom he believed drove a hard bargain with him in taking a lease, who did not pay their rents or proved difficult in some way as tenants, to speak well of those he liked and to notice instances of his generosity or kindness. Several examples may be given to illustrate these aspects of his attitude towards his tenants, and his concise, sharp style of writing. "A tenant in Chapel Street, Thomas Lanclet, is a drunken idle fellow: to this house he hath a fine large croft on the back side. If I could have bought him out of it, there was one would have laid out four hundred pounds on a dwelling . . . this fellow and his wife are two such idle people that they scarce ever pay me either rent or hens." Widow Plome in Castle Street was "a good honest woman. A pretty new house. I did put in her son's life for £9 and the building this house". In Dale Street he wrote of Jane Tarlton, "her husband was drowned at Dublin, and I gave her a lease for three lives in this house for £15, although £30 was named (when I was offered £60), merely out of charity, she having many small children".[29]

He had a number of ways of improving the estate. To derive maximum financial advantage in terms of fines and secure tenants who would pay their various rents, leasehold properties were kept as small as possible. Of one tenant in Old Hall Street, John Lorting, he wrote: "he hath in this lease what may well be made three several dwellings; and fail not to part them whenever you fine them; for if you lease them to several, they will, with the ten lands in the field, give you at least £150, though his fine was but £50 and to build one of these houses, which cost him £50 more." He followed the usual practice of remitting fines wholly or in part on building leases. For a house built by William Bushell in Moor Street he remarked "he never gave me penny fine; he built it". In Castle Street a tailor, John Mornely, paid a small £13 fine and built a house costing at least £100, so that the next lease would be worth a £60 fine.[30] Sometimes to encourage building he paid for one or both gable ends. In Pool Lane he wrote of William Gardiner, Bailiff: "a very honest man. He paid no fine, only built the house: it is a very good house. Let the old rent be raised to forty shillings per annum, and the fine to sixty pounds. Remember, to this house I found him one gable end, which cost me six pounds."

More interesting are his schemes for new streets, of which the document is full. Two new streets had already been laid out on the estate, Moor Street and Fenwick Street. Moor Street was all his own land, in Castle Street field, and it was laid out partly 15 feet and partly 18 feet broad. The making of the street involved his workmen cutting into the rock. He also sank a well for the use of the street, costing about £6. He expected the houses to be similar, and condemned one Robert Wade: "this man should have built two dormer windows, as others did". The first house in the street set the pattern, all the rest of the building lessees engaging to build uniform with the first house. Moore claimed that an apothecary who built the first house on one side "wronged this street five hundred pounds" by building two stories instead of four.[31]

Fenwick Street was also on Moore's land, but there were problems in its layout: he was unable to buy some land belonging to another landowner named Crosse.[32] There was also difficulty in getting tenants to surrender part of their land: of one Joan Holt in Water Street he wrote: "this old woman she did use me very hard when I made Fenwick Street; in a word, she would let me have nothing after me, either as her landlord or a friend. She is the only hindrance for houses on that side Fenwick Street; for the little piece of her back side, she had six times as much land of me in the town field." If all her back property was removed it would have been possible to build houses along Fenwick Street. He describes in an interesting manner the making of the street, which was a costly investment:

> Have in mind I was at the sole charges of freeing and carrying all the rubbish and earth out of this street; that I had two or three carts a day, and four fillers, lusty men, a day, for 17 days together, in carrying and sinking the street from Robert Lion's house to widow Creton's door; for I have taken it near three quarters of a yard deep, or more, all the way, to make the water, God willing, fall that way into the Water Street; and if God permit, after Christmas I am to the same fillers, to fall the rest of the street to the bridge, and then from the bridge to the post and chains. This will cost a great deal of money.[33]

The street was to be paved at the cost of the building tenants, Moore having to pay for sections where no sites had been laid out.

So far as the future was concerned, vacant land adjoining existing streets was obviously suitable for building. Thus of Pit Hey field adjoining Tithebarn Street he wrote: "either keep it to the demesne as formerly, or lease all the front lying to the Tithebarn Street, where you may have several good houses, and lay to each a brave back side, reserving from every house at least 15/- a year".[34] But he had new streets constantly in mind. On the north side of the town two fields called the Parlor-Hay and the Barn-Hey were leased:

> if ever this falls in, and trading as good as now, you may very well make a street; the front of the houses on the West side, standing towards the lane, goes into the town field, and the front of the houses in the Barn-Hey to face the other. Then you may allow to each house, on both sides, large back sides . . . or, if you please, take good advice whether it be not better to cut a street through the Parlor-Hey to the river, which might be no steeper than the Chapel Street, taking it by degrees away.[35]

He was particularly interested in a more ambitious idea for developing the south side of the town involving four closes "you might have a little town there built all on your own land". If the Pool on the south side was made accessible for shipping the trade of the town would be concentrated on this part of the town. "You may have building here worth far more than twenty thousand pounds."[36] The area was built on during the next fifty years.

The Moore "rental" is of enormous interest, as the landowner's attitude is explicitly revealed. The project of new streets and buildings sites, the physical preparation of the roads, the rough design of the houses, the layout of backsides, and the fixing of rents are all described in the document.

The different kinds of documentary evidence for the three towns provide a fascinating insight into some aspects of urban estate development at this early period. Of particular interest are the attempts by landlords to regulate house building and especially to ensure some degree of uniformity in the number of storeys of houses in a street. This is very noticeable both on the Bristol Corporation Estate and the Moore Estate in Liverpool. The Bristol estate reveals a variety of practice in this respect according to the location of the development and (presumably) the type of tenant expected to live in the new housing. The Moore rental shows the difficulty a landlord might have sometimes in enforcing his wishes about the size and style of building. The Birmingham deeds suggest that the practice of using covenants might differ among landlords in a particular town.

Although landlords had a vital part to play, the builders sometimes made their own contributions. In Bristol they appear to have forced the Corporation to grant fixed-term leases of about 50 years; in Birmingham the tenants, not the landlord, were certainly responsible for the construction of houses of a similar type and size in one street, and may have been in many others. The Moore rental shows the importance of the landlord gaining the co-operation of the builders. Sometimes they pressed for the modification of the landlord's terms, sometimes regulated jointly their own work, and sometimes ignored covenants in the leases. In various ways builders might modify or add to the building schemes prepared on the part of the landowner.

Notes

1   C. W. Chalklin, *The Provincial Towns of Georgian England: A Study of the Building Process 1740–1820* (London, 1974), p. 20; P. G. E. Clemens, "The rise of Liverpool, 1665–1750", *Economic History Review*, 2nd ser., vol. 29, no. 2 (May 1976), pp. 211–12, 217.

2   Chalklin, p. 22: the estimated population for 1671 is based on the Heath Tax (741 homes: Warwickshire RO QS/11) which is probably a more reliable source than the Compton Census, 1676; M. J. Wise, "Birmingham and its trade relations in the early eighteenth century", *University of Birmingham Historical Journal*, vol. 2 (1949–50), pp. 58–62.

3   P. Clark and P. Slack, *English Towns in Transition 1500–1700* (Oxford, 1976), p. 52; Chalklin, p. 15; for a detailed study of Bristol trade in the seventeenth century see P. McGrath (ed.), *Records Relating to the Society of Merchant Venturers of the City of Bristol in the Seventeenth Century*, Bristol Record Society, Vol. 17 (1951), and *Merchants and Merchandise in Seventeenth-Century Bristol*, Bristol Record Society, Vol. 19 (1955).

4   These calculations are based on an average of five persons per house.

5   J. A. Picton, *The Architectural History of Liverpool* (Liverpool, 1858), p. 26.

6   Warwickshire Record Office QS/11: this assumes that the houses of people receiving poor relief were almost all only of one hearth.

7   Bristol Record Office: Corporation MSS (hereafter cited as BRO): Common Council Proceedings 1670–87, f.14; R. A. Pelham "The immigrant population of Birmingham 1686–1726", *Transactions of the Birmingham Archaeological Society*, Vol. 61 (1940), p. 62.

8   BRO: Common Council Proceedings, 1649–59, p. 98.

9   E. Ralph and M. E. Williams (eds), *The Inhabitants of Bristol in 1696*, Bristol Record Society, Vol. 25 (1968) p. xxi.

10   BRO: bargain books 1653–63, 1663–72; not all leases were registered in the books; Common Council Proceedings, 1649–59, p. 127; ibid., 1659–75, p. 35.

11   BRO: Common Council Proceedings, 1659–75, fol. 80; bargain book, 1663–72, fols 4–8; bargain book, 1681–94, fol. 82.

12   BRO: bargain book, 1663–72, fols 43, 44, 46; ibid., 1694–1711, fol. 22.

13   W. Ison, *The Georgian Buildings of Bristol* (London, 1952), p. 140; BRO bargain book, 1672–81, fols 5–7.

14   BRO: bargain book, 1672–81, fols 62–3, 66–70, 74–5. There were more leases in 1679 and 1680.

15   BRO: bargain book, 1672–81, fols 81–5.

16   BRO: bargain book, 1681–94, fol. 98.

17   Ison, pp. 141–4.

18   W. E. Minchinton (ed.), *The Growth of English Overseas Trade in the Seventeenth and Eighteenth Centuries* (London, 1969), p. 93; T. S. Ashton, *Economic Fluctuations in England, 1700–1800* (Oxford, 1959), p. 91; J. Evans, *A Chronological Outline of the History of Bristol* (Bristol, 1824), pp. 246, 252–3.

19   Birmingham Reference Library (hereafter cited as BRL): L. Chubb, "Deeds and documents relating to Birmingham in the Reference Library" (typescript, BRL 1925), fols 148, 171–2, 181, 186–7; BRL MS. S. H. B. 25b; *The Records of King Edward's School, Birmingham*, Vol. 2 (1928), pp. 109–10.

20   BRL MS. 372139 and Town Clerk's MS. 2354.

21   BRL Chubb fols 183, 250.

22   BRL Chubb fols 181, 212.

23   BRL Lee Crowder MS. ZZ329; Chubb fols 217, 219, 225, 239, 248, 260.

24   BRL MS. 372137.

25   BRL T.C. 1439; J. Hill and R. K. Dent, *Memorials of the Old Square* (Birmingham, 1897), pp. 10, 17, 80, 119.

26   BRL Chubb fols 181, 183, 186–7, 189, 211–12, 218, 219, 225, 234, 252; Lee, Crowder 344b, 1238, 1540, T.C. 1439, 2051, 2354, MS. 324166, 372137, 372139; the governors of the Grammar School in their leases in the 1680s and 1690s required a specified sum

to be spent within a period of time, but these were mostly rebuilding leases of old property: *Records*, Vol. 2, pp. 95–135.

27   Other individuals owned land in the town or on its edge, notably the Earl of Derby, but also the families of Fazakerley and Crosse. The Corporation acquired the Molyneux estate in Liverpool in 1672, which included the new Lord Street, and were making grants of building land thereafter: J. A. Picton, *Selections from the Municipal Archives and Records from 13th to the 17th Century* (Liverpool, 1883), pp. 285–93.

28   T. Heywood (ed.), *The Moore Rental (Remains Historical and Literary Connected with the Palatine Counties of Lancaster and Chester*, Chetham Society, Vol. 12 (1847), introduction.

29   ibid., pp. 18, 46, 62.

30   ibid., pp. 15, 54, 89.

31   ibid., pp. 84–5, 92–3, 97, 100.

32   ibid., p. 117.

33   ibid., pp. 38–9, 107.

34   ibid., pp. 29.

35   ibid., p. 11.

36   ibid., pp. 48, 80–1.

6 Liverpool Corporation as landowners and dock builders, 1709–1835

JANE LONGMORE

Liverpool's docks were a source of wonder to eighteenth-century visitors. An American tourist who passed through Liverpool in the summer of 1780 wrote: "the docks are stupendously grand, the inner one called Town Dock, lying in the centre of it".[1] At this time there were three docks; two more were to follow in the 1780s and 1790s and another six before 1836. These eleven docks were a vital prerequisite for the prosperity of the great Victorian port: their construction was a financial and engineering triumph as well as a tribute to the tenacity of the unreformed Corporation of Liverpool.

Merely eighty years previously Liverpool had been an unremarkable, if expanding, town on the north bank of the River Mersey. The local historian Enfield estimated that the population numbered 5,145 in 1700.[2] Local authority was vested by a succession of charters between 1207 and the late seventeenth century in the Common Council of the Corporation of Liverpool,[3] a self-elected body of forty-one burgesses. As early as 1700 the Corporation was demonstrating the ability to consolidate their property which was to make them more powerful than any other provincial Municipal Corporation prior to the Municipal Reform Act of 1835. In the confusion of the fifteenth century the Corporation had established prescriptive rights over all of the 900-acre common pasture between Liverpool and the Royal Park of Toxteth to the south. This gave them considerable confidence in their dispute with Lord Molyneux in the 1670s over ownership of this common pasture or "waste". The Molyneuxs, a local family, had taken advantage of Charles I's financial difficulties in 1627 to acquire the freehold of the Lordship of the Manor of Liverpool. However, as a royalist, Lord Molyneux suffered during the subsequent political vicissitudes of the seventeenth century. The Corporation of Liverpool, as supporters of the parliamentarian cause, seized the opportunity to ask Parliament for permission to enclose and improve the waste.

By 1650 the community had expanded to the edge of the 900-acre Corporation Estate and cast its eyes enviously over this land. At virtually no cost the Corporation was then able to increase its revenue from rents quite substantially as burgesses took leases of parts of the waste for agricultural use. It therefore came as a considerable shock when the Restoration of Charles II reinstated Lord Molyneux as landlord of the town and common with renewed control of the manorial rights and petty customs. The town bitterly resented this revived feudal domination after fifteen years of freedom and began a legal fight to contest the lordship of the common in 1669. The expense of the legal contest probably explains the compromise of 1672 whereby the Corporation of Liverpool took from Lord Molyneux a 1,000-year lease of all the lordship at an increased annual rent of £30 per annum. Molyneaux's tenure of the lordship was reduced to a nominal ownership by this long lease and the Corporation was able to enclose further sections of the waste to let it to tenants. Realizing that they had lost effective control, the Molyneux family were to sell the reversion of this lease in 1777 for £2,250.

The waste was to form the bulk of the valuable Corportion Estate: from a mere twenty acres in 1672 it had increased to approximately 900 acres in 1674. Liverpool Corporation was exceptional among corporate land-owners in gaining control of such a huge piece of land at little cost and retaining it as an area for the future expansion of the town. Sheffield and Manchester, for example, never obtained the lordship of their adjoining wastes. Moreover, using both the rent roll and the land itself as security the Corporation was able to borrow money in the eighteenth century to finance ambitious commercial schemes.

It had soon occurred to enterprising councillors that the right to enclose land *on the seashore* between high and low watermarks was an additional benefit of the lordship.[4] Between 1709 and 1835 another hundred acres was added to the Corporation Estate in this way. The Corporation extended its role from landowning to dock-building.

As Okill's conjectural map demonstrates, seventeenth-century Liver-pool possessed a natural inlet or haven for ships in the "Pool", a creek extending inland from the Mersey for a few hundred yards and fed by streams which ran down from the encircling sandstone ridge (see Map 6.1 and Figure 6.1, *c.* 1650). Liverpool's commercial origins lay in the salt and Irish trades: small coasting vessels called in at high tide and found safe anchorage in the Pool. The swiftness of the tides and the rocky bottom of the Mersey estuary would have been particularly hazardous for any vessel forced to anchor in the river.

By 1670 trade was beginning to increase rapidly. Within thirty years Liverpool had broken away from the customs authority of the adjacent port of Chester and built its own customs house to symbolize its commer-cial expansion and independence. The traveller Daniel Defoe noticed the quickening pace of commercial life in Liverpool:

> The town was at my first visiting it about the year 1680 a large handsome, well built and increasing or thriving town, at my second visit, around 1690, it was much bigger than at my first seeing it. . . . I am told that it still visibly increases both in wealth, people, business and buildings. What it may grow to in time, I know not.[5]

The reason for this rapid expansion was partly geographical: late-seven-teenth-century Liverpool was very favourably situated to exploit the trade

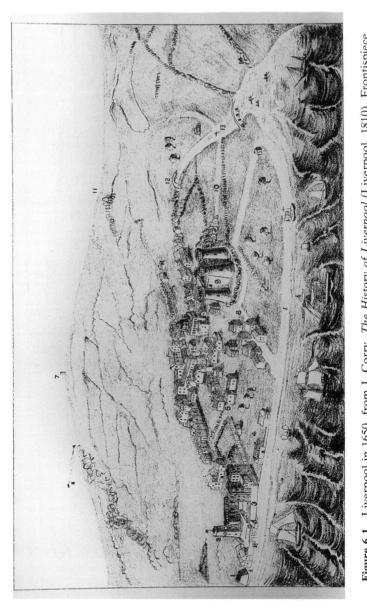

Figure 6.1 Liverpool in 1650, from J. Corry, *The History of Liverpool* (Liverpool, 1810), Frontispiece

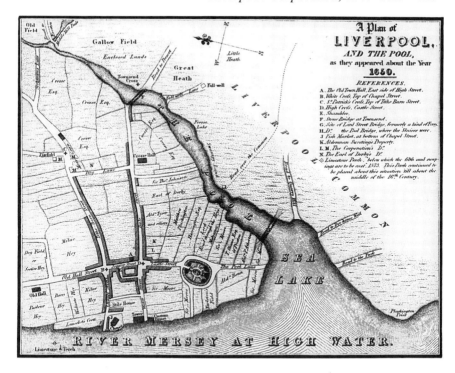

Map 6.1 Charles Okill's Conjectural Map of Liverpool, c. 1650, based on Corporation Leasing Records. By courtesy of Liverpool Record Office.

of the colonies. Hitherto, Britain's trade had mainly looked east to Europe, and the east coast ports and London had been better positioned than Liverpool for these routes. However, as the colonial tobacco and sugar trades began to expand Liverpool took the lead from Chester: the latter was twenty miles up the heavily silted River Dee, while Liverpool was only three miles from the open sea.

Newcomers were attracted to Liverpool by commercial opportunities. In the late seventeenth and early eighteenth centuries, there were immigrants from the Lancashire and Cheshire hinterland;[6] and shipbuilders, such as the Rathbones, established themselves on the wide sandy bank of the Mersey to service the increasing number of shipowners. Richard Cleveland, a London sugar merchant, came to Liverpool with Daniel Danvers, who built a large sugar refinery in 1671–2.[7] By 1702 Thomas Johnson MP could write to a fellow Liverpool tobacco merchant, "we are sadly envied, God knows, especially the tobacco trade, at home and abroad".[8]

Such immigrants were known locally as "strangers": they introduced a new commercial vitality to the little Merseyside community. They quickly saw that congestion in the Pool would limit Liverpool's commercial growth. It is also possible that the gradual silting of the Pool, which acted as the main sewer for the town, was beginning to prevent the entry of larger vessels. These would have to risk the perils of the river anchorage and unloading on the sandy foreshore.

Thus, it was the combination of a commercial need, entrepreneurial vitality and the availability of Corporation land which led to the construction of the first dock in 1709. The explanation for the timing of the dock might also lie in the fact that a dock of ten acres, the Howland Great Wet Dock, had recently been constructed at Rotherhithe. The owners of this docks had claimed that it could accommodate 120 of the largest merchant ships, "without the trouble of shifting, mooring or unmooring any in the dock for taking in or out any other". These claims seemed to be substantiated in the great storm of November 1703 which devastated other shipping in the Port of London: only one vessel in the Howland Dock had been slightly damaged.[9]

This must have made a great impression on contemporaries, who would have avidly discussed the notion of a large wet dock with gates onto the Thames tideway. The advantages of such a haven, especially in foul weather, would have been appreciated by the mercantile community, who faced the prospect of losses from increasingly extensive and valuable cargoes. Hyde calculates that from 1700 onwards merchant voyages saw a net return of double and often treble the original outlay of capita.[10] It is thus hardly surprising that the merchants who comprised the early-eighteenth-century Corporation of Liverpool began to consider the construction of a similar haven. The Town Books of 1709 refer to "a dock being highly necessary for the safety of all ships".[11]

Nothing as large as the Howland Dock was intended, partly because of the geographical limitations of the proposed site on the old Pool. There were also complex engineering difficulties. Rotherhithe was forty miles from the open sea. The dock had been dug out of dry land and then a narrow gut had been made to connect it with the River Thames. The Liverpool site adjoined a fast-flowing tidal river. As Francis Hyde points out:

> The River Mersey is like a bottle with narrow neck. On the north side stands Liverpool, on the south Birkenhead, Wallasey and New Brighton. The estuary is subject to strong tides and the pressure of water into and out of the great pool which forms the main container of the bottle, creates strong currents and a high rise and fall of water. It was precisely at this point in the neck of the estuary that the early sailing ships had to berth and load cargo.[12]

It is to the credit of the Corporation that its councillors were undeterred by the engineering problems of converting the marshy Pool into a wet dock. They marked out a rectangular area of about three acres and, realizing that local expertise was unavailable to cope with the technical problems of constructing such a novelty as a wet dock in a fast-flowing tidal estuary, they sought outside help. In November 1708 the Corporation ordered two councillors who were familiar with London, the Liverpool

MPs Sir Thomas Johnson and Richard Norris, to negotiate there for "a proper person to come to this town and view and draw a plan of the intended dock".[13]

The obvious source for such an individual was Rotherhithe. Nineteen months later, Johnson and Norris were thanked for their services in finding Thomas Steers of the City of London, "who was brought down on purpose" to be Dock Engineer at Liverpool.[14] Mystery surrounds Steers's origins, but it is surely too great a coincidence that a Thomas Steers of the City of London was an engineer living at Rotherhithe during the construction of the Howland Dock. He may have been the principal assistant. He set to work immediately in Liverpool and, having surveyed the site, confidently "staked it four parts nearer to the sea than set out before".[15]

The Corporation tackled the problem of finance in a similarly decisive fashion. Having judged that £6,000 would be necessary for the construction of the dock, it ordered the two MPs to obtain an Act of Parliament "for the raising of a sufficient sum".[16] This was an expensive undertaking but the Corporation did not flinch at having to borrow £1,200 only six months later on security of its property in order to cover the expense of obtaining the Act. Loss of nerve at that point would have had profound consequences for Liverpool's subsequent commercial growth.

The 1709 Act was innovatory. The Corporation was placed in the unique position of Dock Trustees: its dock was to be the first publicly-owned wet dock in Britain. It was empowered to borrow £6,000 to construct a dock on security of dock dues, which it was authorized to levy on ships entering and leaving the docks. It was hoped that the dock would earn about £600 per annum from such dues, thereby making dock bonds a safe investment. The dues were to be levied for twenty-one years from June 1710 and were to be used to build and repair the dock as well as providing security, interest and eventual repayment of the initial loan. After twenty-one years the dues were to be reduced to no more than a quarter and to be paid to the Trustees for the upkeep of the dock.[17] At this point the Corporation could not envisage the subsequent extension of the dock system which prevented repayment within the stated time.

Despite this enthusiastic start the construction of the first dock was a prolonged and difficult operation, both financially and technically. The wide sandy shore of the Pool was entirely covered at the spring tides. The work was therefore carried on behind a wooden stockade and with continuous problems of seepage. The site was soft mud through which the workmen had to take the foundations of the dock to a depth of about eighteen feet to reach the solid sandstone rock.[18] As clay was more readily available than good building stone at this time the sides of the dock were built of brick with stone piers and stone copings for additional strength. In front of the dock entrance gates Steers constructed an octagonal basin and, on the north side of this, a small graving dock for ship repairs. But manual excavation was a slow process; a single horse would pull six to eight loaded wheelbarrows to the top of the dock while empty ones descended. Construction dragged on for five years, so that in January 1716 a further Act had to be obtained to extend the time allowed for building the dock.[19]

The financial problems were as acute as the technical difficulties. The Dock Trustees borrowed money from local investors. With such large sums involved – much of which would have been loaned by the mercantile councillors themselves – reputations hung in the balance. As financial pressure increased, the Dock Trustees ranged further afield in search of funds: an investor from Warrington is recorded as early as 1711. By 1714, the Dock Trustees were trying to raise money to complete the dock by making strenuous efforts to lease the adjoining land on favourable terms.[20] By September the dock dues were no longer adequate security for the loan. The original £6,000 was exhausted and a further £5,000 had already been spent. At this point it would have been perfectly justifiable for the Corporation to have abandoned the whole venture as an over-costly gamble that had failed. It is to its credit that it remained committed to the scheme, mortgaging its own property, the Shambles, as security for a further £300 from a Mr Walker of Manchester.[21] Two years later the Act of Parliament mentioned above let the Corporation off the hook by sanctioning further borrowing of up to £4,000. The scheme was safe and the work was finally completed in 1719, with the shallow "Pool" completely built over, and converted into Liverpool's first deep dock (see Map 6.2, 1725 and Figure 6.2, 1728).

The enterprise and tenacity of the Corporation ensured that Liverpool had the advantage of a modern commercial facility. In turn, the construction of the docks encouraged further transport improvements as Liverpool needed better links with her hinterland to permit continued commercial growth. Hence, in 1720 the Mersey and Irwell Navigation Act authorized the improvement of the navigability of the rivers in an attempt to reach Warrington and Manchester. Steers played a crucial role in the planning of this scheme[22] and lent advice for similar improvements to the River Weaver for the carriage of Cheshire salt to Liverpool. The salt trade was regarded by the Liverpool historian Holt as "the nursing mother" of the port.[23] It was a cheap item of outfreight for the small trader with a reliable market as it was an article of universal consumption. Moreover, Cheshire salt was considered to be of superior quality and whiteness, allowing Liverpool merchants to win expanding markets for salt in Ireland and northern Europe. Baltic timber vessels considered salt as the most suitable outfreight from Liverpool. By 1732, another local historian calculates, out of 202 vessels owned by the Port of Liverpool eighty were sloops and flats carrying salt.[24]

Thus it is hardly surprising that he attributed the need for further dock construction within twenty years of the completion of the first dock to the pressure of the salt trade. However, Liverpool's merchants were also benefiting from the termination of the Africa Company's monopoly of slaving. In 1709 there had been one slave trader in Liverpool; by 1730 there were fifteen.[25] These commercial developments led to severe congestion in the octagonal basin. In bad weather ships were crowding into the basin and blocking access to the dock and dry dock. By 1737 the Corpor-

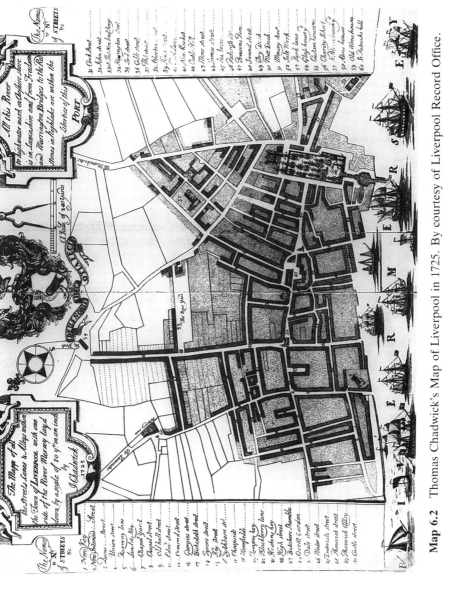

Map 6.2 Thomas Chadwick's Map of Liverpool in 1725. By courtesy of Liverpool Record Office.

Figure 6.2 A South-West View of Liverpool in 1728, from R. Muir, *Bygone Liverpool* (Liverpool, 1913), p. 11. The first dock can be seen to the right of the picture.

ation had accepted the need for further dock space. Its engineer Steers had been heavily occupied since 1730 with the construction of the Newry Canal in Ireland, but he was now ordered to turn his attention to the congestion in the Port of Liverpool.[26] According to Steers's plan and estimate, seven acres of reclaimed shoreline and £12,000 would be necessary for the construction of a new dock and the modificaton of the existing basin. As dock duties were increasing steadily[27] the Corporation felt sufficiently confident to press ahead with the scheme under 11 GEO. II c.32. This Act also revealed that £4,830 was still owing at interest on the previous dockworks – evidence that the dock was already a sound longterm investment.

Unfortunately, it was not a good moment to begin new dock construction. No sooner had the building contract been advertised and settled with Mr Edward Litherland, a local mason who was to build the new dock with stone obtained from a nearby quarry, than the War of the Austrian Succession broke out. During wartime government stocks were always a more attractive investment because of inflated interest rates. It is possible that dock construction at Liverpool was delayed by the consequent inability to procure much of the authorized capital. Steers was busy with the Newry Canal until 1742, as well as with local building schemes such as a theatre. Under the circumstances, the Corporation decided to limit work to the immediate priorities: the construction of a stone pier to replace the flimsy old wooden pier jutting from the south side of the octagonal basin and the remodelling of the latter into a larger rectangular shape. Both measures were intended to relieve the congestion experienced in the port, especially in bad weather.

Steers's death in 1750 probably caused further delays, although Henry Berry, his former clerk, who had overlooked the dock works in his master's frequent absences, was ordered to take over immediately. But locally funds were flowing into another grandiose scheme, the construction of the new Town Hall between 1748 and 1754 to the designs of the foremost architect of the day, John Wood of Bath. The Corporation itself was deeply preoccupied with this scheme which symbolized the burgeoning wealth and confidence of the provincial port.

Thus the new dock works dragged on until 1754 when the four-and-a-half-acre South Dock was completed. Once again, the Corporation dug into its own pocket to complete construction, providing an additional loan of £1,000.[28] There were now eighteen acres of docks and basins and trade was flourishing. The Liverpool Memorandum Book of 1753 lists 101 merchants "trading to Africa".[29] By undercutting their rivals at London and Bristol, Liverpool merchants were controlling half of England's "African trade" by 1764. Few Liverpool merchants were involved solely in the slave trade, but many indulged in a number of speculative ventures: returns varied from 500 per cent to complete losses.

The Corporation of 1709 could not have dreamed of such spectacular commercial growth within half a century. Liverpool had entered the ranks of the major British ports and the new dock space was inadequate virtually as soon as it was provided. A further problem arose from the increasing size of vessels. Tonnage increased steadily over the century. As early as 1748, the Corporation had to compensate a shipowner whose vessel had been so large that he had to wait sixteen tides for sufficient water to float her out of the dry dock after repairs. Six years later the Corporation was to order the construction of another dry dock at its own expense.[30] Once again its members demonstrated their willingness to respond to the needs of the mercantile community: without adequate repair facilities Liverpool would not have been able to compete with her rivals.

In their capacity as Dock Trustees, the Corporation councillors also pursued a forward-looking policy of land management. It was obviously advantageous to embark and enclose as much land as possible from the Strand, especially around the new docks. Such embankment was costly. Thus, the Corporation used attractive inducements to encourage lessees of land on the Strand to enclose the adjoining seashore. Rentals were delayed for up to three years and free stone was provided from the Corporation quarries for such embankment. Mindful of the difficulty of removing leaseholders should the need for dock extension arise the Corporation included appropriate surrender clauses in the leases of embanked ground. Leases of embanked land adjoining the Mersey were particularly attractive to shipbuilders as they were permitted to erect buttresses to the west of the retaining wall to launch their newly built ships. In turn, shipbuilders' yards were a perfect site for subsequent dock extension as they could be converted with ease. There were few buildings to be demolished when a shipbuilders' yard was appropriated for dock works.[31] Only if such incentives failed would the Corporation undertake the considerable expense of enclosing the land itself.

The number and size of vessels using the port by the 1760s forced the Corporation to apply for parliamentary authority to build another dock.[32] Rates and duties were to be continued for a further twenty-one years and no more than £25,000 was to be borrowed. Again the Corporation encouraged the scheme by donating the ground for the site of the dock. Moreover, it continued to counter problems as they arose: the violent storm of October 1762 which destroyed part of the newly built dock wall, the shortage of suitable building stone,[33] and the arguments concerning the layout of the new dock and its surrounding area. At five and a quarter acres the new dock was the most ambitious scheme yet undertaken so that a special committee of the Corporation was appointed in February 1765.

The dock was to be constructed to the north of the existing docks and was to project further into the fast-flowing river than the previous works. It was possibly felt that such a novel scheme ought to be thrown open for consideration by several engineers. Plans were submitted by the builder-architect, Thomas Lightoler,[34] "of the intended dock and other necessary works adjoining thereto", a reference to the most unusual feature of the new scheme, a range of adjoining warehouses. Neither of the earlier docks had purpose-built ranges of warehouses. Indeed for most of the eighteenth century their surrounding quaysides were mainly open and merchants deposited their cargoes for transit by cart to their individual warehouses. The advantages of dockside warehousing were so obvious that this feature was also included in the plans submitted by Berry, the dock engineer. Berry's original plan of 1765 has recently emerged from the archives held by the Mersey Docks and Harbour Board.[35] It clearly shows an arcaded range of warehouses on the eastern quay of the intended dock (see Maps 6.3 and 6.4, 1765). Three years later a payment is recorded to another local architect "for copying and altering the drafts of a set of warehoues intended to be built between Water Street and Moore Street".[36] Yet arguments continued to rage about the form of the warehouses and it was to be another two decades before the Dock Trustees were able to carry out the plan. In the meantime, lessees were encouraged to build their private warehouses.

Financial aspects of the new dock ran smoothly in comparison. The Dock Trustees were able to take advantage of the increasing wealth of Liverpool. Funds were gathered from April 1766 and the dock opened fairly promptly in 1771. But it was now becoming a matter of course for the Corporation to move on to the next extension of the docks as soon as the previous scheme was completed. The port was flourishing; new streets radiated from the town centre and magnificent Georgian houses were being constructed for Liverpool's wealthier merchants. Liverpool had outstripped her former rival Bristol as a port.

From 1774, the Corporation records refer to land "set apart" on the north shore for docks; land on the south shore was being purchased simultaneously for a massive £6,700.[37] The Corporation had possibly formulated a long-term plan for dock development as it became aware of the increasing profitability of its dock estate. The dock duties paid by ships entering and leaving the port had risen from £810 11*s* 6*d* in 1724 to £5,384 4*s* 9*d* in 1775.[38] Thus, it was in the confident expectation of continued growth that the Corporation ordered Mr Berry to mark out a piece of the Strand to be appropriated for the use of the docks in 1774. Such confidence made no allowance for international events. Within a year George III had proclaimed rebellion in the American colonies and Liverpool's trade was greatly disrupted. Income from dock duties began to fall and by 1780 they were bringing in £3,528 7*s* 7*d*. In such an uncertain climate the Corporation shelved its plans and it was to be a full decade before a post-war boom encouraged their revival.

By the time that a new committee was appointed in November 1784 to consider the construction of "one or more docks" the scale of operations had changed dramatically. Trade had been encouraged rather than hampered by the breakaway of the American colonies and Liverpool was in an excellent position to exploit this expanding market. Two new docks were constructed in rapid succession between 1785 and 1796 for the American trade: the five-acre King's Dock and the seven-acre Queen's Dock. Despite the fact that the Corporation was preoccupied with an enormous street improvement scheme in the centre of Liverpool its councillors continued, as Dock Trustees, to devote close attention to the improvement of the commercial facilities. This included the constant maintenance of the existing docks system, an increasingly costly operation as the docks aged, as well as provision of extra dry docks for repairs.[39]

Map 6.3 John Eyes's Map of Liverpool in 1765. By courtesy of Liverpool Record Office.

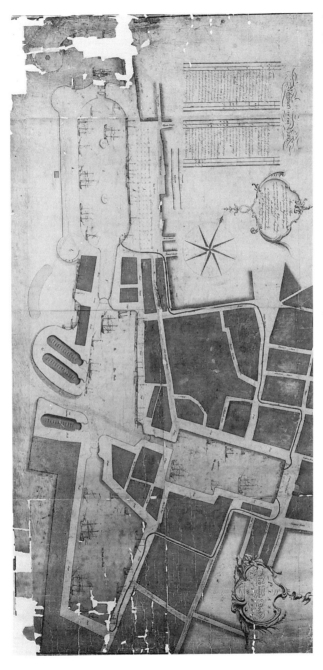

Map 6.4 Henry Berry's Plan of the Docks, 1765. The intended George's Dock and arcaded warehouses are shown on this plan. By courtesy of the Liverpool Maritime Museum.

The Corporation felt that it was appropriate to consider again an overall scheme for the subsequent extension of the docks. It was buying land in the early 1790s with future dock construction in mind, both to the north and south of the town.[40] By March 1792 John Foster, the Corporation surveyor, had prepared ambitious plans for the "improvement and extension of the docks". Unfortunately no trace of this plan now exists, but in February 1793 a permanent dock committee was appointed to execute the scheme and its surviving minutes between 1793 and 1837 enable us to gain some impression of Foster's plan.[41] He envisaged two new docks to the south of the town with a range of arcaded warehouses similar to those planned in the 1760s but running the *whole* length of the docks. This would have given the dock system an impressive visual cohesion but Foster's exciting plan was to be a casualty of the credit shortage during the wars of the 1790s. As the war against revolutionary France proceeded investors once again chose government stocks in preference to the lower interest rates offered by local investment. By 1793 the Corporation was facing a deep financial crisis, having overstretched itself in the improvement scheme and the purchase of vast areas for dock construction. It exhibited considerable skill in engineering a statutory entitlement to issue negotiable notes on security of the Corporation Estate up to the value of £300,000. The immediate crisis was averted, but it was obviously inappropriate to carry out Foster's scheme at a time of financial uncertainty.

Despite the disheartening interruption of its plans the Corporation persevered, helped by the fact that Liverpool's trade continued to increase during the twenty-three-year war. Mercantile confidence returned. The need for further dock space was now pressing. However, Liverpool was a more complex commercial and political community by the end of the eighteenth century and the Corporation found that it was no longer regarded as the automatic arbiter of dock affairs. Powerful vested interests had developed and suspicion was generated by the secrecy of the proceedings of the Dock Committee. By the 1790s many wealthy mercantile residents of Liverpool were not members of the Corporation and hence had no voice on the Dock Committee. The Corporation was a High Tory Anglican body; political or religious dissenters had to voice their opinions through the local press or through membership of the Parish Committee, another arm of local government. Matthew Gregson and Henry Wilckens, both members of the Parish Committee, maintained a vigorous opposition to Corporation efforts to promote further dock building, hinting that the Corporation was using dock construction to increase the value of land they had purchased beyond the Corporation Estate.[42]

Such suspicions do, at first glance, appear to be partially justified. Having obtained an Act of Parliament in 1799 for enlarging two old docks, constructing two new docks and doubling dock duties, the Dock Trustees had exhausted their statutory allocation of funds by 1802 without laying a stone of the new docks. In the same year they petitioned Parliament for authority to levy a futher £20,000 for dock construction. The Corporation claimed that it had used the funds allocated by the 1799 Act to repair the dilapidated state of the docks and to purchase the site of the south dock.

But the closed account books of the Corporation reveal purchases of land for the site of a north dock totalling £3,000 in October 1802. This land was sold to the Dock Trustees in 1806 for £67,406 18s 7d.[43] There was obviously something unethical about the Corporation purchasing land beyond its Estate, then obtaining powers to construct docks and selling the site to themselves as Dock Trustees at considerable profit.

On the other hand, the Dock Estate had drawn heavily on the financial and administrative resources of the Corporation during the eighteenth century, and such a transaction could be regarded as adjusting the balance. The land for the first three docks had been donated by the Corporation but, as land values rose in tandem with the commercial expansion of Liverpool, the Corporation began to regard such donations as unduly generous. Thus, the site of the King's and Queen's docks in the 1780s and 1790s had been sold to the Dock Trustees at cost price. The financial pressures of the late 1790s probably persuaded the Corporation to regard the Dock Estate as a source of profit.

The Corporation had never envisaged the financial complexity of dock construction when it had applied for powers as Dock Trustees in 1709, so that throughout the eighteenth century the funds of the two bodies had been intermingled and administered by their mutual personnel. The Corporation treasurer also managed the Dock accounts until the appointment of a separate Dock treasurer in September 1792. It was not until November of that year that the Corporation decided to open a bank account for Dock funds.[44] Prior to that date it is difficult to disentangle the accounts of the two bodies as money was simply moved around within the Corporation coffers. Much of the finance for dock construction was borrowed locally from prominent merchants such as Sparling, Bolden, Blackburne and Daltera, who were also members of the Corporation. In the 1780s John Blackburne had sold land required for the site of King's Dock for £6,000 but merely accepted the issue of Dock bonds as payment for the land.[45]

Such transactions had been relatively simple when the funds of the two bodies had not been distinct. There had also been a practical reason for unified financial administration. During the eighteenth century the Corporation Estate had been more financially secure than the Dock Estate and Dock bonds had been issued on security of the Corporation Estate. However, by the 1790s, with five wet docks and a range of dry docks and basins the Dock Estate was a valuable concern (see Map 6.5, 1796). Dock rates were increasing annually: by the mid-1790s they were producing over £10,000 per annum and the Corporation no longer felt obliged to nurture the Dock Estate financially. In 1793, the Dock Committee reported "that an account of long-standing now lies open between the Trustees of the docks and the Corporation and that the balance due to the Corporation is supposed to amount to the sum of £10,000 and upwards". The Corporation ordered the settlement of this debt.[46]

To the Dock ratepayers the Corporation justified its failure to implement the 1799 Act and its need for further funding under the 1802 Bill by pointing out that the cost of maintaining and repairing the docks

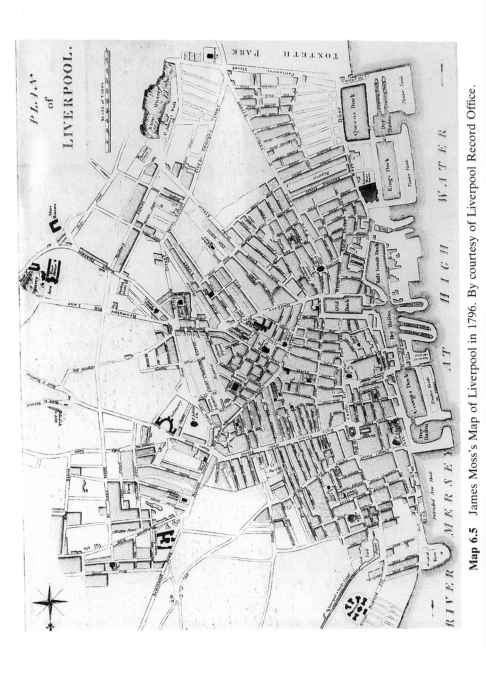

Map 6.5 James Moss's Map of Liverpool in 1796. By courtesy of Liverpool Record Office.

was a heavy burden which had absorbed much of the available finance. It is also possible that its councillors lacked the technical expertise to proceed further. In 1800, an independent expert was summoned to give his advice on the position of the new docks. Mr Jessop, a civil engineer who had designed the layout of the Bristol docks and who had been appointed engineer and designer of the London docks in 1800, presented his professional opinion in a lengthy letter to the Dock Committee.[47] Silting in the river and the increased tonnage of vessels using the port led to a demand for the new docks to be sited to the north of the town adjacent to deeper water. Jessop observed that, in his view, one large dock was preferable to two smaller ones as it involved less expense and subsequent management.

Despite these arguments, local opposition organized by the Parish Committee succeeded in killing the Bill. One critic explained that the Bill was "no favourite measure of theirs (its promoters) but had its rise in the pressing instances of government to adopt a plan for erecting docks upon a similar footing with the London docks".[48] There is indeed little evidence of enthusiasm for the Bill in the Town Books; credit was scarce during the Napoleonic wars and, in 1804, Dock rates had to be increased to the full extent permitted by the 1799 Act to satisfy the pressing demands of creditors and allow the works in progress to continue.[49]

Instead the Dock Trustees limited themselves to the consolidation and rationalization of the existing system during the first decade of the nineteenth century. An urgent consideration was the straightening of the river wall to prevent unequal accumulation of mud. The King's Dock was enlarged by embanking westward and the line of the embankment to the west of Salthouse Dock was also straightened. George's Dock basin was enlarged and repaired and a new basin to the south of Queen's Dock was constructed. Kaye's plan of 1810 reveals the extent of this massive rationalization (see Map 6.6).

Unfortunately, contemporaries failed to comprehend the need for this remodelling of the dock system. Perhaps the Dock Trustees were at fault in not explaining the severe consequences of silting if the river wall had not been straightened. Access to the docks would have become almost impossible. Suspicion of the activities of the Dock Committee continued. When the Corporation applied for another Act of Parliament to enable them to raise funds for the constructon of a much-needed dock in 1811 local opponents ignored the time and expense devoted to rationalization and again grumbled that the Corporation had not commenced either of the docks authorized by the Act of 1799. Resentment was provoked in particular by the clause in the new Bill which established that dock duties should become perpetual. The earlier Dock Acts, critics noted, had stated that the rates would be decreased eventually when the capital was paid off. They also expressed the fear that Liverpool would lose much of her commercial prosperity if she was unable to maintain her low rates. Finally, the Corporation was accused of "an overgrown desire of power and influence in the community".[50]

Stung by the criticism, the Corporation took the unusual step of entering

Map 6.6 Thomas Kaye's Plan of the Town of Liverpool in 1810. By courtesy of Liverpool Record Office.

a pamphlet war in order to present its case. In its view the Bill of 1811 was vital for the future commercial growth of Liverpool. Trying to mollify the cries for greater openness by the Dock Trustees, the Corporation included a clause to authorize the appointment of audit commissioners for the accounts of the Dock Estate. Combined with the pressing need for dock space, this temporarily curbed opposition and the Bill passed into law.

Between 1811 and 1825 dock-water space increased by approximately 80 per cent – almost the equivalent of the whole area of the eighteenth-century docks and basins. When the site of the old Fort and Battery was ordered to be purchased from the Board of Ordnance in 1811,[51] it was possible to begin construction of the first of the northern docks, the eleven-acre Prince's Dock. The size of the dock, which was to be used by corn merchants, illustrated the increasing volume of traffic as well as the advent of much larger ships. For this huge undertaking the Corporation relied once again on the advice of an eminent outsider. John Rennie, the celebrated engineer, was consulted about the problem of carrying the west wall of the new dock out into the river beyond the low water of spring tides.[52]

The docks increased rapidly and their construction became more complex in the post-Napoleonic period. Local expertise was no longer adequate. John Foster, the Dock Engineer, was a local man who had risen from the position of a humble joiner to his monopolistic role as both Corporation and Dock Engineer. Loyalty to a faithful servant may have prevented his earlier replacement but, on his retirement in 1824, the Corporation recognized the need for a better-qualified Dock Engineer. Vast sums of money were now involved in dock construction. Prince's Dock had cost approximately £450,000,[53] a striking contrast with the £25,000 expended on Queen's Dock between 1788 and 1796. A professional was needed and the job was advertised. After extensive interviews Jesse Hartley was selected from a short list of twelve for the post of Dock Engineer in October 1824. The new sense of professionalism was reflected in the allocation of specialized dock offices for the engineer and his clerks.

Hartley was to leave an extremely personal imprint on the development of the Liverpool dock system. A skilled professional engineer, he had drawn up his own plan of the future development of the Dock Estate within three months of accepting the job. In the next thirty-one years, he was to supervise the construction of eighteen docks. His first dock was the completion of Foster's legacy – the Brunswick Dock to the south of the town – between 1828 and 1832. However, Hartley's mind was already turning to the need to cater for the advent of the steam-powered ship. In 1830 the first of the steamship docks was built at a safe distance to the north of the town in order to avoid a fire risk. The docks to the north of Prince's Dock had been intended as conventional longitudinal docks by Foster,[54] but Hartley recognized the ability of the steamship to enter docks placed at right angles to the river. In this way, between 1830 and 1836, he was able to fit four steamship docks – Clarence, Waterloo, Trafalgar and Victoria – into the space intended for a single longitudinal dock. Simultaneously Hartley had provided an ingenious solution to a problem which oppressed the Dock Trustees in the 1830s: the dispute with the Board of Ordnance over the site of the new Fort which was blocking northward development of the docks until its sale in 1839.[55]

Much more serious problems were, however, on the horizon. In 1833 the Whig government established a commission for inquiry into the Municipal Corporations. The self-elected Corporation of Liverpool was to fight a losing battle against the subsequent Act, as the Whig government was determined to push through a reform which, it was hoped, would undermine the Tory nature of local government. In order to justify the reform of the Municipal Corporations they had to be presented to the legislature as essentially corrupt. The label has tended to stick. Both as municipal governors and as Dock Trustees, Liverpool Corporation was vilified during the 1833 inquiry. It is therefore important to offer a balanced assessment of the role of the Liverpool Corporation as dock builders.

The Corporation opposed the Municipal Corporations Bill, claiming that Liverpool could not be compared to any other Corporation due to "the extent and variety of the interests committed to its charge or to the amount and importance of its estates and revenues".[56] It was referring partly to its role as Dock Trustees. Its members pointed out that as Dock Trustees they were spending £180,000 per annum on construction and maintenance and had bond creditors totalling £1.4 million by 1833.[57] This was an important commercial operation on a totally different scale from the trivial dealings of corrupt corporations like St Davids, Pembrokeshire. Unfortunately, the secrecy of the proceedings of the Dock Trustees had continued to fuel local suspicion and there were plenty of critics willing to condemn their administration at the 1833 inquiry. Despite the fact that a Dock Act of 1825 had finally admitted eight merchant ratepayers to the committee of twenty-one members of the Corporation which supervised Dock expenditure, there had been little real alteration of the power of the Dock Trustees.[58] The latter retained the right to annul any resolutions of the committee. Resentment amongst the merchant ratepayers continued to simmer and boiled over in 1833.

Was there any greater substance to criticism of the Dock Trustees than the impotent resentment of merchant ratepayers who were still effectively excluded from the management of the docks whilst paying escalating dock duties? A more sinister criticism focused on the close connection between Corporation and Dock finances and, in particular, the familiar complaint concerning the sale of land at a profit by the Corporation to themselves as Dock Trustees. In the 1833 inquiry it was stated by one critic that the Corporation had sold land valued at over £300,000 to the docks. Analysis of the Corporation accounts does reveal huge profits on land sales to the Dock Trustees after 1800. The sale of the site of Prince's Dock has already been mentioned. The profits on subsequent land sales were even more marked. In 1801–2, the Corporation had purchased the site of the future Brunswick Dock for a total of £18,000; in 1827 this land was sold to the Dock Trustees for £96,000. The land to the north of Prince's Dock was sold simultaneously for £110,000. A year later land to the west of Salthouse Dock was sold to the Dock Trustees – the site of the Albert Dock commenced by Hartley in 1841.[59] It did indeed seem improper for the Corporation to charge the Dock Trustees inflated prices for land which they had often embanked themselves with the soil from dock excavations. Merchants complained bitterly that the Strand on the north shore had improved in value from 6s 8d to 15s per yard as a result of this procedure. Ultimately they feared that the dock rates would have to reflect such inflated expenditure on land.

Discrepancies between the handwritten books of account and the subsequently published accounts of these years add further confirmation that the Corporation were profiting handsomely from land sales to the Dock Trustees. There is, however, no suggestion that *individual* members of the Corporation were privately pocketing the profit from land speculation. It is possible that the increasing complexity of dock administration in the nineteenth century made it impossible for each of the forty-one members of the Corporation to follow the details of land sales. Hartley's brisk spate of dock building was a far cry from the painfully slow construction of the first dock in 1709 in which every merchant of note had been involved administratively, if not financially. Nevertheless, it is difficult to exonerate the Corporation completely from charges of corruption by claiming collective ignorance of the details of land speculation, especially as eight of the thirteen members of the Dock Committee were also members of the powerful Finance Committee which managed the funds of the Corporation.[60] It is probable that the profit of dock-land sales was quietly absorbed by the Corporation treasurer to ease the immense financial burdens of the 1820s, such as the grandiose improvement scheme being undertaken by the Corporation or the huge new Customs House being constructed on the site of the redundant Old Dock.

The Corporation was able partially to justify its inflated prices for land for dock construction by pointing out that it had dealt with all the complex negotiations for the initial purchase of such land and had used its own funds or the security of its own estate for payment at a time when the finances of the Dock Estate were still shaky. It is thus arguable that without this security the Dock Trustees would never have been able to undertake such an ambitious dock-building programme. During the eighteenth century, at least, it had not always been certain that the Corporation Estate would recoup all of this expenditure. It was not until the Dock Act of 1811 that the Dock Trustees were allowed to levy money on security of the docks themselves. The Corporation had not pressed the Dock Trustees for payment for land during periods of credit shortages[61] – perhaps this was an acceptance of reality rather than an act of generosity – and it was not until 1805 that the Corporation decided to start charging the Dock Trustees for hard stone procured from special quarries on the Corporation Estate for dock building. No charge was ever made for stone used for the eighteenth-century docks and basins. The man-made chasm now known as St James's Cemetery behind Liverpool's Anglican cathedral is testimony not only to the quantity of stone required for the docks but also to the liberality of the eighteenth-century Corporation. Moreover, the Corporation also supervised the endless details of dock construction such as contracts with building craftsmen. A rare example of such a contract has survived and is held in the Liverpool Maritime Museum.[62] The agreement between the Corporation and Peter Buxton, stonemason, drawn up on 1 August 1785, was carefully devised and, if typical of closed tenders of this period, shows that the Corporation was conducting its task as dock builder with a high regard for public interest. The specifications, such as size and type of masonry, are extremely detailed and a penalty clause of £500 for late completion is also included.

Not only did the Corporation as Dock Trustees devote much time and attention to the construction of the docks but it also supervised the monotonous and relentless business of raising finance. Dock bonds were generally raised locally amongst the mercantile community which stood to gain most from dock building. In the early eighteenth century the foremost merchants were also members of the Corporation and provided much of the loan capital. Individual members continued to be major creditors of the Dock Estate in the later part of the period. In 1792, for example, bonds totalling £11,150 were received for the use of the docks from, among others, council members Matthew Stronge (£1,000) and Thomas Seel (£630) and dock engineer Henry Berry (£300). At times of credit shortage the Corporation placed advertisements in the press for loans for dock construction[63] and cast a wider net. In 1807, William Yates Esq. of Springside near Bury lent £15,000 to the Dock Trustees.[64] A local historian, Underhill, noted in the late 1820s of the dock bonds "this is an eligible investment of money for persons resident here and far preferable to the chequered risk of the public funds".[65] When funds dried up completely during the Napoleonic wars the Corporation was willing to arrange a Treasury loan of £60,000 to allow vital dock construction to continue.

The extent of the Corporations's financial achievement in developing the Dock Estate is revealed in Table 6.1. The problematic escalation of building costs after the Napoleonic wars is clearly indicated: Prince's Dock cost twenty times as much as King's Dock although only twice its size.

The Corporation had not merely provided docks. There were additional commercial facilities such as the attempt to develop a unified range of dockside warehouses (see Figure 6.3) – a casualty of the credit squeeze of the 1800s.[66] A vast tobacco warehouse was also erected by the Dock Trustees on the east side of King's Dock in 1789 at a cost of £12,309 4s 8d to lodge all imported tobacco until the duties were paid.[67] The Corporation also tried to persuade local merchants to accept integrated warehouses and docks in 1803, 1810 and 1821 to reduce the time lost and the expense of cartage from the docks to scattered warehouses. Fierce opposition from local merchants to such "prison warehouses" and their fears of the reduction in value of private warehouses delayed this scheme until the construction of Albert Dock and its warehouses in the 1840s.

The Corporation also maintained a constant vigilance in their efforts to preserve the value of the Dock Estate. The most outstanding example of this policy was the judicious land purchases by individual Corporation

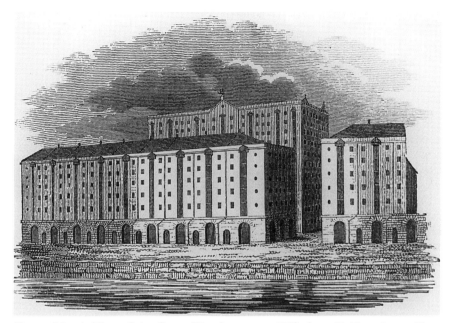

Figure 6.3   A View of the Goree Warehouses, c. 1800, from T. Troughton, *The History of Liverpool from the Earliest Authenticated Period Down to the Present Time* (Liverpool, 1810), unpaginated.

members to stifle the plan to build rival docks at Wallasey Pool on the opposite side of the Mersey in 1828.[68]

The Liverpool survey of 1835 offers a visual summary of the achievements of the Corporation as Dock Trustees (see Map 6.7). It shows the ninety acres of docks constructed by embanking into the Mersey between 1709 and 1835. As well as devoting much time and energy to their construction the Corporation had amassed a vast £4 million to finance them. As a result, the number of ships using the port and the acreage of docks rose in tandem – an elevenfold increase over the period. The dramatic increase in Liverpool's trade is also shown by the rise in dock duties from £810 11*s* 6*d* in 1724 to £103,422 12*s* 5*d* in 1833.

Without the unremitting efforts of the Dock Trustees, Bristol rather than Liverpool might have been the beneficiary of the shift of trade westward in the eighteenth century. They had guaranteed her pre-eminent position as a port in the nineteenth century. The transport historians, Dyos and Aldcroft, wrote of Liverpool's progress: "as the result of the continuous accretion of one dock after another it was a phenomenon which was in every way exceptional in the eighteenth century".[69] Hull did not build her ten-acre wet dock until 1775–8 and two further docks covering thirteen acres until 1807–29. Bristol and Portsmouth both built a wet dock in the early eighteenth century but neither was publicly owned.

Table 6.1   Dock Construction in Liverpool 1709–1836

Name of dock	Date of construction	Cost	Area (acres)	Type of trade
Old Dock and Basin	1709			Irish,
		c. £30,000	*c.* 3.5	Mediterranean,
Graving Dock	1717–18			West Indian and African
Salthouse Dock	1738–53	£21,000	4.5	Corn and timber
Graving Dock 1	1756–57	£1,453 16*s* 2*d*		
George's Dock	1767–71	£21,000	*c.* 5.25	West Indian/American
Enlargement of Graving Dock 1	1775–77	£2,810 5*s* 10½*d*		
Graving Docks 2 and 3	1784–89	£3,260 7*s* 2*d*		
King's Dock and Basin	1785–88	£20,000	*c.* 5.33	American/Baltic
Queen's Dock	1788–96	£25,000	7.25	Greenland fishery/American
Manchester Flats Quay and Basin	1790–93	£5,639 10*s* 3*d*		
Graving Docks 4 and 5	1796	n.a.		
New Basins south of Queen's Dock	1804–11	n.a.	2	
Lengthening Queen's Dock	1811–16	£15,165 2*s* 5*d*	4 added	
Prince's Dock	1816–21	£650,000 inc. land	11	Corn
3 basins and 6 slips on west side of Queen's Dock	1819–24	£19,565 10*s* 10*d*		
Enlargement of George's Dock	1822–25	n.a.	2 added	
Brunswick Dock Basin and 2 Graving Docks	1828–32	£438,000 exc. land	*c.* 14	Timber
Clarence Dock	1830			
Waterloo Dock	1834	£795,000	*c.* 25	Steam ships
Trafalgar Dock	1834–36	excl. land		
Victoria Dock	1834–36			

Sources: H. Smithers, *Liverpool: Its Commerce, Statistics, and Institutions* (Liverpool, 1825), *passim*, and *Liverpool Corporation Accounts, 1773–1854* (Liverpool Record Office, Hq 352.1 and H 352.1 FIN).

Edinburgh town council ran into enormous debt in its attempts to extend Leith docks in the late eighteenth century and was bankrupt by 1833.[70] London, the greatest port in Britain since the medieval period, had constructed a succession of timber wharfs along both banks of the Thames. The first commercial docks in the Pool of London thirty miles up the Thames were constructed by the private West India Company in 1799 and the London Dock Company in 1802. Although six docks were constructed

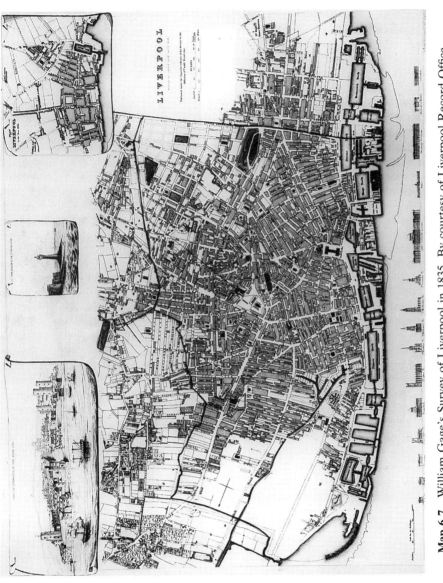

Map 6.7   William Gage's Survey of Liverpool in 1835. By courtesy of Liverpool Record Office.

in London between 1799 and 1828, they were administered by rival companies in frequent conflict. The unified control of dock construction at
Liverpool produced more impressive results.

The conclusion ought to rest with a merchant, Cyrus Morrall, who
had lived in Liverpool since 1797. At the 1833 inquiry he stood up and
proclaimed: "if the merchants had the entire control [of the Dock Commit-
tee] they would be very apt to attend to immediate wants without consult-
ing futurity".[71] Ninety acres of docks were the stone monument to the
vision of the Liverpool Corporation.

Notes

1 Extract from the journals and letters of Samuel Curwen, Judge of the
   Admiralty, an American refugee in England, quoted in R. Brooke,
   Liverpool During the Last Quarter of the Eighteenth Century (Liverpool, 1853), pp. 246–7.
2 W. Enfield, *A History of Liverpool* (Liverpool, 1773), p. 25. His
   figures were based on the parish registers and therefore took no
   account of the Roman Catholic and Dissenting population.
3 Henceforth referred to as "the Corporation".
4 This right was fiercely defended by the Corporation in the Galley v.
   Clegg case of 1748 to 1753 (Liverpool Record Office (hereafter cited
   as LRO), Town Books, vol. 10, fol. 601) against a boatbuilder's claim
   to the shore as a presumptive right. A further threat to the valuable
   site of the docks arose from the Duchy of Lancaster in 1828. The
   Corporation successfully defended its right to the shore and the claim
   was relinquished on 2 April 1828 (LRO Town Books, vol. 16, fols 19
   and 36).
5 Daniel Defoe, *A Tour Through the Whole Island of Great Britain*
   (Penguin edn, 1971), p. 541.
6 Lt Col. Fishwick, "Distribution of surnames in Lancashire in the
   sixteenth and seventeenth centuries", *Transactions of the Historical
   Society of Lancashire and Cheshire*, vol. 17 (Liverpool, 1902).
7 A petition to Parliament from Liverpool in 1699 spoke of men settling
   in Liverpool after the Plague and Great Fire of London in 1665–6:
   LRO, Wakefield Papers: 942 WAK/42.
8 Thomas Heywood (ed.), *The Norris Papers*, Letter 61, Chetham
   Society, Vol. 9 (1846).
9 John Pudney, *London's Docks* (London, 1975), p. 55.
10 F. E. Hyde, *Liverpool and the Mersey* (Newton Abbott, 1971), p. 23.
11 LRO, Town Books, vol. 5, fol. 40, 5 October 1709.
12 Hyde, p. 10.
13 LRO, Town Books, vol. 5, fol. 26, 3 November 1708. Johnson had
   been knighted in May 1707.
14 ibid., fol. 51, 17 May 1710. Henry Peet, *Thomas Steers: The Engineer
   of Liverpool's First Dock* (London, 1932), provides many details of
   Steers' career.

15 LRO, Town Books, vol. 5, fol. 51, May 1710. At this meeting the Town Clerk was ordered to keep a special book for decisions relating to the construction of the dock. This book has disappeared, as have all records of the informal Dock Committees up to 1793. These losses may have been connected with the Town Hall fire of 1795.

16 ibid., fol. 40, 5 October 1709.

17 Act 8, Queen Anne, cap. 12. The dues were levied on tonnage. An Act of 1811 imposed dues on goods as well as tonnage.

18 G. H. Morton, *The Geology of the Country round Liverpool* (London, 1891), p. 216.

19 LRO, Town Books, vol. 5, fol. 142, 25 January 1716.

20 ibid., fol. 105, 7 April 1714.

21 ibid., fol. 112, 1 September 1714.

22 The scheme was completed in 1740.

23 LRO, Holt, Gregson and Okill Papers, 942 HOL/10.

24 H. Smithers, *Liverpool: Its Commerce, Statistics and Institutions* (Liverpool, 1825), p. 79.

25 ibid., p. 102.

26 LRO, Town Books, vol. 5, fol. 540, 1 February 1737.

27 Smithers, p. 174, notes that dock duties totalled £810 11s 6d in 1724 and had doubled by 1752 to £1,776 8s 2d.

28 LRO, Town Books, vol. 10, fol. 642, 3 April 1754. The irregular shape of this dock was due to the configuration of the surrounding streets. It was probably impossible to persuade the adjacent saltworks to move, so the dock was aligned accordingly. It was subsequently known as the "Salthouse" Dock.

29 British Museum, 10349 e.15 (5).

30 Town Books, vol. 10, fol. 680, 18 December 1754. The Dry Dock was not built until February 1756 with the help of a loan from the Seaman's Hospital in Liverpool: ibid., vol. 11, fols 2 and 6, 4 February 1756.

31 See Town Books, vol. 10, fol. 586, 2 May 1753, vol. 11, fol. 20, 2 June, 1756, vol. 11, fol. 14, 14 May 1756 and fol. 228, 7 October 1761 for examples of such leases.

32 Act 2, GEO. III, c.86.

33 In May 1765, the Corporation ordered excavations to be made in fields on the south side of Liverpool to procure another source of building stone for the docks. Massive quantities were also required for the embankment and the Corporation prevented building on Goodwin's Fields in 1769 to allow another quarry to be opened. Town Books, vol. 11, fol. 510, 21 December 1769.

34 H. Colvin, *A Biographical Dictionary of British Architects 1660–1840* (London, 1954), records that Lightoler was responsible for the design of St Paul's Church in north Liverpool.

35 I am grateful to the Liverpool Maritime Museum archivist, Mr J. Gordon Read, for drawing my attention to this valuable recent acquisition.

36 LRO, Town Books, vol. 11, fol. 462, 6 July 1768. Dockside warehous-

ing was constructed by William Jessop at the West India Docks in London in 1799.

37   ibid., vol. 11, fol. 685, 2 November 1774 and fol. 706, 5 April 1775.

38   Smithers, p. 174.

39   Two further graving docks had been constructed between 1765 and 1768. They were lengthened in 1784. Nowhere in Britain have such early graving docks survived with their fittings intact. Two more graving docks were built to the west of Queen's Dock in 1796. The Corporation built the graving docks at their own expense and managed them directly as part of the Corporation, rather than of the Dock Estate.

40   LRO, Town Books, vol. 12, fol. 644, 3 February 1790. Purchase of ground from Lord Derby and including the Strand to the north of the existing docks.

41   LRO, 352 MIN/DOC 1/1–6.

42   LRO, Holt and Gregson Papers, 942 HOL/34.

43   LRO, Town Books, vol. 12, fol. 650, 3 March 1790. Lord Derby was the vendor and received payment on 5 February 1793: Corporation accounts, 352 TRE1/1/8. The land was sold to the Dock Trustees on 2 April 1806: Town Books, vol. 14, fol. 112. The payment was made on 18 October 1810 (352 TRE1/1/9) with interest, although the printed accounts for 1810 reveal a payment of only £7,406 18s 7d from the Dock Trustees: LRO, Corporation and Borough Fund Accounts, 1773–1854, printed by J. Gore and Son, Castle Street, H.352.1 FIN.

44   ibid., vol. 12, fol. 765, 16 November 1792.

45   LRO, Corporation Accounts, 352 TRE 1/1/7.

46   LRO, Town Books, vol. 13, fol. 36, 5 June 1793. It was to be another eleven years before the debt could be settled due to the difficulty of procuring funds in the 1790s: vol. 14, fol. 12, 1 August 1804. In the following May the Dock Treasurer finally paid the Corporation treasurer £13,778 3s 4d "being the balance due to the Corporation for the site of the Queen's and King's Docks': fol. 47, 1 May 1805.

47   Liverpool Maritime Museum, MDHB Misc. (14) 4 (b), Jessop's report 1800.

48   LRO, 942 HOL/34. Printed "Statement of the Petitioners against the Liverpool Docks Bill" (Liverpool, 1804), and "Remarks on the 1802 Improvement and Dock Bills" (Liverpool, 1803).

49   A letter of John Foster, the dock engineer, to the Common Council urging dock extension for increased shipping was completely ignored at the Dock Committee meeting of 14 August 1801, 352 MIN/DOC 1/1.

50   LRO, 942 HOL/34. "An address to the inhabitants of Liverpool on the subject of the new Dock Bill to be introduced into Parliament this present session by Mercator" (Liverpool, 1810). Critics also disliked the proposal to fill in the Old Dock – now heavily silted and too shallow for larger vessels – as warehouses in that area would lose their value.

51   M. S. Partridge, "Cannon or commerce? The case of the Liverpool

Battery, 1824–1855", *Transactions of the Historical Society of Lancashire and Cheshire* (Liverpool, 1987).
52 LRO, 352 MIN/DOC 1/1, 12 July 1812. Rennie was paid £113 8*s* 3*d* for his advice in plans in February 1813. He had been engineer and consultant to the West India Dock Company in 1800.
53 Excluding the cost of the land: LRO, 942 UND/2. Underhill Papers.
54 They are outlined on Swire's Map of 1824.
55 The original North Battery was pulled down in 1841.
56 LRO, Town Books, vol. 16, fol. 544, 25 July 1835.
57 Their income in 1832 from duties on tonnage and goods totalled £103,422 12*s* 5*d*. This included a small amount for lighthouse and graving dock duties.
58 This was in the wake of a scandal in 1823–4 concerning the excessive charges for the supply of dock-building materials. A committee of the Corporation had concluded that there was some justification in the criticisms and it was decided to end the system of supplying materials and labour without public tender: Town Books, vol. 15, fol. 321, 14 January 1823. In October 1824 delegates from the trades associations met with the Common Council to request "a total alteration of the Trust" to admit ratepayers as half of the Dock Committee. The Corporation held that the proposal was "wholly inadmissable".
59 LRO, Town Books, vol. 15, fol. 699, 5 December 1827 and vol. 16, fol. 89, 3 December 1828.
60 *A Copious Report of the Inquiry into the Affairs of the Corporation of Liverpool before His Majesty's Commissioners, George Hutton Wilkinson and Thomas Jefferson Hogg Esq.* (Liverpool, 1833), p. 40.
61 During the Napoleonic wars, for example, the Corporation was willing to wait from April 1806 to October 1810 for payment for the site of Prince's Dock.
62 Liverpool Maritime Museum, MDHB (Outsize Documents), Item 2, Articles of Agreement between Peter Buxton and the Corporation of Liverpool, 1 August 1785.
63 An advertisement in Williamson's *Liverpool Advertiser*, 23 June 1785, requested the loan of money to build docks and noted that loans would be based on security of the Corporation House.
64 LRO, Town Books, vol. 14, fol. 160, 20 January 1807. He was probably related to the branch of the Yates family resident in Liverpool.
65 LRO, Underhill Mss, 942 UND/2.
66 J. Stonehouse, *The Streets of Liverpool* (Liverpool, 1870), p. 18, notes that portions of the projected arcade in Wapping were commenced but abandoned unfinished.
67 A larger tobacco warehouse, covering four acres, was erected 1810–16.
68 LRO, Town Books, vol. 16, fol. 55, September 1828. Despite pledges to the contrary the Corporation took little action to develop the Wallasey Pool commercially for another fifteen years.
69 H. J. Dyos and D. H. Aldcroft, *British Transport: An Economic*

Survey from the Seventeenth Century to the Twentieth (Harmonds-worth, 1974), p. 59.

70   A. J. Youngson, *The Making of Classical Edinburgh 1750–1840* (Edin-burgh, 1966), p. 258.

71   Inquiry of 1833, p. 39.

7 The development of the Crown and Corporation estates at Reading, 1828–60

S. T. BLAKE

Between 1801 and 1861, the recorded population of Reading increased from 9,742 to 25,045, and its stock of houses from 1,783 to 5,018. These figures represent far higher rates of growth than in the preceding century, and reflect the town's considerable economic progress during these years – a progress largely based upon the successful exploitation of its excellent position for transport by road, river, canal and rail.[1] During the eighteenth century, Reading had compensated for the earlier decline in its cloth trade by expanding its role as a marketing and distributive centre for agricultural produce, and particularly for malt.[2] This role was augmented during the early nineteenth century by a growth in its brewing industry and in the manufacture of sailcloth and coarse linen, and by the establishment of several important new industrial concerns. Foremost amongst these were Barrett, Exall & Andrewes' ironworks, Huntley & Palmer's biscuit factory, and Huntley, Boorne & Stevens' tinworks.[3] The success of these and other manufacturing concerns was undoubtedly influenced by the coming of the railway to Reading in 1840, an event which, in particular, reduced the journey time to London from 5 hours to 75 minutes and greatly enhanced the town's existing attractions as a residential and commuting centre.[4]

A comparison between John Speed's 1611 map of Reading and that of Charles Tomkins, surveyed c. 1800, reveals little in the way of outward expansion during the intervening years, even though the population may have doubled between 1600 and 1800.[5] Most of this increase had clearly been accommodated by rebuilding and infilling within the existing urban area, utilizing the town's many orchards and gardens (see Maps 7.1 and 7.2). Although this process of infilling certainly continued during the early nineteenth century, far more important was the expansion of the town, for the first time, beyond its medieval and early modern limits. To the north, south and west of the town, the adjoining fields were held, and subsequently developed for building, in comparatively small blocks by a large number of private landowners. The situation to the east of the town was, however, rather different. There, the ownership of the entire area by just two landowners – namely the Crown and the Corporation of Reading – meant that east Reading had the potential for a more uniform and carefully planned pattern of development than was the case elsewhere

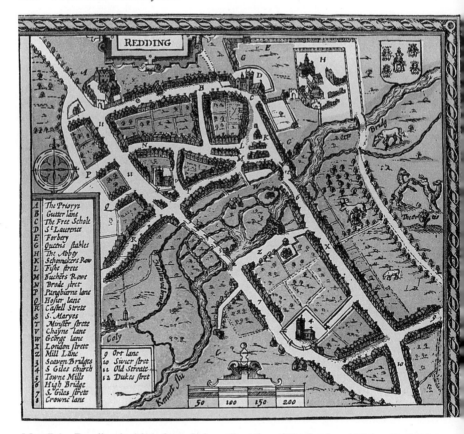

Map 7.1   Reading in 1611, from J. Speed's *Atlas of England and Wales: Berkshire* (London, 1611), unpaginated.

within the expanding town. The extent to which these two landowners managed – or even attempted – to impose such an overall pattern, and the tensions and rivalries that arose between them, are the subjects of this paper.

Until the sixteenth century, the entire area to the east of the town was the property of Reading Abbey, at the dissolution of which, in 1539, the property had reverted to the Crown. A large tract of this former monastic land was granted to the Corporation of Reading under Elizabeth I's charter of 1560.[6] This included the so-called Town Orts, bordered on the north by the River Kennet and Gunter's Brook (the latter also known after 1802 as the New Cut), on the east by Watlington or Orts Lane, on the west by the rear of properties in London Street and on the south by that part of London Road known as New Street.[7] It was this part of its estate, covering an area of approximately forty acres, that the Corporation was to develop for building during the 1830s. To the south of New Street was the second

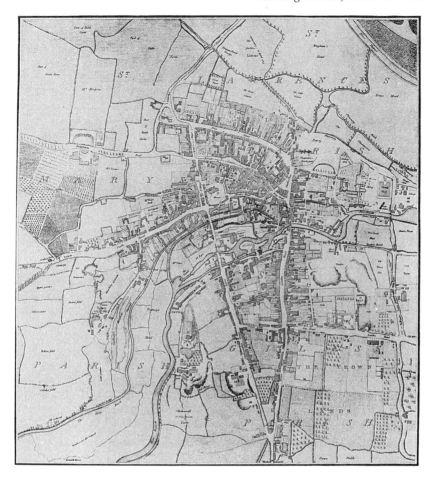

Map 7.2 Reading in 1802, by C. Tomkins. First published in C. Coates, *The History and Antiquities of Reading* (London, 1802), Frontispiece.

part of the Corporation Estate, which was not intensively developed during this period. This was the so-called Crown Fields, purchased by the Corporation from Richard Knollys in 1643, and bordered on the west by Silver Street and on the east by Red Lane.[8]

Immediately to the east of Watlington Lane, and north of London Road, was the major part of the Crown Estate, which by 1800 was administered by His Majesty's Commissioners of Woods, Forests, Land Revenues, Works and Buildings. This consisted of the seventy-three-acre Ort or Orts Farm (also known as Ort Field), plus three other smaller tracts of land totalling thirteen acres, namely two plots of meadowland to the north of

Gunter's Brook, on either side of Watlington Lane, known as Tanhouse Mead and Broken Brow, and a small tract of land immediately to the east of Duke Street, between the Holy Brook (north) and the Kennet (south) (see Map 7.3, 1828). The Crown's possession of these three small tracts of land was to prove crucial to the development of its estate, as it enabled the Commissioners of Woods to construct a line of road from Ort Farm to the town centre wholly within its own property. The Crown Estate also included eighty-two acres of meadowland to the north of the Kennet, although this was excluded from the 1828–33 plans for the development of the estate.[9]

Before the transformation of the Crown and Corporation Estates during the 1830s, the degree of development within each was sparse.[10] Within the Corporation Estate, the only residential development (apart from the late seventeenth-century Watlington House) was along both sides of New Street, where a succession of detached and terraced houses, such as Portland Place (*c.* 1809), The Acacias (1817) and Albion Place (*c.* 1822–5) were constructed by a number of builders on 99-year leases from the Corporation. The area did, however, include two embryonic streets, both of which were later included in the Corporation's plans for the area. These were East Street and Wharf Lane, both of which ran northwards from New Street towards the two large gravel pits that occupied the centre of the Town Orts; Wharf Lane also led to the Quaker Burial Ground. North of the gravel pits, on the south bank of the Kennet, was an area variously known as the Little Orts or as Boult's Wharf, which consisted of a timber wharf and a scatter of buildings, including cottages, sheds, stables and a blacksmith's shop. The name Boult's Wharf, which was derived from the name of its lessee, was later applied to the entire Town Orts area.[11]

Within the Crown Estate, the only developments before the 1830s were in that part of the property immediately to the east of Duke Street, on the Kennet bank opposite Boult's Wharf, where, by 1800, there was a waggoners' depot, a coachyard, stabling, timber yards and cottages;[12] further east, a part of Tanhouse Mead was occupied by basket makers. Within Ort Farm, the only buildings were those of the so-called Collins' Farm, on the east side of Watlington Lane, the site of which is now occupied by St John's Church.[13] Since 1770, the estate had been leased to Messrs Blagrave and Vansittart, who, by the 1820s, had sub-let the agricultural land to Alderman Thomas Garrard and the waterside premises to the ironmongers, Messrs Blandy and Palmer.[14]

The development of both the Crown and Corporation Estates during the 1830s followed a similar pattern. Each was based upon a major new east–west thoroughfare (Kings Road and Queens Road respectively), designed to create a shorter and more convenient route into the town centre than that provided by the existing London Road, which was of uneven width and included a sharp right-turn into London Street at the narrow "Anchor Corner".[15] In addition – and no doubt uppermost in the minds of both Crown and Corporation, and particularly of the former – the land adjacent to each new road would provide ideal building land for a combination of commercial and residential premises, depending on

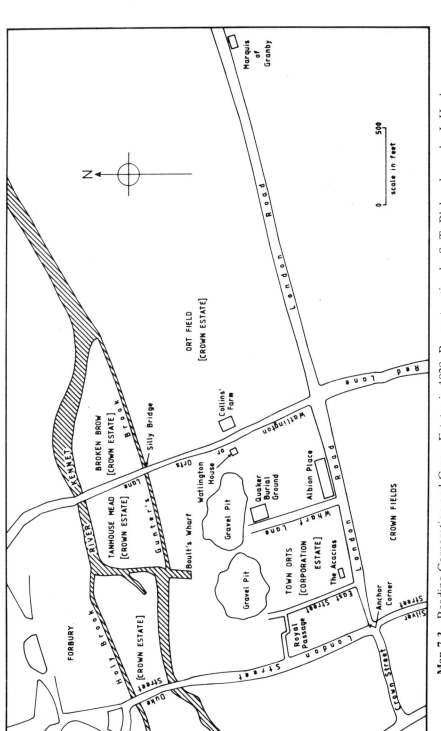

Map 7.3 Reading Corporation and Crown Estates in 1828. Reconstruction by S. T. Blake, drawn by J. Hoyle.

situation. This dual advantage to the landowners and to the town in general was particularly well expressed in an anonymous letter, dated 19 June 1828, from an inhabitant of Reading to the London-based Surveyor of Crown Estates, Edward Driver. It claimed that the proposed new road across the Crown Estate would be "of the greatest benefit to this borough and will increase your revenue fifty fold".[16]

Although it was ultimately the Commissioners of Woods who were the first to put their plans into operation, it is clear that the Corporation had in mind the establishment of a new road across their property, from London Street to Watlington Lane, from at least 1816.[17] In November of that year, they decided to offer premiums of 20 and 10 guineas for the two most approved plans for such a road, which would provide not only a better means of access to and from the town, but also scope for building land, as "the population of the said borough requires an increase of houses to be built for the accommodation thereof".[18] However, although the premiums were awarded[19] and tenders for the work involved were advertised for in 1819,[20] no more is heard of the scheme, which clearly lapsed, for in 1824 the Committee of Leases "renewed consideration" of the project.[21] Even then the Corporation failed to take any action, and it was not until 1829, when they saw an opportunity to turn the Crown's plans to their own advantage, that they were prompted into any positive action.

The moving spirit behind the development of the Crown Estate was Edward Driver, who first suggested the improvement to the Commissioners of Woods in February 1828.[22] His scheme was for a road 50 feet wide (including footpaths) to run for a total of 4,743 feet from the first milestone on the London Road, adjoining the Marquis of Granby Inn, across Ort Farm and bridging both the New Cut and the Kennet to join Duke Street at the "White Hart Corner", thereby lying entirely within Crown land. Although the Commissioners declined to accept his proposals – suggesting instead that perhaps some private speculator might be encouraged to promote such a scheme – Driver persisted, and in November 1828 he wrote to the Commissioners once again, noting that:

> As the whole of the land over which it was proposed by me the road should be made is Crown land, it will be evident no person except the Crown can be likely to undertake such an improvement unless it was the Trustees of the Turnpike Road and it is not likely they would stand forward in such a measure, but the sole object I had in view is to promote a very important advantage to the Crown by enhancing the value of their estate very considerably, as the benefit of the wharfage which would be obtained at the four sides of the new Bridge would I apprehend be quite sufficient to be a remuneration for the whole expense of the road.[23]

On this occasion, the Commissioners instructed Driver to prepare an assessment of the costs involved, which, according to the estimate presented to them by Driver in March 1829, amounted to £1,431.[24] Financially, the scheme certainly seemed an attractive one. By 1829, the annual rental from Blagrave and Vansittart was £530 5s 3d, which Driver admitted could possibly be increased to £800 without any improvement to the land. However, with the creation of the new road, he argued, the annual value of the land would increase to at least £2,000 and its value as freehold land, if sold for building, to a considerably higher sum, Driver being confident shortly before the first sale of land adjacent to the road that well over £30,000 would be realized by the estate.[25] The Commissioners were clearly swayed by Driver's arguments, and by mid-1829 they had given their approval to the scheme.[26]

In the meantime, in December 1828, Driver had persuaded the Commissioners to spend £1,300 purchasing two dilapidated houses adjoining the White Hart Inn in Duke Street, as the western termination of the road, should they decide to proceed with the scheme.[27] Driver also obtained the agreement of Blagrave and Vansittart and their under-tenants to relinquish their leases (which were due to expire in March 1831 anyway), Blagrave and Vansittart on payment of compensation equivalent to two years' profit on their sub-leases (a sum amounting to £136 per annum), Alderman Garrard on receiving compensation for his crops, and Blandy and Palmer on the promise of a direct lease of waterside premises between the new road and the New Cut, immediately west of the proposed Kennet Bridge.[28]

Once the Commissioners' plans for their new road had become known, the Corporation lost no time in petitioning them to adopt an alternative route for the road, to run westwards from the Marquis of Granby as far as Watlington Lane, there to join a line of road to be constructed by the Corporation across the Town Orts, which would enter London Street a little to the south of the High Bridge.[29] The Corporation argued that their route would save the Commissioners the expense of constructing the two new bridges (and the borough that of maintaining them in future), while providing a shorter and more level line of road, with a wider entrance to the town than was possible at the "White Hart Corner". Their arguments were certainly valid, yet they were firmly rejected. In his reply to the petition, Lord Lowther, the First Commissioner, admitted the expense of the Crown's plan, but repeated Driver's argument that the consequent increase in the value of the adjoining land – particularly of the waterside premises – would be ample compensation, and that if the road was not able to pass entirely across Crown land, it would not have been contemplated in the first place.[30] Clearly, both Driver and the Commissioners took exception to what they viewed as the Corporation's attempts to subvert and make capital out of the Crown's plans. According to the Corporation's surveyor, Richard Billing, Driver, on hearing the suggestion at a meeting between Billing and the Commissioners in London on 26 October 1829 "broke out into a horse-laugh and said, 'Now you see, my Lord, the corporation only want to dispose of their own property, and now do not care a farthing what becomes of the Crown property'".[31] Driver himself later spoke of the attempts of

interested parties, aided, and supported by the then Borough Members, to mislead the Commissioners of Woods etc., and prevail on them to abandon their project and adopt another line, for the sinister purpose of improving some extensive property belonging to the Corporation of Reading, and keeping in seclusion the most valuable portion of the Crown property.[32]

Driver even went so far as to suggest that the Corporation, rather than trying to divert the line of the Crown's new road, should have admitted its value to the town and contributed £2,000 or £3,000 towards its cost, particularly as, in his opinion, the line of the new road provided the Corporation with the possibility of continuing it westwards across Duke Street and into Castle Street and Bath Road, thereby bypassing the narrow streets of the town centre and reducing the length of the main road to Bath by one-third of a mile.[33]

Although the Corporation continued to petition the Commissioners in favour of their alternative route throughout the second half of 1829,[34] plans for the Crown's new road went ahead regardless, and by September 1829 its line had been staked out across Ort Farm.[35] Already, however, several problems which were to lead to widespread criticism of Edward Driver had arisen. The earliest involved his negotiations with the Thames Navigation Commissioners regarding the new bridges over the Kennet and New Cut. In August 1829, the Commissioners of Woods sought the approval of the Thames Commissioners for the construction of the two new bridges.[36] The latter responded by suggesting that rather than build a new bridge over the New Cut, the Commissioners of Woods should co-operate with themselves in rebuilding the existing, and wholly inadequate, Orts Lane or Silly Bridge at the top of Watlington Lane, a little to the west of the site of Driver's proposed bridge.[37] However, although Driver admitted to the Thames Commissioners that he had originally planned to incorporate the Orts Lane bridge in his new road, he eventually decided against their offer and submitted to them his plans for the two new bridges. To the Kennet Bridge they made no objection, but they insisted that the bridge over the New Cut (which later became known as Orts Bridge) should be both wider and higher than he intended, to enable the towpath to pass under the bridge, rather than across it, and that its span should be of iron, and not of brick, as Driver had intended.[38] Driver appears to have regarded their demands as excessive, and later accused the Thames Commissioners of acting in a vexatious manner in order to disrupt the entire project, a charge that the Thames Commissioners vigorously denied.[39] Negotiations and a lengthy correspondence continued until January 1831, in which month the Commissioners of Woods finally agreed to the Thames Commissioners' terms "after trying all means to prevail upon them to alter their decision as to the particular description of bridges which they had resolved should be built".[40]

The Commissioners of Woods' decision to accede to the Thames Commissioners' demands exacerbated a second problem facing the scheme, namely that of cost. Driver's original estimate of £1,431 for the construction of the road and bridges had proved hopelessly unrealistic, particularly once Driver had decided not to incorporate the existing Orts Lane bridge. The lowest tender for the construction of the actual road, that of Thomas Collis (accepted on 3 October 1829), was for £1,756 18s 3d, to which a further £598 19s 8d, plus a contingency sum of £100 were added in order to undertake the additional work necessary to raise the level of the road on either side of the heightened New Cut bridge.[41] Eventually even this sum was exceeded, and Collis's final payment amounted to £2,554 18s 10d.[42] The lowest tender for the brick and masonry work involved in the bridges, that of Hugh McIntosh (accepted on 5 April 1831), was for £4,346[43] to which a sum of £120 was added in June 1831, once it was discovered that the land on either side of the New Cut bridge was virtually quicksand and the footings had to be spread and strengthened in order to provide an adequate base.[44] Fortunately, McIntosh's final payment was reduced to £4,087 8s 9d once it was decided – to the chagrin of the Thames Commissioners – to dispense with flood arches on either side of the New Cut bridge.[45] In addition to McIntosh's contract, £115 was spent on the ironfounders' work on the bridges, undertaken by Messrs George Cottam and Samuel Hallen, and £45 12s 6d on forming a flight of steps adjoining Kennet Bridge, undertaken by William Brown. The eventual cost of the road and bridges was, therefore, £7,838 0s 1d. To this sum must be added the £1,300 expended on the two houses in Duke Street, and £20 spent purchasing two other small pieces of land elsewhere in the line of the road. This brings the total cost of the project to £9,158 0s 1d, £2,000 of which, according to Driver, was expense occasioned by the opposition of the Thames Commissioners.[46]

The level of expenditure on the road and bridges was clearly far higher than the Commissioners of Woods had expected, and was the subject of a lengthy investigation by the *Select Committee on the Land Revenues of the Crown*, which took evidence from a number of individuals, including Driver and Billing, during June and July 1833.[47] While Driver maintained that the expenditure was justified by the outcome of the two Crown Estate sales and the increased value of Palmer's Wharf, others – notably Richard Billing, who cannot have been wholly unbiased – argued that the Crown's property had not been sufficiently increased in value by the expense, and that around £5,000 could have been saved had Driver agreed to co-operate with the Corporation in making a joint road in 1829. Several other criticisms were also aimed at Driver, including that the raising of the level of the road on the approaches to the New Cut bridge would prove danger-ous to traffic, and that the laying of 12 inches of screen gravel on the surface of the road was both excessive and expensive, especially as the ground itself was largely gravel. Billing – who had prescribed 4 inches of gravel for the Corporation's new road – claimed that travelling along the Crown road was "like going over a bed of horse beans" and that several of the purchasers had begun putting soft sand on the gravel, in order to bind it.[48] The Select Committee eventually noted in its second report that

the evidence in this matter being of so contradictory a nature, some members of your committee went to Reading and viewed the property;

and the result of the whole investigation was, that your committee, without coming to any formal Resolution on the subject, are of opinion that (although £9,158 was a large sum to lay out in alterations and improvements), as the sale of the property has turned out, the expenditure has not been injudicious.[49]

A third problem encountered by Driver involved the western termination of the new road. The two houses purchased in 1829 were demolished in May 1831 to make way for the junction of Kings Road and Duke Street, and negotiations were opened with Colonel Blagrave to purchase a portion of the adjoining White Hart Inn in order to widen the junction still further. The Commissioners offered £250, but Blagrave would only consider the sale of the entire property for £500, to which, according to Driver "we could not for one moment listen". The Commissioners then proceeded to investigate Blagrave's title to the property, and decided that the freehold was in fact that of the Crown, which Blagrave, not surprisingly, denied.[50] With the Commissioners unwilling to accept Blagrave's terms, but apparently unable to prove their own title, a situation of stalemate ensued, and when the new road was opened, its western termination narrowed to only 25 feet 6 inches. Certainly the Commissioners may be criticized over the matter, for having spent so much on their road an additional £250 would hardly have made a great deal of difference. Their refusal to come to terms with Blagrave on what was clearly a matter of principle alone caused a considerable inconvenience to the road's users for many years, as the junction was not finally widened until 1868–9.[51] That the Commissioners looked purely to their own interests and not to those of the town is particularly clear in this instance, and it is interesting to note that in 1835, when the Paving Commissioners had to expend £200 on removing a particularly dangerous part of the White Hart, the Commissioners of Woods refused any financial help, arguing that their part in the road's construction was complete.[52]

The work of constructing the road and bridges began in 1830 and by September 1832 the road was described as "now completely finished and ready to be opened to the public",[53] although it was not formally opened until April 1833.[54] In addition to Kings Road itself, the Commissioners had constructed three other roadways by the latter part of 1832. Nearest the town centre, a little to the west of Kennet Bridge, the new Abbey Street ran north out of Kings Road, across Holy Brook, to the Forbury. Further east, in Ort Field, two roads were constructed to provide rear access to intended building plots, namely the semicircular Orts Road, to the north of Kings Road, and a narrow roadway running east out of Watlington Lane, to the south of Kings Road, later forming St John's Road and Eldon Terrace (see Map 7.4, 1850).

In the meantime, plans were made for the sale of the land adjoining the road. In March 1832, Robert Palmer had received a 70-year lease, at £310 per annum, on approximately two acres of land on the north side of the New Cut, on which he agreed to spend £1,000 constructing a warehouse and other buildings, subsequently known as Crane Wharf.[55] Driver

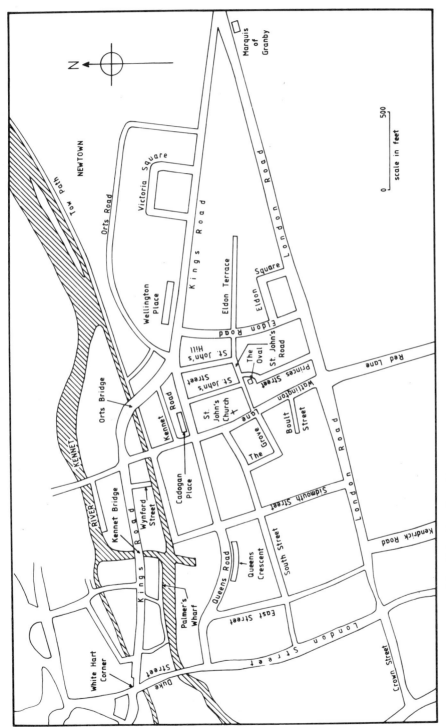

Map 7.4 East Reading in 1850. Reconstruction by S. T. Blake, drawn by J. Hoyle.

then made arrangements to divide the rest of the estate into between seventy and eighty lots of building land, at an estimated cost of between £40 and £45, "it being necessary to hire a plough with horses and men for some days to mark out the lines of the respective lots, and several hundred large stakes which must be furnished and properly prepared by a carpenter, and also the necessary assistance of labouring men, etc.".[56] He was clearly anxious to complete the work as soon as possible so that the plots could be auctioned and all the legal arrangements completed before the start of the building season in February 1833.[57] He did, however, suggest that only a part of the land be put up for auction initially, as to offer the entire property at once would overstock the market, as well as being too much for a single day's sale, a second consecutive day being, in his view, inadvisable, as the attendance was rarely equal to the first day on such occasions, and the competition consequently less sharp.[58] In addition, Driver may have hoped for the rapid development of the property sold, so that interest would be stimulated and the value of the remainder increased.

Consequently, on 21 November 1832, fifty building plots were auctioned by Driver, at the Crown Inn (see Figure 7.1). These comprised the entire western part of Kings Road, to the north of the New Cut, intended for commercial and waterside premises (Lots 1–26), plus fifty acres of ground south of the New Cut, described as

> well appropriate for the erection of Villas, or other Residences, as the soil is remarkably dry and healthy, and noted as the most salubrious spot in the Neighbourhood of Reading, or for many Miles around; and as it presents pleasing and commanding eminences, its value is much enhanced by the beautiful views over Caversham Park, and the intermediate rich Country, with the Thames intersecting the same, so that perhaps no spot could be selected, more appropriate for such purposes.[59]

Unfortunately, Driver's expectations were not fulfilled, the reserve price put on each plot being generally higher than the bids received. Those plots that were sold fetched only £11,124 of their estimated £13,480 value, being sold despite the reduced prices as no better offers could be hoped for by private sale, and, no doubt, to stimulate interest in the area from other potential developers and builders. Fifteen waterside plots were, however, withdrawn owing to negligible interest; in one case a plot with a reserve of £1,000 received a bid of only £100.[60]

In a letter to the Commissioners of Woods two days after the sale, Driver expressed his disappointment at its outcome, despite what was described as "an excellent attendance", and – perhaps in an attempt to exonerate himself – argued that it was very difficult to assess the value of land in what he described as a "new created situation".[61] He had, however, been right to allow some plots to be sold below the reserve price while withdrawing others. A number of building projects were soon underway on various parts of the estate, and when the entire remaining property, including the plots withdrawn at the first sale, was put up for auction on

CROWN  ESTATE,

READING.

SPECIFICATIONS

Of very Important and extremely Valuable

Freehold Property,

BELONGING TO

HIS MAJESTY,

(Tithe Free and Exonerated from the Land-Tax,)

Most advantageously Situate in the Parishes of

ST. LAWRENCE AND ST. GILES,

WITHIN

THE BOROUGH OF READING,

ADJOINING THE

NEW ROAD called THE KING'S ROAD, lately formed as a more Commodious Entrance, into the Heart of

THAT LARGE MARKET TOWN.

COMPRISING

CAPITAL WATERSIDE PREMISES,

WITH EXTENSIVE

FRONTAGES to the RIVER KENNET and the NEW CUT;

Valuable Building Sites for Shops,

Warehouses, a Brewery, or any other description of Premises requiring considerable Space,

MOST ELIGIBLY SITUATE

Near the Entrance into Duke Street;

TOGETHER WITH ABOUT

FIFTY ACRES,

Remarkably well appropriate for the Erection of

DWELLING HOUSES OR VILLAS;

The Soil being dry and healthy, and the Situation noted as the most salubrious in the Neighbourhood, and at the same time commanding most beautiful Views over

CAVERSHAM PARK.

AND THE

INTERMEDIATE RICH COUNTRY

WITH

THE RIVER THAMES

Intersecting the same.

——o——

Which will be Sold by Auction,

By Order of the Right Honourable Lord Duncannon, William Dacres Adams, Esq. and Major General Sir Benjamin Charles Stephenson, K. C. H. Commissioners of His Majesty's Woods, Forests, Land Revenues, Works and Buildings, and under the Authority of the Lords Commissioners of His Majesty's Treasury.

By MESSRS. DRIVER,

AT THE CROWN INN, READING,

On Wednesday, the 21st day of November 1832, at 11 o'Clock,

IN FIFTY LOTS.

Printed Specifications with Plans annexed, may be had at the Crown Inn, Reading; Sun, Maidenhead; Angel, Oxford; York House, Bath; Castle, Windsor; at the Auction Mart, London; at the Office of Woods, Forests, Land Revenues, Works and Buildings, Whitehall Place; of Messrs. Green, Pemberton, Crawley and Gardiner, Solicitors, Salisbury Square, Fleet Street; of Mr. Hawkes, Friar Street, Reading; and of Messrs. DRIVER, Surveyors and Land Agents, 8, Richmond Terrace, Parliament Street, London.

Figure 7.1 Frontispiece of the first Crown Estate Sale Particulars, 1832. By courtesy of Reading Central Library.

12 June 1833, the result was rather more successful, the total reserve price of £12,050 for the thirty-five plots being exceeded by £10, although the waterside plots withdrawn at the first sale and originally valued at £9,870 were finally sold for only £3,720, a clear indication that Driver had over-estimated their value.[62] Inevitably, the sums received for the plots varied considerably according to their location. Those in the eastern part of the estate fetched on average £200 to £300 an acre, while those nearer the centre fetched on average £3,000 an acre, with Lot 2 at the first sale being sold at the equivalent of almost £10,000 an acre.[63] In all, the Crown had received a total of £23,184 from the two sales, as well as still having in hand meadows and two other small plots of land to an estimated value of £7,060, plus the freehold of Palmer's Wharf, which was valued, in 1833, at £7,130.[64]

Amongst the purchasers at the first Crown Estate sale was a local solicitor and former mayor of Reading, John Jackson Blandy, who acquired, for £1,200, Lots 40–2, in order to effect "an improvement of the Corporation property in Boult's Wharf".[65] In January 1833, he offered the Corporation as much of the land as was needed to form "a handsome and commodious communication" between Kings Road and Watlington Lane, from which it could then run westwards across the Town Orts into London Street – for which land he received £294 in April 1833.[66] One week later, Richard Billing had staked out a line of road 510 feet long and 50 feet wide, and a contractor to construct the road, to be called Queens Road, was advertised for, the contract being awarded to John Sowden, on a tender of £198.[67]

The construction of the principal thoroughfare of the Corporation Estate was paralleled by the establishment of a number of adjacent streets. The existing East Street and Wharf Lane (the latter being renamed Sidmouth Street) were extended northwards to Queens Road and the towpath respectively, while South Street was created to the south of Queens Road, as a means of access between Watlington Lane and East Street, from which the existing Royal Passage connected to London Street (see Map 4, 1850). Owing to the uneven terrain, a great deal of levelling was undertaken, and junctions were formed with London Street, Watlington Lane and Kings Road, the first involving the demolition of three houses. The work also involved the removal of the Quaker Burial Ground. Yet as early as September 1833, the work was described as "in such a state of forwardness" that the first auction of building land within the estate could be planned,[68] and on 26 November 1833 sixteen plots suited to commercial premises, and comprising a total frontage of 1,010 feet to the north side of Queens Road, plus an adjoining wet dock and wharf, were auctioned at the Crown Inn. The plots were offered on 99-year leases, at an annual ground rent of £2 10*s* per plot, plus a single cash payment, representing the sum bid at auction.[69] The success of the auction, which realized £2,285, well above the reserve prices, prompted the rapid completion of the project, and on 3 January 1834 Queens Road was dedicated to the public.[70] Five months later, on 24 June 1834, a second auction was held, at which fifty plots were offered, suited to residential or retail premises. Of these, all but eleven were disposed of, lessees being found for the remainder during the following months.[71] By the second half of 1835, the project was, therefore, virtually complete, a total of 4,830 feet of building frontages, comprising the entire northern part of the Town Orts, having been made available for building.

Despite the outward similarities between the Crown and Corporation Estates, the actual pattern and chronology of development within each was to prove very different. At the root of these differences lay the contrast between freehold and leasehold development. Although the Corporation possibly viewed leasehold development as in the best long-term interests of the borough, it is more likely that it was unwillingly hamstrung by the liabilities with which the land was charged at the time of its acquisition, which precluded freehold development. These liabilities included the payment of an annual fee farm rent of £22 (which by the 1830s was payable to a London barrister named Thomas Bros jnr), the payment of the land tax, various obligations towards the upkeep of roads and bridges within the borough, and the payment of a £10 annual salary to the Master of the Free School.[72] An uncertainty as to whether "the Boult's Wharf lessees", as they became known, were liable for these payments arose during 1834, inducing one of the successful bidders at the first sale, a local solicitor named John Weedon, to decline taking up his lease. The situation caused great uncertainty in the minds of many of the inhabitants and prevented a majority of the lessees from finding tenants willing to take building leases on what was soon widely regarded as land of dubious title, especially in view of the general preference for freehold land, which was readily available in Reading, particularly with the development of the Crown Estate.

In order to rectify the situation, the Boult's Wharf lessees soon took the initiative and made a series of attempts to induce the Corporation to obtain the wherewithal to enfranchise the land. They first approached the Corporation in March 1837, requesting that the latter should obtain a local Act of Parliament, under section 94 of the 1835 Municipal Corporations Act, enabling them to purchase the fee-farm rent and to dispose of the property either freehold or on a perpetual fee farm, in fee simple, investing the proceeds in the purchase of other land, on which the remaining liabilities could be charged.[73] In return, the lessees agreed to pay a fair proportion of the expense of obtaining the Act, and to convert their £2 10s per plot annual rental into a perpetual fee farm of £3 10s per annum. The Corporation was clearly in agreement, and in 1839 the Reading Corporation Act was obtained.[74] Yet the problem still remained, as the Corporation apparently did nothing to acquire the fee farm. The lessees therefore petitioned them, once again, in May 1840, offering to pay a sum equivalent to 35 times the annual rental in order to enfranchise their property, if the Corporation would indemnify them against the outstanding fee-farm payment.[75] Once again, the Corporation was in agreement, and the necessary Treasury consent was obtained in January 1841;[76] however, further problems soon arose, for the valuer appointed by the Lords of the Treasury then demanded from the lessees not only a payment equivalent to thirty-five years' rental, but also an additional sum for the reversion of the fee simple. A majority of the lessees rejected these terms, arguing that the sums fixed by the valuer, a Mr Powell, were excessive.[77] The Corporation, however, refused to accept their arguments, or to sanction a petition to the Treasury for a reassessment of the terms, and a state of stalemate ensued, with only six out of the eighteen Boult's Wharf lessees coming to terms with the Corporation before 1858. In that year the Corporation finally agreed to a petition for a revaluation, which was made in 1859, and which reduced the total sum demanded for the unenfranchised plots by almost £1,100.[78] In the meantime, the Corporation had eventually acquired the £22 fee-farm rent, paying Thomas Bros £770 for it on 17 April 1845.[79]

The net result of these difficulties and delays was a marked lack of development within the Corporation Estate in the years after 1834. At the time of the 1839 petition to the Treasury, the Corporation stated that only one house had so far been built upon the land disposed of at the 1833–4 sales,[80] and by 1858 the total was no more than twenty-three.[81] Of these, by far the most important were the fifteen stone-fronted houses forming Queens Crescent, on the south side of Queens Road (see Figure 7.2). These were built in *c.* 1838–40 by a number of builders, on subleases from a linen draper named Thomas Lawrence, who had acquired the land at the 1834 auction and who – perhaps because of the success of his project – was the only one of the Corporation's lessees to agree to their enfranchisement terms without protest.[82] The use of bathstone for

Figure 7.2   Queens Crescent, built 1838 to 1840, photographed in 1975.

these and many other houses within east Reading, was facilitated by the canal and later rail links with Somerset, and Lawrence himself is known to have imported a large quantity of stone into the town.[83]

Given this lack of development, it is not surprising that the Corporation was disinclined to offer the remainder of its estate for building, and until 1860 it was leased out as agricultural land. Apart from the sale by auction, on 21 June 1844, of the four plots on which Weedon had declined to take his lease,[84] it was not until 20 July 1860 that a third major sale of building land, in the south-east corner of the estate, was held, following an improvement in the means of access between London Street and South Street by the widening of Royal Passage in 1859.[85] The Corporation's decision to dispose of the remainder of its estate at that time was no doubt influenced both by the more optimistic mood within the rest of the estate, following the revaluation of 1859, and by the increasing demand for building land and houses within the town as a whole during the 1850s.[86] The printed sale particulars noted that "the plots will form most eligible and appropriate sites for the erection of moderate sized residences, which are much needed in Reading, and several of them are adapted for villas and other houses of a superior class, for which also there is a great and increasing demand"; the particulars also noted that the land was "within 10 minutes of the Reading stations".[87]

Clearly, the terms on which the land was offered in 1860 were designed to avoid the problems that had arisen after the earlier auctions. The land was offered on a perpetual annual fee farm, in fee simple, the amount of which was settled by auction. This was, in effect, equivalent to freehold, without involving the Corporation and its lessees in the question of enfranchisement. It would also serve to provide the Corporation with a regular annual income, while "persons of limited capital desirous of building would be thereby enabled to purchase".[88] From the point of view of the Corporation, it also had an added advantage in that under the terms of the 1839 Act, the Corporation was compelled to reinvest the proceeds of freehold sale in the purchase of real estate, or in low-interest Exchequer Bills, an unfavourable investment.

In all, fifty-six plots were offered in 1860, comprising 1,300 feet of frontages to London Road, Watlington Lane, South Street and Sidmouth Street, as well as to two new streets running west out of Watlington Lane, namely Boult Street and The Grove, both of which were constructed, on behalf of the Corporation, by a builder named Thomas Woodley.[89] All but four of the plots were disposed of, the prices received varying from 2s 9d per foot of frontage for land in South Street to as high as 7s 3d for land in London Road.[90] All that remained unsold after 1860 was a block of land to the east of Albion Place and one small plot in South Street (see Map 7.5, 1861). The outlook for the area's future was considerably brighter than it had been after the 1834 sale, the *Reading Mercury* noting shortly before the 1860 sale that the area would soon be "one of the most populous in the borough".[91] This assessment was well justified by the amount of building which took place within the estate during the 1860s. Already by April 1864, all but nine of the fifty-two plots sold at the 1860

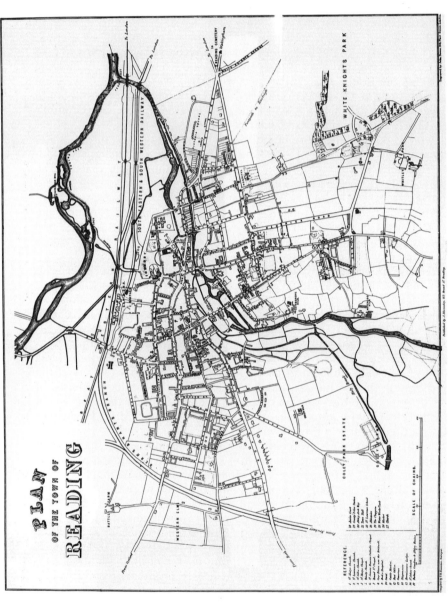

Map 7.5 Reading in 1861, by T. H. Simmons. Reproduced by courtesy of Reading University Library.

sale had been developed, with a total of thirty-seven houses in place and six more in the course of erection,[92] while the remaining 1833–4 lessees gradually enfranchised and developed their plots from 1860 onwards.[93]

One other major contrast between the development of the Crown and Corporation Estates was the extent to which restrictive covenants were imposed within each. Within the freehold Crown Estate, these were minimal. Apart from making a broad distinction between those areas of the estate intended primarily for commercial and residential premises respectively (a distinction underlined by the prices paid for the plots), and the imposition of a 40-foot building line along Kings Road south of the New Cut, the Crown chose not to impose any detailed restrictive covenants upon the purchasers, each of whom was therefore left to decide how best to develop his own land. In so doing, the Commissioners failed to impose any overall design on the estate, and the divided ownership of the area after 1833 resulted in the same varied and piecemeal pattern of development that pertained within other parts of the town, such as west Reading, in which a small-scale and divided pattern of land ownership had long been the norm. In this, the Crown stands in marked contrast to the Corporation, which imposed detailed covenants upon the successful bidders at each of its sales. In addition to the imposition of a building line, a minimum value of £300 per house was imposed on the plots auctioned in 1833–4, along with covenants to keep the properties in repair and to permit the lessor access to view the state of repair at any time. At the 1860 sale, minimum values of between £150 and £500 per house were imposed, depending on situation, and purchasers were to build on their plots within seven years – a covenant no doubt introduced in the light of the problems faced by the estate during the previous quarter of a century.[94]

Within the Crown Estate, the years 1833–60 saw far more building than was the case within the Corporation Estate, including the establishment of several distinct, but diverse, areas of housing.[95] Within the commercial part of the estate, along Kings Road between the New Cut and Duke Street, development was rapid, with the formation of new wharves and the establishment of such concerns as the Cannon Brewery, a tobacco warehouse, the Reading Gas Works, and the short-lived silk-crepe manufactory of Messrs Baylis, the site of which was later (1846) acquired by Messrs Huntley and Palmer for their great biscuit factory. By 1871, the western part of Kings Road was described as "where most of what may be termed the heavy business of the town, such as wharfingers, corn and coal dealers, etc. is carried on".[96] Residential development was not, however, entirely absent, a number of artisans' cottages being built along and adjacent to the road and wharfs, including twenty-four small houses in the new Wynford Street (now Bembridge Place), running south out of Kings Road to the west of Watlington Lane.

The construction of small artisans' houses eventually continued on the south side of the New Cut, and it is here, in the residential part of the estate, that the effects of a lack of any overall control on building are most apparent. Here, the earliest developments were of large detached or semi-detached houses. In April 1833, for instance, the *Reading Mercury* noted that "a spirited gentleman has already commenced building six houses of handsome elevation in one of the most eligible situations in kings Road",[97] almost certainly a reference to the large bathstone houses of draper Thomas Lawrence's Wellington Place, contemporary with which was the creation, also by Lawrence, of the imposing new Eldon Road and Eldon Square (see Figures 7.3 and 7.4). Within a very few years, however, houses of a far lower quality had begun to intrude. By 1835, John Weedon had established the narrow Kennet Road, between Kings Road and Watlington Lane, immediately north of Queens Road, and had begun building artisan housing on its north side. It is interesting to note that in

Figure 7.3　Wellington Place, Kings Road, c.1840. By courtesy of Reading Central Library.

Figure 7.4　Eldon Road, looking northward from Eldon Square, c.1840. By courtesy of Reading Central Library.

October 1835, Weedon sold the entire southern side of Kennet Road to John Blandy, the owner of the larger Cadogan Place and Penrhyn Lodge on the north side of Queens Road; Blandy promptly added the land to the gardens of the latter houses, and may have been motivated by a desire to avoid his properties being overlooked by artisan dwellings.

Thomas Lawrence's Eldon Road was itself soon adjoined by an area of predominantly artisan housing, namely St John's, which may in fact have originally been intended for the construction of villas. On Kemp and Nichols's 1834 plan of Reading,[98] the area immediately west of Eldon Road (now occupied by the St John's area) is shown as a projected development with a central oval, from which four wide roads radiated. Although not a part of Lawrence's property, this may well have been planned by its owners, John Blandy and James Wheble, as an integral part of Lawrence's exclusive "villa-suburb". However, such a plan was clearly not adhered to, and – particularly in the northern half of the St John's area, which was owned by Blandy – small red-brick houses were built from *c.* 1836 onwards, with only the large detached house known as "The Oval", on the south side of St John's Road, as evidence of the original plan (see Figure 7.5). A similar situation also pertained further east, where John Blandy's exclusive Victoria Square, laid out on the north side of Kings Road as "a highly ornamental suburb" in 1845–6 was soon adjoined (and no doubt prejudiced) by the artisan streets of Newtown, between Orts Road and the canal, an area intensively developed after 1850.

Figure 7.5 "The Oval", St John's Road, built 1841 to 1851, photographed in 1975.

By 1860, virtually all the land that had been intended for building by the Crown and the Corporation in the 1830s had been disposed of, and many residential, retail and industrial premises had been built, particularly on the Crown Estate (see Map 7.5, 1861). Like many landowners, neither the Crown nor the Corporation had undertaken any actual building itself; that was left to the many individuals who acquired the land. Within the Crown Estate, several men purchased sufficiently large areas of land to enable them to establish their own independent building estates, including further new streets, in which they in turn transferred smaller plots to builders, who constructed the actual houses. In this way, several distinct areas were created within the Crown Estate, and the already-mentioned contrast between, for instance, Thomas Lawrence's Eldon Road and Square and John Blandy's adjoining St John's area is still apparent in the present-day townscape (see Figures 7.6 and 7.7). Certainly, the Crown Estate owes far more of its layout and street plan to the purchasers than does the Corporation Estate, in which all the new roads were constructed by the Corporation and the land was auctioned in far smaller plots, being acquired (with the exception of Thomas Lawrence in his Queens Crescent development) directly by builders rather than by developers. In this way at least, the Corporation may be said to have exerted a greater overall control on the future development of its estate, even though its own record of initiative and positive action during these years leaves much to be desired.

The fact that the Crown and the Corporation failed to co-operate with one another in the late 1820s may well have been to the ultimate disadvantage of both landowners, in terms of initial costs and the fact that the marketing of two major estates virtually at the same time, in addition to developments elsewhere within the town, may well have overstocked the market and depressed demand and prices, at least temporarily. From the point of view of the town, however, there was no such disadvantage, for the development of the two estates provided ample freehold and leasehold land, including valuable canalside premises, and resulted in the building of a wide variety of housing, for all classes of inhabitant. Furthermore, the construction of both the Crown and Corporation roads, rather than a single new road, gave the inhabitants and travellers a choice of routes to and from the town; as the local banker Henry Simonds remarked to the 1833 *Select Committee,*

> we have the advantage of two roads, and in my opinion so eligible for building that they must both be a benefit to the town; I should say it would be more advantageous to the Corporation if there was no competition and less land for building on, and for the Corporation it would be better there should be only one road, but for the town it is better there should be two.[99]

Despite their failure to co-operate, therefore, indeed because of it, the joint enterprise of the Crown Commissioners and Reading Borough Corporation operated to the great advantage of the town, and resulted in

Figure 7.6   The three westernmost houses of Wellington Place, Kings Road, built 1835 to 1840, photographed in 1975.

Figure 7.7   The north side of Eldon Square, built 1835 to 1840, photographed in 1975.

the development of what remains even today as one of the most handsome parts of Reading.

Acknowledgements

I should like to thank Dr C. F. Slade and Dr C. W. Chalklin for their generous help and advice during the preparation of the thesis on which this paper is based, and the staffs of Reading Central Library and the Berkshire Record Office for their practical help at all times. I would also like to thank Jon Hoyle for drawing the two maps of east Reading in 1828 and 1850.

The former Reading Borough Archives, which are a major source for this paper, are now part of the collections of the Berkshire Record Office, and are currently (1988) being catalogued. Where a particular document has not yet received its final catalogue reference, it has been cited in the footnotes to this paper as "Berks RO, Reading Archives, uncatalogued documents".

Notes

1　A general survey of the town's economy during this period and a detailed account of its growth is contained in my unpublished PhD thesis, "The physical expansion of the Borough of Reading 1800–1862" (University of Reading, 1976; hereafter cited as Thesis). See also W. M. Childs, *The Town of Reading During the Early Part of the Nineteenth Century* (Reading, 1910), and E. W. Gilbert, "Reading: its position and growth", *Transactions of the South-Eastern Union of Scientific Studies*, Vol. XII (1934), pp. 81–90.

2　C. F. Slade, "Reading", in M. D. Lobel (ed.), *Historic Towns*, Vol. 1 (Lovell Johns-Cook, Hammond & Kell Organization, London, 1969), pp. 4–5.

3　For details of these concerns, see T. A. B. Corley, *Quaker Enterprise in Biscuits: Huntley & Palmer of Reading 1822–1972* (London, 1972); T. A. B. Corley, "Barrett, Exall & Andrewes' ironworks at Reading: the partnership era", *Berkshire Archaeological Journal*, vol. 67 (1973–4), pp. 79–87; T. A. B. Corley, "Simonds' Brewery at Reading 1760–1960", *Berkshire Archaeological Journal*, vol. 68 (1975–6), pp. 77–88.

4　Thesis, pp. 37–8. The *Reading Mercury* (hereafter cited as *RM*) noted on 23 June 1860 the "constant demand for villas . . . of which we are assured by house agents that the supply is by no means adequate to meet the requirements of parties whom the facility of railway transit and the attractions of the neighbourhood lead to seek a residence near our town".

5　Speed's map was included in his *Atlas of England and Wales* (1611); Tomkins's map was first published in C. Coates, *The History and Antiquities of Reading* (London, 1802). According to J. M. Guilding, *Notable Events in the Municipal History of Reading* (Reading, 1895), Appendix A, the estimated population in *c.* 1600 was 4,700, although on what basis this figure was arrived at is not stated.

6　C. Fleetwood-Pritchard, *Reading Charters, Acts and Orders 1203–1911* (London, 1913), p. 15.

7　Topographical details based on the map of Reading surveyed by Charles Tomkins, *c.* 1800.

8　*Reading Corporation Terrier, 1807–9* (Berks RO R/578), pp. 31–4. The only notable development within the Crown Fields in this period was the establishment of Kendrick Road in *c.* 1842 (Thesis, p. 359).

9   The acreage of the Crown Estate is stated in a letter from the surveyor Edward Driver to the Commissioners of Woods, 20 April 1829 (Public Record Office (hereafter cited as PRO) Cres. 2/35/1082).

10 Thesis, pp. 294–300.

11 *RM*, 26 June 1820.

12 The premises are described in the *Report from the Select Committee on the Land Revenues of the Crown*, 1833 XIV 677 (hereafter cited as *Report*, 1833), p. 86.

13 W. S. Darter, *Reminiscences of Reading by an Octogenarian* (Reading, 1888; reprinted with an introduction by D. Phillips, Countryside Books, 1985), p. 6.

14 Rental agreements in Crown Estate papers: Reading, Orts Estate Miscellaneous (PRO Cres. 2/32).

15 Anon, *The Stranger in Reading – Letters to a Friend* (London, 1810), p. 21.

16 Letter, 19 June 1828 (PRO Cres. 2/35/3770).

17 *Corporation Diary* (hereafter cited as *CD*), 22 March 1816, recording an instruction to its Committee of Leases to "report on the best mode of letting the same . . . and . . . to see whether any communication can be made with the above from London Street, or any other improvements" (Berks RO R/ACa 1/25).

18 *CD*, 18 November 1816 (Berks RO R/ACa 1/25); *Memorial from the Corporation to the Lords of the Treasury*, 1819 (Berks RO Reading archives, uncatalogued documents).

19 *CD*, 25 August 1817 (Berks RO R/ACa 1/25).

20 *RM*, 11 October 1819.

21 *CD*, 27 March 1824 (Berks RO R/ACa 1/25).

22 As quoted, along with the Commissioners' reply, in a letter from Driver to the Commissioners, 17 November 1828 (PRO Cres. 2/35/3770). Edward Driver, the Surveyor of Crown Estates, was also Receiver of Crown Rents in sixteen counties and was a founder member of the Land Surveyors' Club in 1834; see F. M. L. Thompson, *Chartered Surveyors: The Growth of a Profession* (London, 1968), pp. 94, 101.

23 ibid.

24 Letter, Driver to Commissioners, 7 March 1829 (PRO Cres. 2/35/741).

25 Quoted in letters, Driver to Commissioners, 14 June 1832 (PRO Cres. 2/35/1143); 22 September 1832 (PRO Cres. 2/34/2176).

26 Letter, Driver to Commissioners, 13 May 1829 (PRO Cres. 2/34/1277).

27 Letter, Driver to Commissioners, 16 December 1828, endorsed with the Commissioners' approval (PRO Cres. 2/34/4051).

28 Letter, Driver to Commissioners, 7 April 1829 (PRO Cres. 2/35/1082).

29 *CD*, 23 July 1829 (Berks RO R/ACa 1/26); also a letter, Driver to Commissioners, 20 August 1829, enclosing a letter from the Town Clerk of Reading, dated 26 July 1829 (PRO Cres. 2/35/2084).

30 Letter, Lord Lowther to the Corporation, 23 September 1829 (Berks RO, Reading archives, uncatalogued documents).

31 *Report*, 1833, p. 85.

32 ibid., pp. 79–80.

33 ibid., p. 83.

34 *CD*, 2 October–16 November 1829 (Berks RO R/ACa 1/26); the Corporation's efforts included the preparation of a plan of their proposed road and a meeting between Billing and the Commissioners in London on 26 October.

35 *Berkshire Chronicle* (hereafter cited as *BC*), 5 September 1829.

36 Letter, Driver to Commissioners, 28 August 1829 (PRO Cres. 2/35/2044); *Thames Navigation Commissioners Minute Book* 1822–31 (Berks RO D/TC 9), p. 267.

37 As reported by Edward Law, one of the Thames Navigation Commissioners in *Report*, 1833, p. 92.

38 ibid.

39 ibid., p. 82 (Driver's evidence) and pp. 93–4 (Law's evidence).

40 Letter, Driver to Commissioners, 22 May 1832 (PRO Cres. 2/35/901).

41 ibid.

42 ibid; also *Report*, 1833, p. 255, giving a full financial account of the scheme.

43 Letter, Driver to Commissioners, 5 April 1831 (PRO Cres. 2/35/7083). McIntosh was

one of the leading bridge contractors of his day, and was responsible for, amongst other works, Marlow Bridge.

44   Letter, Driver to Commissioners, 1 June 1831 (PRO Cres. 2/35/7536).
45   *Report*, 1833, p. 134.
46   ibid., p. 255.
47   *Report*, 1833, and *Report from the Select Committee on the Land Revenues of the Crown*, 1834 XV 459 (hereafter cited as *Report*, 1834).
48   *Report*, 1833, pp. 85–91.
49   *Report*, 1834, p. 463.
50   Letters, Driver to Commissioners, 23 August 1832 (PRO Cres. 2/34/1894); 24 September 1832 (PRO Cres. 2/35/2177). Also *Report*, 1833, p. 80.
51   Documents relating to the eventual widening of the junction are contained in Berks RO Reading archives, uncatalogued documents.
52   *Paving Commissioners' Minute Book* 4, 10 July–6 November 1835 (Berks RO R/Sp 4).
53   Letter, Driver to Commissioners, 22 September 1832 (PRO Cres. 2/34/2176).
54   *RM*, 1 April 1833.
55   Conveyance, 1 March 1832 (PRO Cres. 2/36/4490).
56   Letter, Driver to Commissioners, 4 October 1832 (PRO Cres. 2/34/2288).
57   Letter, Driver to Commissioners, 22 September 1832 (PRO Cres. 2/34/2176).
58   Letter, Driver to Commissioners, 22 October 1832 (PRO Cres. 2/34/2458).
59   Printed sale catalogue in Reading Central Library (hereafter cited as RCL), QR/NL Acc. 11095; also *BC*, 13 October 1832 *et seq*.
60   Letter, Driver to Commissioners, 23 November 1832 (PRO Cres. 2/34/2746). The sale catalogue is annotated with the prices fetched; these are tabulated, with names of purchasers, in Thesis, pp. 364–5.
61   Letter, ibid.
62   Printed sale catalogue, RCL QR/NL Acc. 11095; tabulated in Thesis, pp. 366–7.
63   *RM*, 26 November 1832.
64   *Report*, 1833, p. 255.
65   *CD*, 11 January 1833 (Berks RO R/ACa 1/26).
66   ibid., 26 April 1833.
67   ibid., 3 May 1833; 27 September 1833.
68   ibid.
69   Printed sale catalogue, RCL QR/NL Acc. 11095. The various purchasers are listed in *CD* 27 September 1833, 26 December 1833 and 17 January 1834 and are tabulated in Thesis, p. 368.
70   *BC*, 3 January 1834.
71   Printed sale catalogue, RCL QR/NL Acc. 11095; *CD*, 4 January–10 October 1834. *BC*, 28 June 1834 noted that "the competition was very spirited and the whole of the lots were disposed of at exceedingly good prices". Tabulated in Thesis, pp. 369–70.
72   Fleetwood-Pritchard, p. 15.
73   *Council Minutes* (hereafter cited as *CM*), 17 March 1837 (Berks RO R/ACa 2/1).
74   Fleetwood-Pritchard, pp. 184–210. The Reading Corporation Act 1839 (2 and 3 Victoria c.40), which became generally known as the "Boult's Wharf Act" was 'to enable the Mayor, Aldermen and Burgesses of the Borough of Reading . . . to sell certain Real Estate Discharged from certain Liabilities and to invest the purchase Monies arising from such Sales in the Purchase of other Real Estate, to be charged with such Liabilities".
75   *CM*, 8 May 1840 (Berks RO R/ACa 2/1).
76   *CM*, 21 January 1841 (Berks RO R/Aca 2/2).
77   ibid., 7 May–6 August 1841.
78   Valuation by Robert Driver, 4 March 1859 (Berks RO Reading archives, uncatalogued documents).
79   Conveyance, 17 April 1845 (Berks RO Reading archives, uncatalogued documents).
80   Undated [1839] "Epitome of evidence on petition" (Berks RO Reading archives, uncatalogued documents). The petition noted that 2,035 feet of frontage had been built upon within the Crown Estate during the preceding five years.
81   Plan showing houses built within the estate, along with enfranchised and unenfranchised plots, 1858 (Berks RO Reading archives, uncatalogued documents).

82 Thesis, pp. 353–4 and Appendix 9, p. 377.
83 Thesis, pp. 106–7. In September 1836, Lawrence agreed to transfer a plot of Crown Estate land adjoining the canal to a Somerset bargemaster named Aurelius Drewe, in exchange for bathstone to the value of £1,640 (agreement contained in deeds of 3–7 Albert Terrace, seen by courtesy of Reading Corporation). *RM* 1 April 1833 noted that stone could be obtained in Reading for less than the cost of brick.
84 Printed sale catalogue in Berks RO Reading archives, uncatalogued documents.
85 *CM*, 5 May 1859 (Berks RO R/ACa 2/4).
86 Thesis, pp. 111–14.
87 Printed sale catalogue in Berks RO Reading archives, uncatalogued documents.
88 *CM*, 8 May 1856 (Berks RO R/ACa 2/3).
89 *CM*, 31 July 1860 (Berks RO R/ACa 2/4).
90 *RM*, 23 June 1860; tabulated in Thesis, pp. 378–80.
91 *RM*, 23 June 1860.
92 List of houses built or building on land sold in 1860, compiled by Borough Surveyor, William Woodman, and dated 23 April 1864 (Berks RO Reading archives, uncatalogued documents).
93 Details in *CM* 1859 onwards (Berks RO R/ACa 2/4–6).
94 Information from printed sale catalogues 1832–60.
95 The following account is based on Thesis, p. 319ff., the main sources for which are maps, newspaper advertisements and the available title deeds.
96 G. Hillier, *The Stranger's Guide to the Town of Reading* (Reading, 1871), p. 49.
97 *RM*, 1 April 1833.
98 *RCL*, LMC 621.
99 *Report*, 1833, p. 130.

8 A Devon family and their estates: the Northcotes of Upton Pyne, 1660–1851

P. J. KEELEY

Much has been written in recent years concerning the great English landed estates, their owners and management, but comparatively little has been recorded to date about the more numerous small estates.[1] The main reason for this neglect is a lack of evidence. For demographic as well as financial reasons the smaller units tended to break up more readily and more frequently than the larger ones, and the extensive legal and economic evidence generally preserved for the great households is comparatively rare at gentry level.

We are fortunate, therefore, in having the title deeds, leases and rentals which comprise the substantial archive of the Northcote family, deposited in the Devon Record Office by the second Earl of Iddesleigh in 1950.[2] The archive includes sporadic leasehold evidence from the sixteenth and seventeenth centuries, outline rental evidence from the earlier decades of the eighteenth century, an almost complete series of the estate rentals from 1748 to the present century, and details of the family's involvement in commercial and industrial ventures at the end of the eighteenth century.

This essay will sketch the Northcotes' success in the Devon cloth trade from the mid sixteenth century and their simultaneous establishment as landed proprietors; their landed income to the mid eighteenth century is also examined.[3] The tenure of the seventh Baronet Northcote (1784–1851) forms the principal part of the study.

Cloth, land and office

The establishment of the Northcote family as landed proprietors in the first half of the sixteenth century was a result of the rapid growth of the cloth industry in Devon, and more particularly to the trade in high-quality kersey. Crediton, nine miles north of Exeter, was the Northcotes' home town for over a century; like nearby Tiverton it had enjoyed prosperity long before 1550 when Walter Northcote and his eldest son, John, were firmly established as large-scale clothiers. Standing between the processes of spinning and finishing the Northcotes exported "white" (undressed) cloth through London. Crediton enjoyed an unrivalled advantage as the only regular market in Devon for wool, yarn and cloth until 1540, when a proposal to establish a weekly mart at Exeter was finally confirmed by the Privy Council, albeit in the teeth of opposition from local merchants.[4] Nevertheless, the quality of Crediton kersey and the buoyant cloth trade promoted favourable economic conditions in the town until late in the century; the Northcote family, likewise, continued to prosper.

Walter Northcote was assessed at only £2 in the lay subsidy return of 1524.[5] By 1547, when Edward VI granted the church of Crediton to his parishioners for £200,[6] Northcote was residing in the former Deanery (renamed Northcote Court) which was to be associated with the cloth trade for the next three centuries. Cloth manufacture depended on both town- and country-based labour, so the acquisition of a "mansion-house" – part of which was probably given over to small-scale "factory" production, as were certain Essex clothiers' homes – and the purchase of individual tenements in and around Crediton doubtless gave the clothier closer control over the manufacturing processes.[7]

Trading profits enabled Walter Northcote to buy land on an increasingly ambitious scale from the mid sixteenth century. The manor of Henstil, in north-east Crediton, was probably acquired at about the same time as Northcote Court; like all but three of the twelve former prebendal manors Henstil had been farmed out by its secular canons to gentlemen- or yeoman-clothiers since at least the time of the *Valor*.[8] Tenements in Honiton were acquired by Walter Northcote in 1552.[9] The cost of these properties is unknown.

Northcote's principal landed acquisition at this time – in which purchase he joined with his son, John – was of the manor of Newton St Cyres bought in August 1557 for £936; Newton was formerly the property of Plymton Priory.[10] The rectory of Newton was acquired by the Northcotes in 1560 for £402.[11] A prosperous semi-urban village in the valley of the Creedy, Newton lay midway between Exeter and Crediton. Almost immediately the Northcotes divided the manor with the Quicke family (substantial yeoman-clothiers) as co-lords until 1761, when the Quickes acquired the whole manor. In 1570 Walter Northcote successfully petitioned for a grant of arms, following further purchases of local tenements.[12]

In the early seventeenth century the Northcote estate was expanded to include the manor of Kennerleigh, three miles north of Crediton, bought in 1609 for £800 (probably payment for a gaming debt); further farms in Newton St Cyres in 1609 for £1,800, among which was included the mansion of Hayne Barton, from thence the seat of the family until 1734; Uton Barton, immediately south of Crediton, which had been leased since 1582, but was bought in 1626 for £861; and smallholdings in Poughill, Washfield Pyne and Witheridge in the 1620s and 1630s for £200.[13] In 1639 a moiety of the manor of Iddesleigh, in central north Devon, was acquired (for an unknown sum) from the Copleston family, an ancient Devon gentry house then in decline.[14]

There were few great landowners in Devon. This was an important factor in the establishment of the numerous small estates by the gentry and wealthy merchants; some lived on the resources of one manor, while others held several. From the sixteenth century competition between merchants, the expansion of the cloth trade and the resulting scramble for land combined to produce a pattern of scattered landholding which typified the acquisitions of other local mercantile dynasties besides the Northcotes; the Tuckfields, for example, established themselves in and around Crediton, and the Blundells in Tiverton.[15]

Walter Northcote's success probably secured his appointment as one of the twelve Governors of Crediton Church, a self-perpetuating oligarchy whose dominion extended into every corner of life in the district; his son, John (d. 1587) was a Governor from at least 1573.[16] Crediton was principally Puritan in ambience, and adherence to these ideals and practices survived in the senior line of the Northcotes until the late seventeenth century, when the first baronet was portrayed in old age in Puritan garb.[17] The third clothier in the senior line, John Northcote (d. 1633), in addition to inheriting his father's seat as a Governor, also acquired a seat on the Bench in 1598, and was elected sheriff of Devon in 1626.[18]

John Northcote III (1599–1675) sat in the House of Commons from 1640, representing Ashburton in the Long Parliament and Barnstaple in the Convention; he acquired a baronetcy in 1641 but his sympathies lay with the parliamentarians during the Civil War.[19] Thanks, no doubt, to the continued diligence of the numerous members of his family and to his residence on the estate from about 1647 – a moderate, he was turned off the County Committee by the dominant radicals – the patrimonial inheritance seems to have escaped the depredations that might have been expected in an area crossed and recrossed by both armies during the hostilities.

This turbulent period saw not only political but also family problems for Sir John. His eldest son, Arthur, was a keen dice-player; the result of his excesses was exemplified by a deed of 1649 in which the entire Northcote estate was to be conveyed to trustees for 99 years to raise £4,000 unless Arthur paid that sum in three annual instalments immediately following his father's demise.[20] Sir John lived for another quarter of a century but the sum was still unpaid at his death in 1675 and the trust terms came into being. There ensued many years of petitioning between Sir Arthur, his son the third baronet, and the legatees of the first baronet's will concerning their respective rights and interests in the estate; even hearings before the Lords did not put an end to the rancorous exchanges.[21]

Estate income and expenditure, to 1783

The Northcote family was wealthy by the close of the sixteenth century. Walter Northcote the elder died about 1570. His son John Northcote I settled the estate on his eldest son, Walter, but the young man died the day after his father in 1587 (when an outbreak of plague followed a year of dearth in the locality) and the estate passed to his younger brother, John II. This John Northcote left £1,000 to his second son, John III (the first Baronet Northcote), who also inherited the estate following the premature death of an older brother.[22] Sir John Northcote was said to have been worth £1,500–2,000 p.a. at the Restoration.[23] Unfortunately, no detailed financial evidence of the Northcote estate has survived before 1748.

The 1649 trust deed may have been inaccurately drawn; its terms deprived Arthur Northcote, probably unintentionally, of any income. A large property that Sir Arthur acquired through his first marriage was quickly sold,[24] and in 1679 a deed of partition exempted the profits of Hayne and Uton (about £200 p.a.) from the payment of his debts. The income from Hayne, Uton and New Place, Kingsnympton (a property acquired about 1660 from the indebted Sir Hugh Pollard, father-in-law of the first baronet), was the sole landed revenue enjoyed by Sir Arthur;[25] he had no power of leasing. The third baronet, Sir Francis Northcote, whilst apparently also fond of gambling had, nevertheless, a little more financial leeway than his father, but even with power of leasing and mortgaging (and a penchant for borrowing from substantial tenants) Sir Francis died in debt, his wife renouncing claim to his personalty and dependent on her brother-in-law (the fourth baronet) for an income due under the terms of her marriage settlement but never paid.[26] The total demesne income enjoyed between 1679 and 1709 was *c.* £280 p.a.; we do not know whether tithes were paid to the baronets during this period, but these were worth *c.* £80 p.a.

Dr Henry Northcote (1659–1730) had pursued an academic career in medicine at Exeter College, Oxford, prior to his tenure of the baronetcy from 1709. He also lived away from the ancestral seat, residing on his wife's estate in Tawstock, two miles south of Barnstaple.[27] Although we lack detailed knowledge of the Northcote estate revenue for this period, the demesne income was about £700 p.a., including tithes. In addition, he had collected at least £1,100 in entry fines and other "casualties" by 1730.

The resurgence of prosperity which had occurred during the tenure of the fourth baronet was apparently consolidated when Sir Henry's son, also named Henry, married an heiress in 1730.[28] Bridget Maria, daughter of Hugh Stafford, inherited one-third of her grandfather Kellond's estate – a dozen demesnes and 300 lifehold tenements – in the rich South Hams area, and her father's manors of Upton Pyne (contiguous with Newton St Cyres to the east) and Dowland (north of Iddesleigh) in 1734. We do not know the annual value of the Kellond estate since the only remaining survey is incomplete; the Stafford estate was worth £600 p.a.[29] The annual value of the Northcote estate was increased by £100 (to about £800) thanks to the substitution of rack-rent leases for lifehold tenements. In addition to his vastly increased landholding, which possibly doubled to 8,000 acres, the extent of the estate, Sir Henry (MP for Exeter, 1735–43) took more than £3,000 in entry fines from his patrimonial estate during his brief tenure of the title.

Lady Northcote's inheritance proved, however, to be encumbered with bond debts and portions totalling £18,000. Hugh Stafford had sold small parcels of the Kellond estate, but the money realized was insufficient to relieve his debts. As well as being a generous settler the young Sir Henry doubtless spent freely during his sojourns at Westminster, so that at his death in 1743 (at the age of 33) his trustees were faced with the necessity of further sales. New Place Barton was sold in 1744 for £4,700; Honiton tenements fetched £1,200 in 1751; and further parts of the Kellond estate were sold in 1749 and 1752 for £3,738.[30] During the fourteen-year minority of the fifth baronet, income from the Northcote estate averaged £623 p.a.

The institution of a regular system of accounting pre-dated the Northcote estate case (which came before Lord Chancellor Hardwicke and was finally decreed upon in 1746) but sequential rental volumes survive only from 1748.[31] Between 1749 and 1757 outgoings (£6,332) roughly equalled income (£6,599).

During Sir Stafford's tenure (1757–70) income averaged £996 p.a. Again, a rough balance was maintained between income and expenditure.

Table 8.1   Income of Sir Stafford Northcote

Year	Rents(£)	Fines(£)	Tithes(£)
1757	717	50	135
1758	732	0	137
1759	744	0	144
1760	600	105	135
1761	600	0	137
1762	780	49	146
1763	780	4	124
1764	780	31	149
1765	799	703	125
1766	799	0	151
1767	799	0	133
1768	844	358	147
1769	844	0	133
1770	844	45	142
Total	10,662	+1,345	+1,938 = 13,945(£)

Table 8.2   Expenditure of Sir Stafford Northcote

Year	Cash(£)	Rates(£)	Other(£)
1757	440	462	56
1758	633	518	62
1759	1,038	510	54
1760	1,865	402	95
1762	819	113	0
1765	1,850	173	0
1768	1,883	141	0
1770	1,764	328	0
Total	10,292	+2,647	+267 = 13,206(£)

Further sales of land were necessary during this period to ease the burden of debt which lay upon the estate; all that remained of the Kellond estate was sold by 1766. Together with the disposal of parts of the Stafford and Northcote estates (including most of Newton St Cyres) these sales totalled over £12,000. Sales between 1744 and 1766 realized £26,000.

The Northcote estate once more reverted to the care of trustees between 1770 and 1783, following the death of Sir Stafford at the age of 34. The sales of land had satisfied the debts of both Hugh Stafford and Sir Henry Northcote. The average income during this second interregnum was £907 p.a., and careful management achieved savings of £600 p.a., even after provision had been made for the dowager Lady Northcote. Tables 8.3 and 8.4 detail income and expenditure for this period.

Table 8.3   Estate Income, 1771–83

Year	Rent(£)	Fines(£)	Tithes(£)
1771	844	12	129
1772	844	5	128
1773	824	6	149
1774	822	none	162
1775	843	7	144
1776	1,021	148	144
1777	1,094	none	133
1778	1,128	none	163
1779	1,094	115	150
1780	1,128	20	153
1781	1,128	120	140
1782	1,232	30	156
1783	1,232	none	158
	13,234	+463	+1,909 = 15,606(£)

Table 8.4   Estate Expenditure, 1771–83

Year	Cash(£)	Funds(£)	Rates(£)
1773	955	0	90
1774	340	400	46
1775	380	0	61
1776	380	486	389
1777	0	537	0
1778	0	219	0
1779	1,196	79	412
1780	0	61	0
1782	1,704	0	889
1783	500	0	300
	5,455	+1,782	+2,187 = 9,424(£)

The first purchase of land by the family since the seventeenth century was undertaken in 1774 when Sir Charles Bingham's moiety of the manor of Iddesleigh was acquired: it was financed by two loans totalling £7,000. The substantial rates figure above includes interest payments on this sum: maintenance for Lady Northcote and her children accounts for the cash totals, and investments in the funds are also detailed.[32]

By 1640 the Northcote estate was a little over 3,600 acres in extent; the estimates of the first baronet's income in 1660 probably represent the annual value of the estate, since until 1688 the two principal Bartons, which furnished the greater part of the subsequent rack-rent income, were occupied by the family itself and the majority of the estate was probably let on beneficial leases. This valuation figure (10*s* per acre) parallels that paid for the high-rented pastures of north Wiltshire at about the same time.[33]

It would be a mistake, however, to equate acreage with annual value and rental income.[34] On the Northcote estate, out of 111 tenements comprising 3,619 acres valued at £1,865 in 1763, only 25 were rack-rented, and the income from these amounted to a little less than £600 p.a.[35] But the individual valuations of these ancient demesnes were twice the annual value of the life-leasehold tenements. Hayne Barton (eighty-three acres) was valued at £89 in 1743, when the tenant had been there nearly twenty-five years.[36] The same valuation (£1 per acre) was applied over all the rack-rented hill and valley farms in the rich redlands by the River Creedy. The rent of Hayne was advanced little until 1800 when the farm was thrown together with Court Place (Newton St Cyres) and the 283 acres were let for £295 p.a. The value of the very numerous life-leases on the estate in the mid eighteenth century was about 10*s* per acre, though this figure was subject to great variation, depending on land use and location.

The tenure of Sir Stafford Henry Northcote, 1784–1851

Pound Living Mine, Upton Pyne

The long tenure of Sir Henry Stafford Northcote saw a great enhancement of the estate's agricultural income, and in addition the seventh baronet was involved in two commercial ventures: he developed a manganese mine on the estate and was a director of a bank in Exeter. Further purchases of land took place which resulted in the consolidation of the core of the estate at Upton Pyne and Brampford Speke (the parish contiguous with Upton to the north). Attention will first be paid to the non-agricultural ventures, which began in the late 1780s; agricultural income and changes in the area of the Northcote estate will be treated last.

Shortly after entering upon his inheritance, Sir Stafford began negotiations to exploit a lode of manganese in Upton Pyne; Samuel Kingdon, the Unitarian ironmaster (and later the Mayor of Exeter), was the projector of this venture. A letter from Kingdon outlines the negotiations over the initial lease for the mine.[37]

Kingdon wrote to Northcote at the beginning of 1788 that he had been "for several years past . . . endeavouring to gain a complete knowledge of the different uses and qualities of manganese" and had been looking at a lode in Huxham to which he "paid little attention . . . in expectation I should agree with you for [Upton]". A price had yet to be agreed for the raising of the ore, and Kingdon wished to assure himself that there was a sufficient quantity of the metal as to make it worth the raising "being the same trouble to sell fifty ton as to sell two hundred when brought into a regular course of trade".

Northcote proposed to charge Kingdon 15s a ton, but the undertaker demurred. He begged a little time to await the return of a sample "box of manganese" from the lode at Upton which he had sent to a Mr Band (probably of Bristol) "who sells the most of any known person in this kingdom"; Kingdon was aware of Band's "price and situation for the markets", and wanted to strike the right bargain so as to sell "to outdo him, and without doing that a trade . . . from Exeter would be very confined". Kingdon offered "on receipt of the box either [to] take the management of the whole business, and account with you for half the profit . . . or make you such an offer to take it on myself as I think will afford me a small profit, but enable me to do something extensive".

An agreement was reached but the details of the (undated) draft are rather different from the original proposal. Northcote granted Kingdon "a right to dig, search for and raise manganese" at Upton for ten years, entrusting to him sole management but reserving the right to inspect all the relevant documents concerning the venture. After the expenses of the undertaking had been met Kingdon was to pay half the profits of the trade to Sir Stafford. Kingdon had a largely free hand on the site, Northcote merely stipulating that should it "be thought necessary [to pull down any buildings] for the proceeding in and carrying on the work the tenant shall be made all reasonable satisfaction which shall be discharged by Sir Stafford and S. Kingdon equally". It was held that the death of either party should not end the term, and that Kingdon's brother Zachary could carry on "in the same manner as if S. Kingdon was living".

Kingdon had proposed to pay 25s a ton for the ore "when delivered at Exeter Quay and so properly cleaned as shall be thought . . . advantageous for sale, and if not so cleaned S.K. to be at liberty to get it so . . . and deduct the expense from the . . . 25/- per ton". Northcote was

> always to keep at least ten ton clean and fit for immediate sale and to deliver it at Exeter Quay in four days after ordered for [*sic*] and constantly to supply S.K. with so much as he shall want supposing so much can be found, and none to be sold to any other person for fourteen years . . . S.K. obligating himself not to sell manganese raised on any other person's estate without . . . approbation.

This clause suggests how important the availability of cheap water transport was to Kingdon's venture.[38] It further suggests that Sir Stafford Northcote not only allowed the development of the mine at Upton, but also that he directed mining operations there.

Northcote gave Kingdon leave to raise ore at his own expense and to pay 10s per ton after cleansing; the landlord was to pay the cost of

> repairing all injuries that may take place to buildings . . . in raising and carrying away the manganese and obliging S.K. only to fill up the pits

with the earth, gravel, stone etc. that shall raise out of the same in sinking for the manganese, and likewise to grant him leave to sink or cut a drain or audit thro' any part of the ground that may best suit to carry off the water from being an obstruction in raising the [ore].

The onus for recording the correct weight of ore raised was to be on the undertaker, though either party had the power to consult the "wharfing books at Exeter Quay". Ore not merchanted through Exeter was to be accounted for by Kingdon as to quantity and method of transport, "S.K. not to pay for the manganese before he removes it from Upton Pyne".

Of the operations themselves we have an account book from March 1788 to May 1795.[39] Payments to Northcote of the moiety of the annual dividend are recorded; no record of payment into the Northcote estate account exists from this first venture.

The account of Kingdon's exploitation of Pound Living Mine begins dramatically towards the end of March 1788 with the expense of 1s 8d "horse hire to Upton Pyne to give directions to throw down the house." The purchase of basic materials – and local labour, a carpenter and a mason – followed; a shed was erected over the first pit from which the ore was to be taken. The mine was open-cast. A traveller in 1794 described the operations at Upton: "It is improperly called a mine . . . the top being open, it is merely a pit. The deepest part . . . seemed to be about twenty feet. There is no occasion for a shaft as the ore diminishes so much in richness in proportion to its depth that it is worked only in a horizontal direction."[40] Granting a further licence in 1802, this plot was described as measuring 40 by 22 feet, the workings perpendicular "under such extent of surface".

Nowhere does Kingdon set down the number of men employed to raise the ore, but, judging by the wage payments, there seem to have been fewer than six at any one time. It is also impossible to ascertain whether the men had temporarily left agricultural pursuits to work the mine and return to the land later, though the grant made in 1802 particularly obliged new undertakers to keep eight men fully occupied.

Regular extraction of manganese got quickly under way. On 21 April 1788 the first ton of ore was raised. Table 8.5 summarizes the results of six years of exploration.

The average price paid per ton of ore was 55s, with a range from 45s to 60s; 50s per ton was most usually charged. The ore was transported

Table 8.5   Manganese Raised at Upton Pyne, 1788–95

Date	Debit(£)	Credit(£)	Gross profit(£)	Quantity(tons)
12.1789	265	607	321	222
12.1790	282	675	393	238
12.1792	413	1,066	653	365
6.1794	243	847	604	295
5.1795	102	266	164	91
Total	1,305	3,461	2,156	1,211

from Upton Pyne in wooden casks, and the quoted price was net of packing and freight which were charged to the customer at cost. William Maton reported that Exeter and London were the principal destinations of the ore. The account book lists forty-five customers supplied by Samuel Kingdon; Boulton & Watt, and the Northumberland Glass Company were among the many small buyers, taking about three tons each. But by far the largest quantity was sold to a single customer, William Coulburn, who took 555 tons. Coulburn was probably an agent, and we may hazard (despite Maton's remarks about Exeter and London being the principal destinations of the shipments) that Liverpool was the destination of most of the ore raised, given the utility of manganese in the process of glassmaking and the development of that industry which was under way (thanks in part to the operation of a canal system) in south-west Lancashire at this period. Sir Stafford's grandson, who succeeded him in 1851, sold shares in the British Plate Glass Manufacturing Company in the 1840s, and these were probably given to him by his grandfather who doubtless obtained them during the time when he was engaged in the industry himself.[41]

Kingdon's investigations prior to his undertaking at Upton confirm that the ore was already well-known. We do not know how he discovered the Upton lode, but from later descriptions of the ore it may have been visible on the surface and easily detectable once the appropriate geological features had been pinpointed. Two forms of manganese ore were known at Upton: oxides (in three configurations) and a silicate. The oxidic structures were: "manganite, a grey manganese . . . in fine prismatic crystals; pyrolusite [which occurred] in association with other manganese ores; and was found in earthy dark-brown masses. . . . Rhodonite was a silicate of Manganese, red in tone." Kingdon does not distinguish between types in the account book. William Maton "observed that the ore was in nodules of various dimensions and generally crystallized in the inside . . . [It] was used in the glass-houses formerly established at Exeter, but it is now sent chiefly to London." He goes on to speculate about the formulation and to observe the properties of manganese.

> Judging by the colour . . . and the martial earth with which its surface is often covered, several minerologists have supposed it to be a meagre ore of iron, but from the experiments of Bergman, Gahn and others, and from its appearing to possess properties common to no other metallic substance, it should certainly be considered as a peculiar semi-metal . . . The black oxide is used in glass houses to take away the yellow, green or blue tinge from glass intended to be of a clear white. Too large a proportion of it gives a violet colour.[42]

On his second visit to Upton Pyne in 1796 Maton reported that the manganese mine "had been filled up and another opened at Newton St Cyres . . . The matrix of the ore is the same in both places."[43]

Our knowledge of the exploitation of the Upton deposits is sketchy following the close of Kingdon's account book in the summer of 1796. This first grant still had several years to run, but Maton's comments suggest that Kingdon had extracted what he could and closed the first pits down.

Clauses in a second grant, however, suggest that Kingdon's widow (Jane) and son (Samuel) were apparently still active at Pound Living in 1802; no mention is made of the manganese venture in the will of Samuel (senior) in 1798 or that of Jane Kingdon in 1811, although she does refer to shareholdings in mines near Dartmoor.[44]

The second licence granted other parts of the Pound Living to Nicholas Williams (an Exeter cornfactor) from August 1801 to March 1806, but a release executed between the seventh baronet and Williams in 1802 suggests that this venture came to nought and that Williams had better luck in Newton St Cyres.[45]

In the same year Sir Stafford made a third grant, this time to a consortium of six men (four from London, two from Peterborough) to exploit ninety-six acres near the original site in Upton Pyne. Northcote requested one-sixth of the raw ore or 30s per finished ton from these venturers. Work probably proceeded; the estate rental for 1802 records the receipt of £700 from the sale of manganese, though we do not know whether this was for one year or more, or whether it was paid by more than one projector.[46] Presumably in response to problems which had arisen during the previous explorations, Northcote inserted into the third licence a clause forbidding the neglect of the workings; he specified a requirement "to have eight men continually employed". But the consortium was said to have mined with less than the "expected degree of skill or activity" and Sir Stafford seems to have attempted to buy into the mining ventures of Mr Williams ("the most experienced, adventurous and opulent [local] miner") who held a licence to explore for manganese for ten years in Newton. In the river valley very considerable deposits of ore were discovered, as production figures for the 1870s can testify.[47]

Our sketchy knowledge of the subsequent operations at Upton Pyne may be the result of an action taken in response to a legal opinion obtained in 1808 as to the validity of breaking the contracts already granted for mining in the village. Counsel advised that Sir Stafford could not make any new concessions in the same fields until the old grants had expired, and that his demand to inspect the books of the undertakers was unlawful. Evidence that might have survived about the ventures which followed Kingdon's presumably disappeared with the undertakers.

No evidence survives to connect Sir Stafford Northcote with an ambitious mining venture in 1826, though he must have been aware of it. That year saw the promotion of a company formed "to work with effect . . . invaluable lead, tin and manganese mines extending over upwards of four thousand acres". A vividly coloured advertisement – showing sections through Dartmoor (where tin was to be sought) and a scaled map and pictorial representation of the Creedy valley manganese lode – launched the company.[48] Optimistic promises of a net return from manganese of £5 a ton ("at little or no expense as the lode is within a few feet of the surface") were detailed in a note which also stated that the large area under consideration, stretching from Newton and Upton to Poltimore, had already yielded 20,800 tons of manganese (including 2,000 tons from Upton Pyne). We do not know what became of the projected enterprise, but the mining shares mentioned in Jane Kingdon's will may have been issued by this new company.

In 1843 Sir Stafford seems to have got the itch to explore once again at Pound Living, but in the surviving correspondence regarding this new undertaking a Colonel Williamson was "not sanguine as to further prospects for the mine at Upton Pyne".[49] This is the last we hear of mine undertakings on the Northcote estate.

It has been stated that the vein of manganese at Upton was the first in the country to be exploited;[50] but this is uncertain, given that Samuel Kingdon knew of Mr Band's involvement in exploiting the ore. The lode at Upton was successfully exploited for a few years; but it may have been the tail end of a seam which was richest in the Creedy valley and less extensive on the surrounding hills, to judge by the subsequent success of the Newton lode. Newton and Upton mines seem to have yielded similar amount of ore each year; by 1873 the price was £6 per ton, though it fell back to £2 per ton in 1878 due, perhaps, to declining quality – as observed by Maton in 1796.[51]

We can best summarize Sir Stafford Northcote's brief (though profitable) brush with the first "industrial revolution" by saying that the evidence for mining operations at Upton goes some way to support the thesis that this initial period of industrial activity was remarkable for the "invisibility" of its effects on the surroundings. The extraction of manganese ore at Upton led to no dislocation of the surrounding agricultural activities to the advantage of "industry" but rather the opposite, in that a small area of land was temporarily subtracted from and later returned to agricultural use. Indeed, the ultimate advantage may have accrued as much to the farmer as the landlord; Maton observed that the effects of the discarded ore on fields in Newton was to increase their fertility.[52]

The Western Bank, 1793–8

The Western Bank opened its doors to the public on 1 January 1793. Sir Stafford Northcote was one of the four partners, who raised £2,000 as joint stock with a further £500 available from each in case of necessity. The bank was situated in the house of one of the partners, Henry Waymouth of Exeter. Waymouth was allowed £84 p.a. rent, but had to adapt the building to an appropriate form for which he was allowed £30; this meant partitioning off "the front part of the . . . house by a strong wall".[53]

Each partner of the bank was to enjoy an equal quarter-share in the profits of the venture. Sir Stafford was specifically named as "not obliged to attend to the . . . business, but use his own will and pleasure in that respect"; presumably his interest was purely financial. An absent partner, but likewise bound to the agreement as were the others, was Richard Kennaway; he was in the East Indies at the time of the proposed partnership. The partnership could be dissolved at the end of the first two years or at the end of any year following, provided that a year's notice in writing was given. Mutual releases "and bonds for each others indemnity" were to be exchanged between the men to "get in the debts standing out" and these agreements, "as are usual and reasonable between partners on . . . determination" were used when, in June 1798, the operation was unaccountably wound up.

During the few years it operated the Western Bank seems to have been successful. "Within three weeks of opening the bank, the interest on deposits at twenty days notice was raised from two and a half to three per cent". The bank issued its own notes, and at the closure in 1798 "the partners announced that 'any notes of theirs that might be in circulation' would be discharged by Messrs Barings, Short and Collyns at the Devonshire Bank. Five guinea notes were specifically mentioned." Interest and depository notes were also known to have been issued and these were offered for redemption, with principal, from the same bank. That this arrangement was able to be carried out suggests that no financial problems were connected with the closure of the Western Bank.

No clerks were to be hired or fired without the consent of all the partners, and the wages of the clerks and all other business expenses were to be paid before the dividends due the directors. None of the partners was to act in a similar capacity in any other banking concern, or on his own account. Account books were to be kept, and a balance was to be struck "every night, week or month . . . as is usual in other banks". A general accounting was to be held every year, and the partners or their heirs were to be then entitled to their share. All directors had an equal voice in the business, and none were to trade independently, or to advance more money into the Western Bank, without the consent of the others.

It was thought necessary "that a correspondence should be established with some banking house in London" and "that one of the partners in . . . London be . . . a member of the House of Commons". It may be that Sir Stafford Northcote was the prime mover behind the winding up of the Western Bank. Only four years after its closure he entered into a large bond (in October 1804) with the partners of another Exeter bank, in which his father-in-law, Charles Baring of the Devon Bank, was one of the four partners. These men were "jointly and severally . . . bound to Sir Stafford . . . in £10,000". Mr Ryton may be correct in guessing that the motive behind the closure of the Western Bank was Northcote's desire to avoid undue competition with a close relative. Perhaps Northcote bowed to pressure from the expansionist policies of his father-in-law.

Landed income, 1784–1851

At the accession of the seventh baronet the Northcote estate comprised: Court Place, Newton; lifehold farms in Marsh and Henstil; Uton Barton; Hayne Barton; the manor of Kennerleigh (all these having been in the family for at least two centuries in 1783); the Stafford estate; and the Lovett (Winscot) estate. But the seventh baronet's income from land greatly exceeded his ancestors' receipts from this source. In addition to the favourable economic conditions for agriculture during the French wars, there occurred an increase in the rack-rent returns from Iddesleigh as a result of the acquisition of the Bingham moiety of the manor; there was added the full revenues from the manor of Winscot and from the Stafford estate after the death of the dowager Lady Northcote; and changes in the area of the Northcote estate occurred thanks to sales and purchases undertaken by Sir Stafford himself during the first third of the nineteenth century.

The acquisition of Sir Charles Bingham's moiety of Iddesleigh greatly increased rack-rent income from this part of the estate. Many more Bingham than Northcote tenants held termly leases; although a farmer might hold his property in moieties, one from Bingham at rack and one from Northcote on life-leasehold terms. During the course of Sir Stafford's tenure, especially during the postwar depression, there occurred a gradual reversion to life-leasehold grants; by the 1830s only four farms were held on rack-rent leases, compared with more than a dozen after 1775, though enhanced rentals on one or two of the larger farms sustained the levels of receipts. The last life-lease was granted by Northcote in 1829. At nearby Upottery the last life-lease was sealed in 1844, but in Dorset this form of tenure has survived into the present century.[54]

A more dramatic and a permanent change in agricultural income occurred following the death of Lady Catherine Northcote in 1802. She had enjoyed the Stafford and Lovett estates as dower from the death of Sir Stafford's father in 1770. From 1803 the rentals record this expansion of revenue and territory, which was held until the end of the nineteenth century. Winscot had been surveyed in 1763 but had thereafter been accounted for separately from the Northcote estate; at survey the Barton and its dozen satellite lifehold tenements were estimated to contain a little less than 600 acres. The Stafford estate has been described above; the northern portion had been slightly reduced in area in the sales of the first half of the eighteenth century, whilst Upton Pyne had remained intact; its total area was about 1,000 acres. The Northcote estate at Lady Day 1803 comprised 5,500 acres, with an annual rental value of £2,669 p.a.

Some property had been sold between 1806 and 1815, including Northcote Court, Marsh Farm (Poughill) and a few north Devon tenements, and these sales had netted £2,050. A more concerted policy of change was instigated in 1822; farms and fields near Pynes House were acquired and eventually comprised a compact block of property around the villages of Upton Pyne and Brampford Speke. Sales of land between 1822 and 1836 realized £39,194; the money was applied to further purchases of land (£6,530) and securities (£28,594), while the balance (£4,070) remained in hand.

Table 8.6 Northcote Estate Rents, 1803–51

	Rent Due(£)	Allow.(£)	Rent Paid(£)	Arrears(£)	Income(£)
1803	3,069	422	2,285	45	2,682
1813	4,809	850	2,579	16	3,967
1823	4,278	163	2,916	556	3,668
1833	4,412	195	2,703	244	3,459
1843	3,529	209	2,676	98	3,008
1851	4,767	215	3,565	44	4,379

Space permits illustration of only decennial figures, but these conceal a number of interesting features. As might be expected net rents during the French war greatly increased (as did receipts from such "casualties" as entry fines on life-leases, and sales of timber): in 1810 net rents totalled £4,450 (£1,583 fines); in 1815 £4,068, and in 1818 £5,026 (£1,098 fines). Receipts declined to £900 in 1820, and £2,960 in 1822; thereafter, income was sustained at around £4,000 p.a. until the 1830s when we encounter a range from £3,273 in 1832 to £2,988 in 1839, with peaks of £3,700 in 1834 and 1837. The early 1840s saw a further fall in net income which was £3,000 in 1842; from 1846 rents totalled about £3,700 p.a. The sales and purchases referred to above had no dramatic effect on total agricultural revenue: in 1823 this was £3,526, in 1837 £3,469.

Allowances to tenants increased markedly from 1803. In the late eighteenth century they had averaged about £250–300 p.a. Peak years following were 1805 (£654), 1809 (£734), 1813 (£676), 1816 (£527), 1817 (£584); thereafter they were maintained around £200 p.a., a level to which they returned in the 1830s following marked increases between 1825 and 1827 (£378, £508, £349). In 1836 £470 was allowed against total rent due. Income tax of *c*. £100 p.a. was paid from 1846.

Arrears also varied greatly. Negligible in the 1800s and early 1810s, they began thereafter to accumulate: 1814, £207; 1815 £146; 1816 £759; 1817 £427; 1818 £332; 1819 £242. In 1822 £814 was owed, in 1823 £556, 1824 £230; in 1829 £511, 1830 £931, 1834 £389, 1835 £559. Between 1836 and 1851, however, they averaged only £72 p.a.

In notes written in 1753 preparatory to his survey of Devon parishes, Dean Milles remarked on the possibilities of "improving" the immediate vicinity around Pynes House.[55] We do not know if the sixth baronet was aware of Milles's comments but neither Sir Stafford nor his successors saw fit to throw down the intervening walls and empark the fields between the house and the Exe. The mansion stood (and stands) not at the centre of a vast pleasure park but at the heart of a small working estate; cattle from the Home Farm grazed within sight of the house. But agricultural returns from the rich pastures of the Exe valley and its environs were subject to fluctuations which reflected both the family's circumstances and general economic changes. When we contrast the tenure of the seventh baronet with his father's and grandfather's, the part played by personality stands out markedly; though Sir Stafford's opportunities to increase and expand sources of income must in some degree have been due to the economic advances connected with the French wars.

The role played by the baronets' agents deserves mention. Despite two long minorities and a brief recession in the mid-1750s, the administrative machinery of the estate ran smoothly. The institution of a thoroughgoing accounting system in the mid eighteenth century has been noted; its maintenance was the responsibility of the family lawyer, John Jones of Exeter, and the accountant John Reed of Chulmleigh (and after his death his daughter, Anne[56]) . The accession of the business-minded Sir Stafford in 1783 was paralleled by the appointment of a substantial tenant, Henry Osmond (whose father had been one of the surveyors of the estate in

1763) as accountant. The Osmonds only relinquished their duties when the second Earl of Iddesleigh's surviving child, Lady Rosalind Northcote, handed the accounts over to a professional firm in 1927.

The Northcote estate survived intact until the end of the nineteenth century. Following the (albeit delayed) impact of agricultural depression in the mid-1880s and the swingeing taxation of the 1910s and 1940s, substantial sales halved its size, and a number of tenants took the opportunity to become owner-occupiers. But the estate had undoubtedly been at its most prosperous in the late eighteenth and early nineteenth centuries, when commercial enterprise had been blended with sound agricultural management under the judicious stewardship of the seventh baronet.

Notes

1 J. V. Beckett, *The Aristocracy in England, 1660–1914* (Oxford, 1986) for a recent bibliography of landed families. The annual retrospective bibliography in the *Agricultural History Review* is comprehensive.
2 Devon Record Office (hereafter cited as DRO) 51/24.
3 P. J. Keeley, "A Devon family and their estates: the Northcotes of Hayne, *c.* 1520–1783" (Oxford DPhil thesis, 1987), details the economic history of the family. W. Jones, "The early Northcote pedigree", *Exeter Notes and Gleanings*, vol. 4, no. 45 (15 Sept. 1891), pp. 134–43.
4 W. T. MacCaffrey, *Exeter, 1540–1640* (Cambridge, Mass., 1958), pp. 75, 161.
5 T. L. Stoate, *Devon Lay Subsidy Returns 1524–27* (privately printed, Bristol 1979), p. 60.
6 G. Oliver, *Monasticon Diocesis Exoniensis* (Exeter, 1846), pp. 77–9.
7 E. Power, *Medieval People*, 8th edn (London, 1946), pp. 153ff., 157; F. Crouzet, *The First Industrialists* (Cambridge, 1985), p. 5.
8 *Valor Ecclesiasticus*, Vol. 2 (London, 1814), pp. 324–6. Henstil returned to the senior line in 1562–3; Oliver, p. 88, prints the quit-claim of John Waldron to Robert Northcote.
9 DRO/51/24/102.
10 J. Youings (ed.), *Devon Monastic Lands: Calendar of Particulars for Grants*, Devon and Cornwall Record Society, new series 1 (Torquay, 1955), Grant No. 131.
11 *Calendar of Patent Rolls, Elizabeth I*, pp. 295f; Public Record Office (hereafter cited as PRO) LR1/3/65.
12 Jones, op. cit., p. 142.
13 ibid, p. 143.
14 PRO C2/N11/5, Feb. 1639.
15 W. G. Hoskins, "Estates of the Caroline gentry"; in W. G. Hoskins and H. P. R. Finberg, *Devonshire Studies* (London, 1952), pp. 334–65. DRO Z1/10 for the Tuckfield estate; W. Harding, *Memoirs of Tiverton*, 2 vols (Tiverton, 1845), pp. 27ff, 32.
16 DRO 1660A/207.
17 J. T. Cliffe, *The Puritan Gentry* (London, 1984), pp. 59, 250 n. 62; the dustjacket reproduces the engraving of Sir John Northcote.
18 Bodleian Library (hereafter cited as Bodl.), Ms Gough Devon 3, fol. 57.
19 *The Notebook of Sir John Northcote*, ed. A. H. A. Hamilton (London, 1877), introduction, *passim*; G. E. Cockayne (hereafter cited as GEC), *The Complete Baronetage*, Vol. 2 (Exeter, 1902), pp. 106–7.
20 DRO 51/24/102.
21 The main hearings: PRO C33/260/544 (1683); C33/262/262 (1683); C33/264/123 (1684); Lords' Journal XV, 79a (1691); C33/280/662–4 (1692); *L. J.* XVII, 297b (1702); C33/300/302–3, 478, 547; C33/302/118 (1703); C33/304/9 (1704).
22 Jones, op cit., pedigree appended.
23 PRO C33/262/262; *Devon and Cornwall Notes and Queries*, 18 no. 7 (1935), p. 316.

24 Bodl., Ms Top. Devon c 15, fol. 224.
25 DRO 51/24/123.
26 DRO 51/24/126, 127.
27 DRO 51/24/39.
28 GEC, loc cit.
29 DRO 51/24/39.
30 DRO 51/24/30, rental 1748–60 (unpaginated) includes details of sales and application of purchase money, usually under the appropriate year.
31 DRO 51/24/1, rentals from 1761.
32 DRO 51/24/54, Iddesleigh; DRO 51/24/1, rentals 1774–80.
33 J. R. Wordie, "Rent movements and the English tenant farmer, 1700–1839", *Research in Economic History*, vol. 6 (1981), p. 214.
34 Cf. W. G. Hoskins, "The ownership and occupation of land in Devonshire, 1650–1800" (unpublished Ph.D. thesis, University of London, 1938), p. 87.
35 DRO 51/24/7/3. The remains of the Northcote estate, less the Winscot estate, roughly equalled the acreage in 1660.
36 DRO 51/24/2/1, rough notes of agistment rents due.
37 DRO 51/24/100, letter from Kingdon; Kingdon's proposals; draft agreement.
38 Cf. G. Turnbull, "Canals, coal and regional growth during the industrial revolution", *Economic History Review*, 2nd ser., vol. 40, no. 4 (1987), p. 545.
39 DRO 51/24/129.
40 W. Maton, *Observations . . . of the Western Counties . . .* , 2 vols (Salisbury, 1797), Vol. I, p. 94. For Maton, see *Dictionary of National Biography*.
41 DRO 51/24/129. Turnbull, op. cit., pp. 550, 554. W. Coulburn of Liverpool left about £50,000 in 1811, though his will does not mention mining assets.
42 *Reports and Transactions of the Devonshire Association* (hereafter cited as *TDA*), Vol. 2, n. 2 (Exeter, 1868), p. 339. Maton, I, pp. 93–5. On manganese cf. *Encyclopaedia Britannica*, 3rd edn, Vol. 10 (London, 1797), pp. 528–31; the ore was isolated by Gahn in 1774, *Encyclopaedia Britannica*, 15th edn, Vol. 7 (1986), p. 772.
43 Maton, 2, p. 47.
44 PRO PROB 11/1303, Samuel left £5,500; PROB 11/1583, Jane carried on the business and left over £14,000.
45 DRO 51/24/100.
46 DRO 51/24/1 1802 rental. The only lacunae in the long series occur during the period of mining activity. P. Keeley, "The Northcote Estate, 1851–1948", unpublished essay; the study of the Northcote estate in the first half of the present century is possible thanks to the generosity of Lord Iddesleigh in supplying the rentals from 1922 to 1948.
47 R. Burt *et al.*, *Devon and Somerset Mines* (Exeter, 1984), pp. xxvii, 78, 87.
48 DRO 3665Z.
49 DRO 51/24/29/1.
50 W. G. Hoskins, *Devon* (London, 1954), p. 140.
51 Burt, p. 87; Maton, I, p. 93.
52 ibid, p. 47. Sir Stafford held shares in the British Cast Plate Glass Manufacturing Company; these were cashed by his grandson in the 1840s.
53 DRO 51/24/29/2 Draft agreement. J. Ryton, *Banks and Banknotes of Exeter, 1769–1906* (privately printed, Exeter, 1980), pp. 67–9. The present account follows Ryton, but makes greater use of the draft agreement.
54 DRO 152M/Box 67/Estate 4/16, Sidmouth Estate; W. L. Williams, *A West Country Village, Ashworthy: Family, Kinship and Land* (London, 1963), p. 30.
55 Bodl. Ms Gen. Top. Devon, fol. 185.
56 The estates of Maria Edgeworth's father in Ireland were administered by her in the late eighteenth century: Maria Edgeworth, *Castle Rackrent*, ed. G. Watson (Oxford, 1980), unpaginated biographical note.

9 Aristocrats and entrepreneurs in the Shropshire mining industry, 1748–1803

J. R. WORDIE

It was during the second half of the eighteenth century that the rural county of Shropshire earned itself a place in history as the cradle of England's Industrial Revolution. The county's days of glory were short-lived, for predominance in the drive for industrialization soon passed to other regions, but in 1775, when the entire national production of pig iron has been estimated at only 32,000 tons a year, Shropshire alone was producing some 12,000 to 13,000 tons, or about 40 per cent of the whole. By 1806, however, although Shropshire's iron output had risen to 55,000 tons a year, this figure then represented only 22 per cent of the national output of some quarter of a million tons.[1] In terms of coal production, it has been claimed that in the late seventeenth century Shropshire was second in importance only to the Northumberland and Durham region, but by 1800, when England alone was producing roughly 10 million tons of coal a year, Shropshire's contribution was a mere 260,000 tons annually, or about 2.5 per cent of national output.[2] This amount was, however, more than enough to supply Shropshire's local needs, and to enable the county to move into the technical vanguard of many industrial processes. Coalbrookdale is well known as the site of the first successful attempt to smelt iron ore with coke rather than with charcoal, but the county also saw the introduction of long-wall mining, and the first use of wooden and then iron "rail ways" for the movement of coal wagons. Shropshire could also boast of the first iron bridge (1779), the first "inclined plane" for raising canal barges up steep slopes (1788), and the first steam-powered blast furnace, operated by John Wilkinson at New Willey in 1776.[3] Indeed, the county was the first to make use of Boulton & Watt engines in a variety of roles, for pumping water, winding pit shafts, and even grinding corn. It was here that John Wilkinson developed his "boring engine" for the manufacture of accurate cannon barrels and steam-engine cylinders, an invention of vital importance to Boulton & Watt themselves. Here too Henry Cort of Fareham developed his famous puddling process, building on the work of the Cranage brothers of Coalbrookdale. He demonstrated his process for the first time at Ketley in 1784.[4] In addition, the county was in the vanguard of canal development, and for a few decades could claim pride of place as the most innovative and dynamic region of industrial Britain. Yet all of this activity took place within a surprisingly small area. A narrow strip of land running north and south from Ketley to Willey, a distance of only 8 miles, and with a width of only 3 miles, delineated physically the area in which all of these important innovations took place.

The whole story of the Industrial Revolution in Shropshire has been well outlined by Barrie Trinder in the two editions of his book of that title (1972 and 1981), and further details are provided in the *Victoria County History of Shropshire*, particularly in Volume I (1908) and Volume XI (1985). But because these works are broad surveys, they have not been able to investigate in any detail the nature of the relationship between the owners of the land from which the minerals of Shropshire were extracted, and the entrepreneurs who provided the enterprise and the working capital which made the mining ventures possible. Some members of this latter group are very well documented and hence very well known, but others remain shadowy figures. One such was Richard Hartshorne, the leading Shropshire coalmaster of the early eighteenth century who died in January 1733, and of whom Barrie Trinder has written: "If it were possible to discover as much about Hartshorne (or in a later period about John Onions, Edward Blakeway, Richard Jessons, or Alexander Brodie) as is generally known of the Coalbrookdale partners, the history of the Shropshire Coalfield might appear in a very different light."[5]

What follows here is an attempt to sketch in the background of some figures similar to those named above, and to throw some light upon their relationships with aristocratic mineowners, through an examination of the records of the Leveson-Gower family over several generations. The main seat of this titled line was at Trentham Hall in north Staffordshire, but the bulk of their landed property was held in eastern Shropshire, lying mainly between the townships of Wellington and Newport, just a few miles to the north of Ironbridge and Coalbrookdale.[6] This property straddled the northern reaches of the east Shropshire coalfield, and also contained deposits of other minerals which were essential for the promotion of industrial processes, such as clay for bricks, sand, limestone for the smelting furnaces, and limestone of a better quality, suitable for carving into building blocks. In addition, the three large manors of Ketley, Lilleshall and Sheriff Hales also held deposits of iron ore in the form of iron oxides and sulpher stone, or iron pyrites. The parish of Wombridge even provided tar springs and salt deposits.[7] Three generations of the Leveson-Gower family showed themselves to be particularly interested in the direct exploitation of this mineral wealth, represented by four individual aristocrats. They were John, the second Baron Gower, created Earl Gower in 1746 (1694–1754), Granville, the second Earl Gower, created Marquis of Stafford in 1786 (1721–1803), George Granville, the second Marquis of Stafford, created Duke of Sutherland in 1833 (1758–1833), and the latter's half brother Lord Granville, created Viscount Granville in 1815 and Earl Granville in 1833 (1773–1846). These men are all well documented, as is typical of members of their class.[8] Less well known, however, are the families of entrepreneurs with whom they had close dealings, five families in all: they were the Barbors, the Darbys, the Gilberts, the Reynolds and the Bishtons.

Until 1748, the Leveson-Gowers had been content to lease out mining concessions on their Shropshire property to local entrepreneurs such as Richard Hartshorne, Edward Dawe and George Sparrow, who mined the Leveson-Gower lands with varying degrees of success during the first half of the eighteenth century.[9] The year 1748 marked a significant turning point in the industrial history of the Shropshire estates, however, for it was then that John, recently created the first Earl Gower, decided to embark upon the direct exploitation of the mineral resources of his Shropshire lands, employing his own capital and his own colliery managers. It was this venture in direct landlord exploitation which proved to be instrumental in opening up the full mining potential of the Donnington Wood, Wrockwardine and Ketley areas, ensuring a significant emergence of industry in this part of Shropshire. The aim of the first Earl was to amalgamate this wide area into one great mining concern, but between his own lands in Ketley and Donnington Wood lay the manor of Wrockwardine, which incorporated the parishes of Wombridge and Wrockwardine Wood. This manor was held in 1748 by no fewer than three joint lords, Samuel Hill of Shepston, Sarah Revell of Shifnal and the Earl of Shrewsbury. To obtain mining rights in this manor, the agreement of all three lords had to be secured, but this proved to be no easy task. The Revell family, while remaining joint lords of the manor, had sold their interest in its mining rights to the Charlton family in 1673. St John Charlton of Apley Castle had in turn leased his rights to Walter Stubbs of Bockbury in 1737 for a term of 21 years. It was, therefore, with Stubbs that the immediate negotiations had to be carried out.[10] The manor had been mined for coal and ironstone since medieval times, but the pits were in a poor and dilapidated condition by 1747, and clearly needed heavy investment. Before embarking on this, however, Earl Gower needed the security of a lease from the three lords, and this he went to a great deal of trouble to obtain. As Robert Barbor, Earl Gower's chief agent, explained to Samuel Hill with reference to the Wrockwardine Wood Colliery, "as the mine is now in very bad condition and will require a large sum of money to put it in order, my lord desires to have the lease executed before his entry on that expense".[11]

The saga of the leasing negotiations is too involved for narration here, but a number of points arising from them need to be stressed. First, their success depended heavily upon the social standing and financial resources of Earl Gower himself: it is very doubtful whether a humble coalmining contractor without the earl's connections could have carried through to success such a complicated set of negotiations. Secondly, few contractors would have had either the courage or the resources to take on such a large range of mines in such poor condition in any case. Thirdly, the acquisition of sole mining rights in the manor of Wrockwardine was of vital importance to the whole area as an integrated mining region. This timely injection of landlord initiative can be seen in retrospect as the practical opening up of what proved to be a highly productive mineral-producing belt. A leasing agreement was eventually signed on 16 February 1748, originally for a term of 21 years only,[12] but from this point onwards the Leveson-Gowers continually renewed their lease of the mining rights in this manor, and as far as mining operations were concerned they acted as the lords of Wrockwardine until the end of the nineteenth century. In 1771 the second earl bought land in the manor, and by 1900 the Leveson-Gowers owned most of the collieries in the area.[13]

Between 1748 and his death in 1754 the first earl invested a total of £13,534 in coal and ironstone mines in this area, extending the workings and installing capital equipment. He succeeded in making a very small overall profit of about 1 per cent on his investment. The main ventures, in Wrockwardine and Donnington Wood returned a profit of 14 per cent on an average yearly investment of £1,714, but a new mine opened up in Ketley proved to be a less sound speculation, returning a heavy loss of 45 per cent on an average yearly outlay of £575.[14]

The question immediately arises of why a landed aristocrat like Earl Gower should have chosen to invest these very considerable sums of money in so risky a venture as mining. Clearly he hoped for a profitable return in financial terms, but this answer merely raises further questions. How was this profit to be achieved? Was it to be obtained in the short term, or only over the longer run? Had Earl Gower acted on advice, or had he invested on his own initiative? Finally, why had he chosen this moment to move from the role of *rentier* to that of entrepreneur?

The last of these questions is perhaps the easiest to answer. In 1748 Earl Gower was short of money, and ready to explore any new financial avenue. The main reason for his financial embarrassment had been his involvement in very heavy election expenses from 1742.[15] The chief agent of the estates at this time was Robert Barbor, charged with the thankless task of finding the money to pay for the first earl's election expenses in, of all decades, the 1740s, when years of low agricultural prices and mounting rent arrears were rounded off by a severe cattle plague in the Midland counties. Not surprisingly, he too was ready to clutch at any financial straw by 1748. In turning to industrial investment, the hope was for immediate rather than long-term financial returns, and this hope was not entirely ill-founded. The 14 per cent profit margin which the first earl made on his £10,284 investment in the Wrockwardine Wood mines was a good one by any standards, and only his simultaneous involvement with the Ketley mine reduced his overall profit level to 1 per cent. However, Earl Gower's profit margin had also been reduced as a result of his expansion and re-equipping of the mines while they were under his direct control, and this raises another interesting question. Did the landlord take over the direct running of his mines periodically in order to re-equip them, and so make them a more attractive proposition for future lessees? The new capital stock installed was later leased out with the mining rights. Something of the same development had taken place in this same area between 1695 and 1715 when the Leveson-Gowers had previously taken direct control of mining operations, and had left behind in the mines a very valuable stock of capital equipment when they were leased to Richard

Hartshorne in January 1715.[16] In all probability, however, the original intention of Gower and Barbor had not been to make heavy investments at Ketley or Donnington Wood, but once direct control of the mines had been taken over, the temptation to improve them in the hope of future larger profits had proved irresistible.

As to the final question, on whose initiative was this move made, the answer is that the initiative was probably Robert Barbor's. The heavy pre-occupation of the first earl at this time was with politics, and his concern was only for the procurement of money. How to raise that money was a problem for Robert Barbor, estate agent and, in later life, industrial entrepreneur. Biographical information on Barbor is scarce: the aristocrats of Shropshire are inevitably better documented than the entrepreneurs. Barbor's baptism does not appear on surviving parish registers, but he was born in or around the year 1698, probably locally since a number of other Barbors figure in the history of Staffordshire at this time. Henry Barbor, colliery bailiff for the Leveson-Gower estates, was Robert's brother, and no fewer than three other Barbors were also employed in minor positions in the collieries and on the estate, all of them probably related to Robert. A Mrs Jane Barbor had served as postmistress at Stone between 1699 and 1721, while another member of the family, Thomas, acted as postmaster at Lichfield for a few months in 1708. These positions generally ran in families: the Rathbones, for example, looked after the post at Lichfield from 1698 to 1733, and therefore the fact that Robert Barbor took over from Jane as postmaster at Stone in 1721 suggests that he was closely related to her. Thomas and Jane Barbor may in fact have been Robert's parents. Robert acted as postmaster at Stone from 1721 to 1746, and during this period he showed himself to be keenly interested in improving the communications of Staffordshire which, at this time, meant the construction of turnpike roads. Several members of the Leveson-Gower family, and all of their chief agents, were frequently named as trustees in Staffordshire Turnpike Acts,[17] but Robert Barbor seems to have shown a greater interest than most, urging the Committee of Inquiry set up in 1728 to proceed with a second Staffordshire turnpike, from Canal Gate to Stone.[18]

Barbor's parents had found the means to provide a legal training for their son at the Inner Temple, and he first appears on the records of the Leveson-Gower estates in 1722 as a qualified lawyer assisting the then chief agent, William Plaxton. In 1730 he took charge of the Shropshire estates of the Leveson-Gowers, and in 1742 he became chief agent of all their properties. During the 1730s he was described in legal documents as "Robert Barbor of the Inner Temple, London", but in 1744 he was described for the first time as "Robert Barbor Esquire of Somerford", very close to Brewood in Staffordshire, where a substantial country house may still be seen to this day. Barbor very probably kept up a private legal practice in addition to acting as chief agent for the Leveson-Gowers. He had been named as a trustee in the Turnpike Acts of 1728 and 1735, and between 1746 and 1748 had served as Clerk of the Peace for Staffordshire, an office for substantial and respected gentlemen.[19] At his death in 1761 he left his widow lands at Tittensor, Stone and Newbury worth £300 a year, in addition to land and colliery interests at Bradley and Bilston returning an unspecified annual sum.[20] After 1742 he was being paid a salary of £200 a year by Lord Gower, and had also purchased from him an annuity worth a further £200 a year. In all, these documented income sources came to £700 a year, and with his Bradley and Bilston colliery returns and his legal work, Barbor's total income may have approached £1,000 a year towards the end of his life, equivalent to the rental returns of a substantial landowner.

But Robert Barbor was only the head of a large clan of local Barbors. His younger brother Henry was not only colliery bailiff to the Leveson-Gowers, but was also prepared to invest directly in their mines in the role of lessee and entrepreneur. He was soon to be given the opportunity to do so, for in December 1754 the first earl died and his heir had, at that stage, very different views on the question of estate management from those of his father. He was not interested in continuing with the direct exploitation of the coal and ironstone mines into which his father had directed so much investment, but instead leased them all to Henry Barbor in 1756 as part of an extensive package deal. Barbor was to have nothing to do with the new pits which the first earl had sunk in Ketley and which had proved to be so unprofitable, but instead he was to take over the mining rights to the whole manor of Lilleshall. Until 1755 these rights had been held by one George Sparrow of the Glasshouse, Wolstanton, a prosperous local coalmaster, under the terms of a lease of 1734.[21] Sparrow was charged the high rent of £450 a year for this concession, but he had managed to complete the full term of his lease, apparently without financial difficulty. This was no mean achievement, for mining was a notoriously risky venture, at the mercy of fault lines, flooding and explosion hazards, and sharp variations in market demand. A high level of managerial and entrepreneurial skill was required to make a success of such projects, but it would seem that Sparrow as an entrepreneur and Henry Barbor as a manager had proved themselves equal to the task. No doubt, therefore, Henry Barbor felt very confident in 1756 when he took on the heavy commitment of both Sparrow's concession and the mines in Wrockwardine and Donnington Wood which had been worked by the first earl. Indeed, since both concerns had proved to be profitable in the past, their leasing to Henry Barbor was a mark of Leveson-Gower favour towards their former colliery bailiff, who no doubt considered himself to be a fortunate man in 1756, despite his commitment to a high rent charge for a period of 21 years. While Sparrow had paid £450 a year for the Lilleshall concession alone, Barbor now paid £650 a year for the extended enterprise. He stuck to his last as a colliery expert, however, sub-leasing the ironstone mining rights of the area to Abraham Darby II for a rent of £150 a year and a term of 20 years from 30 November 1756.[22]

Henry Barbor probably could have made a success of the venture in view of his long experience as a colliery bailiff, but fate took a hand and he died in 1760, leaving his son James to inherit his lease. James Barbor unfortunately lacked his father's managerial skills. Sensing this, he took in two partners in the June of 1761, Joseph Taylor, who tenanted a brickworks in Muxton which belonged to Earl Gower, paying £40 a year at will, and Richard Hurd, a wealthy local landowner. But neither the former's skill nor the latter's capital was enough to save the partnership. After a turbulent four years of serious financial difficulties, during which Taylor was obliged to withdraw from the venture, the two remaining partners were at last forced to sell their lease back to Earl Gower, who paid them £605 in all for the remaining thirteen years of their mining rights, helping them to clear their debts.[23]

Earl Gower's repurchase of the partners' mining concessions marked a significant watershed in the industrial history of the Shropshire estates. The mines had obviously not been returning a profit under their previous management and normally the landlord was content, in these circumstances, to allow the lease to be assigned to some other entrepreneur who had remained undeterred by the failure of his predecessors. On this occasion, however, Earl Gower not only took over the lease himself, but went on to enter into partnership with his chief agent Thomas Gilbert and Gilbert's brother John, four years younger than Thomas and himself acting as estate agent and colliery manager for the third Duke of Bridgewater. Within a few years he had taken over to a very great extent the duties of chief colliery bailiff on the Leveson-Gower estates as well, filling much the same position as had once been occupied by Henry Barbor.

Thomas Gilbert (1720–98) was a figure of national stature who has earned himself a place in the *Dictionary of National Biography*. He achieved this, however, mainly through his work as a parliamentarian and poor law reformer: his entrepreneurial activities are less well known. Thomas and John Gilbert were both born at Ipstones in Staffordshire where their father, Thomas Gilbert snr, was a small squire with an income of some £300 a year and a seat at Cotton Hall. His association with the Leveson-Gower family dated back to at least 1735 when he had negotiated with the second baron for lead and copper mining rights at Grindon in north-east Staffordshire, where Lord Gower was a joint lord of the manor.[24] His eldest son and heir was sent for legal training at the Inner Temple, was called to the bar in 1744, and returned to Staffordshire. Almost at once he was involved with the Leveson-Gowers in their opposition to the Young Pretender, accepting a commission in a regiment raised by the second baron to check the southward march of the Highlanders in 1745. He remained in the service of the Leveson-Gowers after Culloden, giving them legal advice on political affairs, and it seems that after 1747, when the newly created Earl Gower began his purchase of burgage tenements in Lichfield, Gilbert came to devote more and more of his time to the Leveson-Gowers' political concerns. The death of the first earl in 1754 did nothing to alter Thomas Gilbert's standing with the family. Throughout that year he remained in regular correspondence with both the first and second earls on the political management of Lichfield.[25] From 1753 Thomas was also acting for Francis Egerton (1736–1803), the young third Duke of Bridgewater, taking care of his legal affairs until the duke reached his majority in 1757, at which time Thomas withdrew to a more advisory role, leaving his brother John in charge of the practical day-to-day business of running the duke's estate.[26] Thomas served in Parliament from 1763 until 1795, representing first the Leveson-Gower pocket borough of Newcastle-under-Lyme, and from 1768 their other very safe seat at Lichfield. He held two government sinecures, procured for him by the second earl, the offices of Comptroller of the Great Wardrobe from 1763 to 1782 and Paymaster of Pensions to the Widows of Officers from 1769 to 1795. He also enjoyed a revenue of £300 a year from his own estate at Cotton, and was paid a further £300 a year by the Leveson-Gowers for his services as chief estate agent. By the 1770s his industrial investments and entrepreneurial activities were also returning him substantial profits, and he continued in private legal practice. Like Robert Barbor, therefore, Thomas Gilbert was a man of substance with capital of his own available for investment. Lawyer, soldier, parliamentarian, social reformer, political manager, estate agent, canal promoter, road improver, country gentleman and industrial entrepreneur, Thomas Gilbert led an extremely full life, and was something of a latter-day Renaissance man. His place in the *Dictionary of National Biography* was well deserved.

His brother John (1724–95) began life with all the usual disadvantages of a younger son. Instead of receiving a legal training, he had been apprenticed at the early age of 12 as a silversmith to the Birmingham works of Matthew Boulton snr. He grew up with his master's son, Matthew Boulton jnr (1728–1809) of later steam engine fame. When he was still only 18, however, John was obliged to return to Staffordshire in order to manage the Cotton Hall estate on the death of his father in 1742, while his elder brother completed his legal training in London. The small patrimony included a lease of some valuable limeworks, and his father's interest in the lead and copper mines at Grindon.[27] It was presumably in these years that John Gilbert acquired his skills in estate management, and his interest in mining operations. His opportunity for employment in these capacities came through the close personal connections of the Leveson-Gower and Egerton families who were linked both by marriage and by bonds of genuine affection.[28] The third duke (1736–1803) had spent much of his rather troubled youth in the refuge of Trentham Hall following the death of his father Scroop in 1745. It was therefore natural enough that he should give employment to the younger brother of Thomas Gilbert, chief agent of his old friend and boyhood companion, Earl Gower, and indeed his own chief accountant, who continued to audit the accounts of the Bridgewater estates until 1795. John proceeded to take full advantage of the opportunities which his position now offered him. In 1757 he carried out a survey of Bridgewater's Worsley mines, and Malet argues very convincingly that it was he who conceived the original idea of building the famous Bridgewater canal, and who engineered its early and later stages. James Brindley's importance in the middle years of the canal's construction has been, argues Malet, highly overplayed.[29] But John Gilbert was more than an estate agent, engineer and canal builder. Malet writes of him:

He farmed his own demesne at Worsley, and in 1760 he bought with his usual foresight, the Golden Hill estate on what would later be the route of the Trent and Mersey Canal, in partnership with his brother Thomas, James and John Brindley, and Hugh Henshall, the brother of James Brindley's future wife. John Gilbert owned and directed a black-lead mine at Borrowdale in the Lake District, and a factory for it at Worsely in partnership with his brother; he owned salt works at Marston, near Norwich, limestone quarries at Caldonlow and Astbury; a colliery at Meir Heath . . . limekilns at Hernheath and Ecton, a colliery at Clough Hall, as well as silver and copper mines near Alton, Potterdale, Keswick and Stanhope, carried on by his firm of Earl Carlisle & Co., in which the duke [of Bridgewater] held shares, the earl after whom it was named being Francis' nephew and heir. About 1765 the duke also helped to buy John the estate at Clough Hall immediately above the Harecastle tunnel, as a reward for his services, for he treated his staff as generously as his workmen, and there Gilbert built himself a comfortable country house with some twenty bedrooms and the luxury of mahogany in all the downstairs rooms.[30]

From this staggering catalogue of John's achievements, it would appear that he was no less remarkable a man than his much more famous elder brother, and yet, impressive as Malet's list appears to be, it is not complete, for Malet has overlooked John's investment interest in the Trent and Mersey canal (£2,000 by 1770) and his partnership in Earl Gower & Company. This was the title of the new concern which appeared on the Leveson-Gower rent rolls for the first time at Michaelmas 1764. Thomas and John Gilbert had taken a lease from the second earl on 7 September 1764 of the same mining concessions which had been granted to Henry Barbor eight years earlier, and at the same rent: for Donnington coal-works, £600 per year; for Lilleshall lime works, £50 per year; for taxes, £6; total annual rental, £656. The following day, 8 September, Earl Gower had signed articles of partnership with the Gilberts, so that his role as a landlord was always kept quite distinct from his role as a partner. Half of the working capital to float the new company was put up by Earl Gower, while the two Gilbert brothers were to provide a quarter share each. The Darby family again featured in this transaction, this time in the person of Abraham Darby III, then only 14 years old, whose father had died in 1763. The executors of his father's will took, on his behalf, a 13-year sub-lease of all the ironstone mines in Donnington Wood from Thomas and John Gilbert. This too was signed on 8 September, and the rent agreed was £250 p.a.[31]

With his 50 per cent interest, Earl Gower was now the dominant partner in the new venture, as well as its landlord, and this development represented a remarkable example of direct aristocratic exploitation of mineral resources on a quite unprecedented scale. The development of Ketley and Wrockwardine, begun by the second earl's father, had involved a yearly income and expenditure of roughly £2,300. In the single year of 1774, however, the expenditure of Earl Gower & Company was £10,290, and its receipts were £13,307. By 1798, when the name of the enterprise had been changed to the Marquis of Stafford & Company, its annual receipts were £27,263, and its expenditure £24,365.[32]

Once again, the question must be asked, why this change of landlord policy, and why at this particular time? The Seven Years' War had just ended, in 1763, and the prices of coal and iron were good, but in all probability this was only a marginal consideration. Earl Gower and Thomas Gilbert were still deeply involved with political affairs: the only one of the triumvirate with real mining skills and an interest in purely economic affairs was John Gilbert. The balance of probability is that the venture was his idea. The legal skills, the practical approach, and the shrewd business acumen were provided by Thomas Gilbert. The skills in mining and colliery management were supplied by his brother John. The courage to invest, most of the capital, and the premises themselves were contributed by Earl Gower. The combination was very well planned, and it proved to be highly successful.

At this point in the story Earl Gower emerges as both aristocrat and entrepreneur, so that he deserves rather closer consideration. In 1764 he was 43 years of age, and unlikely to be tempted into rash or risky ventures. His investment in Earl Gower & Company was no doubt inspired partly by his confidence in his two partners, but also by his own long-standing interest in local transport and industry. In 1758 he had co-operated with Josiah Wedgwood and Lord Anson of Shugborough Hall, his neighbour and close political ally in Lichfield, in having a survey made by James Brindley along the course of a proposed canal to run from Etruria in Staffordshire to King's Mill in Derbyshire.[33] The enterprise proved to be too formidable and it was abandoned, but Earl Gower's interest in canals was maintained. In 1765, he allowed Trentham Hall to be used as the headquarters of the promoters of the Trent and Mersey canal scheme, and in the following year he was instrumental in securing the passage of the Trent and Mersey Canal Act.[34] By the end of 1770, Earl Gower and Thomas Gilbert had each invested £4,000 in the Trent and Mersey Canal, and John Gilbert a further £2,000, so that between them the partners held £10,000 worth of stock.[35]

With all three partners so deeply interested in canals, it was hardly surprising that one of the first ventures of Earl Gower & Company was the construction of a private canal across the Leveson-Gower manors of Lilleshall and Sheriff Hales. Its purpose was to link the Ketley and Don-nington Wood mines with an isolated deposit of coal and limestone situated at Pave Lane, an island of Leveson-Gower property just a quarter of a mile north of the manor of Lilleshall. There is no mention of Pave Lane in the rentals, prior to 1764, so the property may have been purchased that year expressly for the purpose of mineral exploitation by Earl Gower & Company.[36] The accounts show that some coal was taken from Pave Lane, but the mines of this area certainly produced far more limestone than coal, the sale of which represented a major part of the company's receipts. The Pave Lane canal was later linked with the Shropshire

Union Canal and the River Severn, greatly extending the potential markets of Earl Gower & Company.[37]

During the first ten years of its life, the profits returned by Earl Gower & Company were very small, with income and expenditure running at about £10,000 a year each. Nevertheless, the company was being very efficiently managed and there was a good reason for the low initial profit levels. During these ten years, Earl Gower had sunk £8,363 17s 9d into improving the facilities of the company, most of this money going on the construction of the Pave Lane canal. Thomas Gilbert had invested £4,310 17s 11d of his own money into the same projects. John Gilbert had invested nothing apart from his mining expertise during these ten years, but had been content to receive negligible profits for that considerable period of time, while the earl and Thomas Gilbert were repaid their investment before overall profit levels were calculated. The year 1774 was a triumphant one for the company, when the two investors were finally repaid in full, and for the first time a profit remained for division among the partners. Earl Gower and Thomas Gilbert had evidently charged the company no interest on their investment, although their meticulous accounting system would have enabled them to do so very easily. Each section of the company was carefully credited and debited for its contributions to and receipts from the others. The annual account for 1774 is reproduced below in full as an illustration of their accounting system.[38] (Thomas Horwood was the auditor of Earl Gower & Company, and also chief agent for the north Staffordshire estates from 1774).

Perhaps the most interesting feature of these accounts is the close integration of a farming unit into the mining operations which they reveal. It is a perfect illustration of the very close links which existed between land and industry in these, the early days of the Industrial Revolution. The importance of farm supplies to the early industrialists becomes obvious enough upon consideration, but it has been a much neglected aspect of eighteenth-century industrial history. We should remember that our Industrial Revolution was launched with water power and with horse power, while steam engines played only a minor role until well into the nineteenth century. In the same way, much more timber than iron was consumed by eighteenth-century miners and manufacturers: farm supplies were therefore crucial to both. Horses were vital to many aspects of mining, such as turning engines or drawing wagons and also, in Earl Gower & Company, for hauling barges. If a miner chose to rear his own horses, and to grow fodder for them, then he had already committed himself to some degree of agricultural enterprise. Moreover, at Ketley, Lilleshall and Donnington Wood, it was usual to lease a number of cottages with the mining rights on land to be worked by the entrepreneur. These cottages were presumably occupied by the labour employed in the mines: certainly the cottagers paid their rents to the lessees rather than directly to Earl Gower. Miners regularly employed on a full-time basis would have been dependent upon outside sources for their food, and this may have been another reason for industrialists turning to farming. As local food producers, they could have supplied their workers directly,

Table 9.1 Thomas Horwood's Account with the Rt Hon. Earl Gower & Co., for the Year 1774

Receipts	£	s	d	Payments	£	s	d
				Colliery			
Of Lord Gower and Mr Gilbert				Paid for getting coals	2,188	3	2½
towards carrying on the works	330	0	0	Paid for rents, sinking pits, driving			
Lime sales not entered in 1773	176	14	6	levels, headings, laying and			
Miscellaneous receipts not entered				repairing railways, carrying and			
in 1773	51	12	3	unloading coal, ropes, iron;			
				salaries	1,900	11	6
Colliery				Paid to Navigation Account for			
For coals and coke sold at Pave Lane	4,231	3	4	carrying 16,709 tons 6 cwt of coal			
For coals and coke sold over				to Pave Lane at 1s per ton	835	9	4
Donnington Wood machine	283	16	3	Paid Thomas Ashley and Richard			
For coals sold over Pave Lane's				Vickers on account of getting			
machine	165	12	3	coals for next year	56	17	3½
From Lime Account for 4,286 tons							
11 cwt of lime coals at 2s 4d per							
ton, including 811 tons of slack				*Lime*			
from Pave Lane	500	1	11	Paid for rent, weighing, getting			
For coal pit wood from the colliery	41	16	11	stone, burning lime, driving			
Lord Gower's annual allowance for				levels, building and repairing			
coal pit wood	40	0	0	kilns, other contingents	2,961	2	4
Of Reynolds & Co. a year's rent for				Paid Farm Account for carrying lime			
ironstone	250	0	0	and slack	69	15	9
				Paid Farm Account for horses			
Lime				drawing limestone at the gins	72	0	0
For lime sold £170 2s in arrears				Paid to Colliery Account for 4,286			
(299,659 measures)	5,448	10	1½	tons 11 cwt. of lime coals at 2s 4d			
For lime coals sold from kilns	6	10	0	per ton including 811 tons			
				received from Pave Lane Colliery	500	1	11
Navigation				Paid to Navigation Account for			
For loading coals at Pave Lane, the				conveying the above coals at 8d			
wages of the men employed being				per ton	142	17	8
charged to the Navigation							
Account	159	1	8½				
From Colliery Account for carriage				*Navigation*			
of 16,709 tons 6 cwt of coals from				Paid rents, repairing boats, steering			
Donnington Wood to Pave Lane				and discharging coals, loading			
at 1s per ton	835	9	4	teams at Pave Lane, repairing			
From Lime Account for carrying				banks and towing paths	424	5	2½
4,286 tons 11 cwt of lime coals at				Paid to Farm Account for horses to			
8d per ton	142	17	8	haul boats with coals to Pave			
				Lane and lime coals	78	10	11½
Farm				Paid proportion of contingent			
For rents, ley of cattle, grain and				expenses.	90	0	0
cattle sold	354	17	3½				
For carrying lime stone, lime coals,							
and horses drawing lime stone at				*Farm*			
the gins	141	15	9	Paid rents of land, cattle and corn			
From Navigation Account for				bought, expenses of husbandry			
hauling coals to Pave Lane and				and improvements of land	640	11	9
lime coals	78	10	11½				
By three articles of work with teams				*Repayment of Advances*			
and horses at various places	68	16	0	Paid Lord Gower his money			
charged to contingents				advanced	220	0	0
				Paid Mr Gilbert his money advanced	110	0	0
Total receipts	13,307	6	3				
Total payments	10,290	6	11		10,290	6	11
Remains profit	3,016	19	4				
Owing to Lord Gower from 1764–74				*Division of Profit among Partners*			
£114 0 0				Lord Gower's Moiety	1,425	18	8
Owing to Thos Gilbert from 1764–74				Mr Thos Gilbert's fourth part	712	19	4
51 2 0	165	2	0	Mr John Gilbert's fourth part	712	19	4
	2,851	17	4		2,851	17	4

Source: Staffordshire Record Office, D593/G/4/3/32.

especially in years of high prices, and thus kept the labour force uniformly well nourished, even in years of scarcity. Payment in kind of this sort may indeed have been the well-meaning forerunner of the notorious "truck shops" of the early nineteenth century.

The farming industrialist was a figure with a long history in this region. Obadiah Lane, one of the leading Foley partners who died in 1707, owned land at Longton close to a furnace site at Meir Heath, and also leased a farm from the first Baron Gower.[39] In 1733 Richard Hartshorne, a local coalmaster, had renewed his lease of Lord Gower's coal mines in Ketley, agreeing to an increase in his rent from £50 a year to £150. At the same time, he took on a 144-acre farm in Ketley, which he tenanted at will for £45 a year.[40] This farm became so much a part of the Ketley industrial enterprise that it was taken over by Abraham Darby II on 28 October 1756 just two years after his leasing of the mineral rights of Ketley on 18 September 1754. The farm lease was renewed in 1775 by Richard Reynolds, Abraham Darby's successor.[41] This farm must have been run as a closely integrated part of the Darby–Reynolds enterprise at Ketley, but no mention of it appears in the histories of these families which have so far been written.[42] By 1813, when the first comprehensive survey of the entire Shropshire estate of the Leveson-Gowers was carried out, it showed industrial tenants to be in occupation of 346 acres of land in the manor of Ketley, most of it devoted to farming, while in the nearby manors of Lilleshall and Sheriff Hales the extensive mines, large farmed area and canal lands between them occupied no less than 1,508 acres.[43]

In 1774, Earl Gower & Company had returned a profit margin of almost 28 per cent on that year's outlay, a very satisfactory result. Until 1778, net profits remained high, with the partners sharing an annual average dividend of £2,749, on roughly the same level of turnover. In 1778, however, the company's rent was raised to £1,000 per annum, in accordance with the terms of the original lease of 1764. This lease had been granted to the Gilbert brothers for the term of three named lives, one of them that of Thomas Gilbert's son, then aged 2, and the other two sons of John, then aged 12 and 16. The 1764 lease was renewable at 14-year intervals, when new lives could be inserted if any had dropped out. This clause favoured the lessees, but on the other hand the whole agreement was to lapse and be subject to renegotiation on the death of Earl Gower, and after the first 14 years the rent was to rise from £650 to £1,000 per annum, whether a new lease was negotiated or not. In 1778 the Gilberts did in fact take out a new lease, replacing the life of John Gilbert's eldest son, who had died in the interval.

Up to this time, Earl Gower had been given no reason for complaint about the company which bore his name. Since 1764, he had netted some £17,000 in rents and profits from it. In 1779, however, the partnership suddenly sustained an overall loss of £716. The reasons for this loss remain totally unexplained: detailed accounts for this year have not survived, and the loss was recorded only in the general series of rentals and accounts.[44] There was certainly no catastrophic fall in coal prices at this time, but again in 1780 company profit levels were down, at only £624, not even covering the loss of the former year. However, in 1781 profits once again rose to over £1,000, and in the seven years from 1781 to 1787 averaged £1,691 per annum. There then occurs a gap in the company's records until 1795, but in this interval the estate lease register reveals the granting of a remarkable new lease to the Gilbert brothers in 1792, this time for a term of three lives or 99 years, just fourteen years after the renewing of their original lease in 1778. At first sight, this lease renewal appears to be rather a futile gesture, for all the parties to it were well advanced in years. Earl Gower, who had been created first Marquis of Stafford in 1786, was 71 years old in 1792, while Thomas Gilbert was 72, and died soon afterwards in 1798. Even John Gilbert was 68 in 1792, and in fact he predeceased his elder brother in 1795. It can only be assumed that the Gilbert brothers secured this lease, as they were perfectly entitled to do under their original terms of 1764, with an eye towards assigning it in the near future in return for a cash payment, which could be used for the benefit of their heirs. Some clue as to their plans for the future may be found in the three lives named in the 1792 lease. They were Thomas Gilbert jnr, Richard Hill jnr of Stallington and Lord Granville Leveson-Gower (1773–1846).[45] The latter was the younger son of the first Marquis by his third wife, Lady Susannah Steward, daughter of the sixth Earl of Galloway, and half-brother to George Granville, who succeeded to the estates as second Marquis of Stafford in 1803. It was to him that the heirs of Thomas and John Gilbert assigned their rights under the 1792 lease on 25 March 1802. The transaction is referred to in a later lease of 1807, together with the fact that in 1798, just after the death of Thomas Gilbert, the capital stock of the then Marquis of Stafford & Company had been valued at £52,706.[46] On 19 April 1802, Granville's father transferred to him his own half share in the Marquis of Stafford & Company, which was thereupon disbanded as a Shropshire concern, although it continued to operate several mines in north Staffordshire. The future of the Shropshire enterprise now clearly lay in the hands of Lord Granville Leveson-Gower, and he made the decision to run it as a partnership as his father had done before him. On 24 June 1802, therefore, a second partnership agreement was signed, using for the first time a new company title, that of the Lilleshall Company, a most durable enterprise destined to trade under the same name on the same site until the third quarter of the twentieth century.[47]

The assignment of the Gilbert brothers' lease provides another interesting example of aristocratic enterprise in Shropshire industry. In the eighteenth and early nineteenth centuries, family ties and personal connections remained of supreme importance in the business world, and it was these that now came to the fore. Although debarred from succession to the ancestral estates, younger sons always had to be provided for in one way or another, and Granville's taking over of the Marquis of Stafford & Company was an illustration of this principle at work. In the four years from 1795 to 1798, the company had returned an average annual profit of some £1,500 p.a., and so was quite a valuable patrimony.[48] The decision to take responsibility for this concern must, however, have been Granville's alone, reflecting his personal interest in the development of industrial resources. His close family ties with the landlord of the property on which his company stood, together with its good financial record, must have inspired potential partners with confidence in the future of his concern, so that there would be no shortage of applicants for partnerships should Granville choose to advertise them. He would be able to pick and choose his partners, but this too would be done on the basis of personal acquaintance.

The leading partner chosen by Granville was in fact his father's own chief estate agent, John Bishton of Kilsall in Shropshire, who had been officially in charge of all the Leveson-Gower properties since January 1789.[49] Like Thomas Gilbert, John Bishton was the eldest son of a family of minor gentry with a modest seat at Kilsall, near Tong. Born in February 1735, John Bishton married on 24 January 1765 a Miss Betty Jellicorse, from a family similar in standing to Bishton's but ten years his junior. The couple had eleven children, all of whom survived into adulthood, and some of whom later featured as local entrepreneurs, notably John, the eldest son, born in 1766, and William, born in 1773. John Bishton snr's first claim to fame was, however, as an agriculturalist. On the basis of his (largely self-proclaimed) successes as an improver, he was selected by the Board of Agriculture to write the first report on Shropshire.[50] It was his professed skills in the agricultural field that first recommended him to the Leveson-Gowers as their chief estate agent, but in 1793 he began to diversify his interests. On 7 February, he took a lease of mines of coal and ironstone at Priorslee for a term of 21 years from Henry Beaufoy, Bishton's first recorded venture into industrial enterprise. On 18 February 1794 his eldest son, John Bishton jnr took over the nearby Snedshill ironworks, in conjunction with three partners, obviously intending to work in close co-operation with his father. Their partnership was made a formal one on 14 February 1795, and William Bishton, a younger son, was later brought into the newly created family firm with a one-eighth share in the enterprise.[51] On 6 February 1797, the Bishtons went on to take over the Donnington Wood ironworks and the ironstone mines at Donnington Wood and Wrockwardine Wood from William Reynolds, who had been leasing them from the Leveson-Gowers since 1775.[52] By 1802 they had erected three new blast furnaces in the area, but they had done this only with the help of three partners, William Phillips of Donnington, ironmaster, John Onions of Bethnall in Shropshire, also an ironmaster, and James Birch Esq., of the Inner Temple, London.[53] It was these three men who, on 24 June 1802, joined Granville and the elder Bishton as the five original partners of the Lilleshall Company. They each held only a one-sixteenth share in the new venture, however, while John Bishton held five-sixteenths. Domination of the company was secured by George Granville himself, who retained the remaining half share in the new enterprise, just as his father had kept a 50 per cent share in Earl Gower & Company, thirty-eight years before. Again like his father, George Granville did not launch into his industrial venture single-handed. By 1802, a close partnership with one or more professional entrepreneurs was regarded as a *sine qua non* for all such undertakings, especially if the aristocratic partner had expansion in mind. Prior to 1802, there had been no extension of the company's premises since 1774. Under this new form of management, however, the stage was set for a further phase of growth in this region of industrial Shropshire.[54]

Just a mile to the south-west of the Lilleshall Company's headquarters, the Leveson-Gowers held another valuable industrial property in their manor of Ketley. Apart from the first earl's brief and unprofitable attempt to sink new coalmines here between 1748 and 1754, however, there had been no direct landlord exploitation of the coal seams in this manor. Instead, the mining rights had been held by the Hartshorne family since at least 1698.[55] After the death of the first earl in 1754, however, the long association of the Hartshornes with the estate came to an end. On 18 September 1754, all the mines in Ketley were leased to Abraham Darby & Company, for a term of 21 years. Whereas Richard Hartshorne had paid a rent of only £150 per annum, however, Abraham Darby was now charged £400, suggesting that Hortshorne had expanded the mines since his last lease renewal of 1733, and also that the new pits recently sunk by the first earl were included in the deal with Darby, who was seeking a regular supply of coal and ironstone for his works at Coalbrookdale, a mere 4 miles to the south of the Ketley mines. The lease gave him specific permission to "lay a rail way towards Coalbrookdale" across the manor of Ketley, a route destined to carry one of the first iron "rail ways" ever built.[56] After the death of Abraham Darby II in 1763, the Ketley mines were managed by his son-in-law, Richard Reynolds, and the Leveson-Gower rent rolls note the change in rent receipts from Darby & Company to Reynolds & Company.[57] In 1775 the old lease of 1754 lapsed, and was replaced by a new 21-year agreement signed on 29 September. This time, however, the lease was based not on a fixed annual rental, but on royalty payments. The scale of these royalty payments is of some interest, for their terms remained unchanged when the Reynolds' lease was renewed 21 years later, on 19 January 1796.[58] Coal and iron prices had already begun their marked upward movement by 1796, but there was of course no guarantee that this trend would continue. Nevertheless, the royalties charged to Reynolds appear to allow him generous terms. They were:

Pyrites (sulphur stone)	3s a dozen
Ironstone (iron oxide)	3s a dozen
Coal for outside sale	1s per ton
Coal for iron or pyrites smelting	8d per ton
Refuse coal for fire engine	Free
Clay and sand for furnaces	Free
Rough stone for building	Free
Building stone (limestone blocks)	1s per ton

The 1796 lease defined a "dozen" of ironstone as consisting of "40 hundred weight, each hundred weight to contain 120 pounds". This meant that each "dozen" would weigh roughly two tons. In 1796, "midland forge pig iron" was selling for a price of about £6 a ton or 120s as against the mere 1*s* 6*d* duty per ton charged for the ore. London coal prices averaged 35*s* a ton in 1797, so that the duty charged on coal was comparatively higher than that on ironstone, but of course the coal required much less processing before its sale. Price levels of this order were sustained throughout the Napoleonic wars, and for almost the whole term of the Reynolds' lease.[59] The agreement therefore appears to have been something of an act of generosity on the part of the landlord. The duties were light, and the leasing terms were flexible – so flexible indeed that they were open to potential abuse by the lessees. But on the other hand, we must remember what a risky and uncertain business eighteenth-century mining was. This point is well illustrated by the royalty records of the Reynolds' Ketley mines which have survived (sporadically) for the years 1776 to 1793.[60]

Table 9.2 Total Royalties paid by Reynolds & Co. 1776–93

	£ *s d*		£ *s d*
1776	639 8 10	1785	Not worked
1777	746 5 2	1786	Not worked
1778	1,108 5 8	1787	185 1 3
1779	1,397 7 2	1788	Missing
1780	1,150 12 2	1789	Missing
1781	1,041 15 4	1790	Missing
1782	955 7 6	1791	Missing
1783	487 19 1	1792	373 14 10
1784	Not worked	1793	612 2 10

The fluctuating fortunes of the Ketley mines were completely out of phase with those of the Lilleshall mines, which were less than a mile away. Earl Gower & Company returned its largest recorded annual profit, £3,043, in 1776, a year of quite low output for the Ketley mines. On the other hand, the two years of 1779 and 1780 which saw the Lilleshall partners making an overall loss were the very years of highest recorded output from the Ketley mines. No documentary material has survived to account for these fluctuations, but the most likely explanation for them would be technical difficulties with the mines themselves. However, the terse note "not worked these years" which appears from 1784 to 1786 inclusive against the Reynolds' royalty entries, is of particular interest, for this could have been the result not of technical, but of financial difficulties. In 1783 Reynolds & Company had borrowed £2,000 from Earl Gower as part of a wider transaction, made possible by a new lease taken on by Earl Gower & Company. On 20 August 1783, the three Lilleshall partners had gone to a new 21 year agreement with the three lords of Wrockwardine, from whom Earl Gower had been leasing the area of land between Lilleshall and Ketley since 1748. The security of this new agreement enabled Earl Gower to extend the Pave Lane canal towards Ketley, and later to link it with the Shropshire Union Canal. It also enabled him to sub-let part of his mining rights in the manor of Wrockwardine to William

Reynolds and his partner Joseph Rathbone. On 1 September, thirty-six acres of land in Wrockwardine, close to Ketley, were leased to Reynolds & Company, expressly for the purpose of their erecting blast furnaces and other buildings, including workers' cottages, on the land. The term agreed upon was 20 years and 6 months, so that it would be safely within the term of the 21-year lease from the three lords of Wrockwardine.[61]

How generous were the terms of this agreement? The rent to be paid for the thirty-six acres of land, £27 per annum, was reasonable enough, but the interest rate upon the £2,000 borrowed by Reynolds was to be 6 per cent, a high level by eighteenth-century standards. On the other hand, 1783 was the last year of the war against America, and English interest rates were therefore higher than usual. In addition, the security of Earl Gower's money was questionable. William Reynolds was only 25 years of age in 1783, and his father had just been involved in a heavy financial outlay in his efforts to save the faltering Abraham Darby & Company.[62] His loan of £2,000 to the young William must be seen as a brave and generous gesture on the part of the second earl, at a time when the fortunes of Reynolds & Company, in Ketley at least, were at a low ebb. Although the interest rate was high, William Reynolds was allowed to defer his interest payments in difficult years. The Lilleshall accounts show Reynolds paying a lump sum of £480 in interest in 1793 after a lapse of three years in his regular payments.[63] Certainly John Bishton, recently appointed as chief agent to the Leveson-Gower estates, thought that the first Marquis had been more than generous to Reynolds & Company.[64] In 1789, when one of the lives in a Reynolds lease dropped out, Bishton wrote to the first Marquis: "It strikes me at present that putting in a new life will be worth a considerable sum, and from a view of that company and what your Lordship has already done for them, no pecuniary compliment remains due to them."[65]

From the terms of later leases, it appears that William Reynolds erected three blast furnaces, a few cottages and some other buildings on the Wrockwardine land between September 1783 and February 1797, when he assigned his lease to that enterprising chief agent, John Bishton of Kilsall.[66] This assignment again suggests that William Reynolds was in financial difficulties. However, on the same day (6 February) that he assigned his Wrockwardine lease, Reynolds signed a new 18-year agreement with Lord Gower for mining rights in Ketley, paying the royalties already mentioned. These were to average a minimum of £600 p.a. taking one year with another, and it seems that Reynolds felt this to be enough of a commitment in 1797. Drawing in his horns, he pulled out of his Wrockwardine Wood works with their three blast furnaces leaving them to John Bishton who, in 1802, joining with Lord Granville Leveson-Gower, merged them into the newly created Lilleshall Company. It was at this point that the Wrockwardine Wood lands of the three lords were swung away from their connection with Ketley, and permanently into the orbit of the Lilleshall Company, with its headquarters at Donnington Wood.

In 1807, the Lilleshall partners negotiated a new lease of their lands from the second Marquis of Stafford, and the Marquis, for his part, took advantage of a clause in the 1783 agreement with the three lords which allowed him to extend his term for another 30 years after 1804 if he so desired.[67]

It is interesting to notice that William Reynolds carefully renewed his lease of the family's 144-acre farm in Ketley in 1797, even although he had felt obliged to assign the valuable furnace lands in Wrockwardine. This farm had been leased to Abraham Darby II on 28 October 1756, for the three lives of Abraham Darby III, Richard Reynolds and Robert Gilpin of Coalbrookdale, gentleman. It was renewed in September 1775 by Richard Reynolds, who inserted the life of his son William to replace that of Robert Gilpin, which had fallen out. William still remained in need of this farm to support his Ketley mines and his three blast furnaces within the manor of Ketley. His father Richard had assigned all of his shares in Reynolds & Company to his sons in 1789, and before his own lease assignment of 1797. William's responsibilities had been heavy, as the head of the family firm.[68] To the first Marquis of Stafford he had been making no fewer than four separate payments: his royalty dues on the produce of his mining rights in Ketley, a total of £147 p.a. for the Wombridge land and works, £45 p.a. for his Ketley farms, and a further £28 5s for an unspecified amount of land adjoining the farm in Ketley, referred to simply as "the Allmoors", located in the north-west corner of the manor of Ketley. From descriptions of this area in leases, it seems to have been of some thirty acres in extent, and to have been a holding of particular significance. Abraham Darby took a lease of "the Allmoors" on 28 October 1756, the same day as he took occupation of his 144-acre farm, and very probably some of the Allmoors land was incorporated into the Darby's farming enterprise. Unlike the farm land, however, the Allmoors were leased not for lives but for an unconditional term of 99 years, with Darby clearly intending to install very costly capital equipment on the premises. Abraham Darby II died in 1763, leaving Richard Reynolds in charge of the Ketley works, and on 17 September 1764 Reynolds negotiated a new lease of the Allmoors with Earl Gower, "it being apprehended that the said Granville Earl Gower had not a power under his marriage settlement to make a lease of the said premises for 99 years absolute". The new lease was for the three lives of Richard Reynolds jnr, Abraham Darby jnr and Samuel Darby, his younger brother. It mentioned that three blast furnaces had been erected on the Allmoors by Darby since 1756, and also, "fire engines, houses, warehouses, buildings, pools, drains, weirs, soughs, and other erections".[69] Since all this building had been carried out on Earl Gower's land by the lessee, however, his successor was still charged only the ground rent of £28 5s p.a. for what was by then a very valuable tenement. William Reynolds renewed this lease on 19 November 1796, inserting new lives and receiving a promise from the first marquis that any of the three lives could be renewed on request during the first marquis's lifetime. The year 1803, in which the first marquis died, saw the Reynolds family in full control of the industry of Ketley. William Reynolds enjoyed mining rights over the entire manor, operated three blast furnaces in addition to an extensive range of other capital equipment, and was in direct occupation of some 175 acres of land, most of it farmed, an area that had increased to 315 acres by 1813.[70] In 1803, however, Reynolds paid for all this a mere £73 5s p.a. to the first marquis, in addition to his mining royalties. The Wrockwardine Wood lands with their three blast furnaces, leased from the three lords, had been detached from the Reynolds' enterprise in 1797, and in 1802 swung permanently over into the camp of the Lilleshall Company under John Bishton. But the operations of Reynolds & Company in Ketley remained very extensive, under the direction of William's half-brother Joseph after the former's death in 1803.

The year 1803 is indeed an appropriate one with which to end this study, for it was then that many of its leading characters were swept from the stage. The Duke of Bridgewater died on 8 March, William Reynolds on 3 June, John Bishton on 9 August, and the first marquis himself on 26 October. The enterprises which they had founded, however, lived on, and continued to prosper.

The Leveson-Gowers were by no means unusual among landed families in their direct involvement with industry, and neither was Shropshire untypical as an industrial county.[71] Here, the links between the landed and industrial classes could scarcely have been closer. Indeed, so close were they that the same individual often fell into both social categories. Robert Barbor, Thomas Gilbert and John Bishton were gentlemen landlords as well as being entrepreneurs, while the first Earl Gower, his son and two grandsons were all actively participating entrepreneurs, as well as being members of the landed aristocracy. Eighteenth-century Shropshire in fact illustrates a very interesting transitional stage in the development of English capitalism. When the first clearly recognizable entrepreneurs (in our modern sense of the word) made their appearance upon the English scene, during the time of J. U. Nef's "Industrial Revolution", they were all members of the landed classes.[72] In the words of J. W. Gough, "our first entrepreneurs did not themselves form a class: rather, that entrepreneurship was one of the outlets for the restless energy of the upper class".[73]

Gradually, however, as the seventeenth century progressed, a more distinct and purely entrepreneurial class began to emerge in England, represented by families like the Foleys and the Crowleys in iron, the Briscoes and Dupins in paper, and later in the eighteenth century by the Darbys, Wedgwoods and Crawshays. It was these generations of entrepreneurs who worked most closely with the landed classes, intermarrying with them, and indeed often swapping roles with them. The distinction between the landed and industrial classes was still blurred, but it was becoming more sharply defined. The completely amateur landed "adventurers" of the late sixteenth century, men like the sixth Lord Mountjoy or Sir Francis Willoughby,[74] had disappeared from the scene by the early eighteenth century. The landed classes were still prepared to adopt an entrepreneurial role, but now only by working in the closest co-operation with the "new breed" of wholly professional entrepreneurs which had only recently emerged, typified by men like Richard Hartshorne and George Sparrow in early-eighteenth-century Shropshire.

By the early nineteenth century, however, the scene had changed again, and the landed classes were beginning to disengage themselves from direct involvement in industry, leaving this role entirely to the professional entrepreneurs who, it must be said, had become even more professional with the passing of the years, and who were, by 1815, much better qualified to take over this job in any case. Political and social reasons prompted the landed classes to disengage from direct industrial involvement, but they retained a most important role in industry as *rentiers* and investors. It is not true to say, as Eric Richards does, that their social withdrawal from an entrepreneurial role represented "something close to a haemorrhage of capital" from the industrial sector.[75] In 1813, 72 per cent of the first Duke of Sutherland's net English income came from his industrial investments, and in 1833 this proportion was still 70 per cent.[76] Far more serious from the point of view of a "haemorrhage of capital" from industry were the very large sums of money withdrawn from the industrial sector by the most successful of the eighteenth century's professional class of entrepreneurs, as families like the Peels, the Strutts, the Arkwrights and the Whitbreads decided to buy their way into the landed classes, using money that might have been ploughed back into their industrial enterprises.[77]

But even this outflow of capital was not enough to slow the pace of England's Industrial Revolution. It is now well established that the Industrial Revolution was, in the main, self-financing. Most of the capital required was provided by the entrepreneurial classes themselves, who ploughed back their profits or, at worst, borrowed from family or friends. Essentially, however, they pulled themselves up by their own bootstraps, for in any case the working or circulating capital of our earliest industrial enterprises was always of greater importance than the fixed capital invested in plant. Even if the landed classes had withdrawn from the industrial sector as investors as well as in their role of entrepreneurs (which they did not), this would still not have represented a serious "haemorrhage of capital", for the self-financing process was very firmly established by the early nineteenth century, and banking services were well developed.[78] By 1832, the landed classes were no longer essential to England's industrial welfare, and they could afford to retire into the background.

The picture was very different, however, in 1748. At this time, the infant industries of England could very easily have been strangled at birth by a hostile landed class which wielded, at that time, virtually the whole of the nation's political power. In addition, small landowners and owner-occupying farmers held only a low proportion of England's acreage: their share was a mere 15–20 per cent in 1748. All the rest of the land was held by large owners, some of them corporations but for the most part landed aristocrats and gentlemen.[79] These were the people who decided whether canals and turnpike roads should be allowed to cross their property, and who secured the necessary Acts of Parliament to make them possible. They decided which commodities should be taxed, and how heavy those taxes should be. They decided whether the minerals beneath their land were to be exploited, and what industrial plant was to be allowed upon its surface. The investment of the landed classes in eighteenth-century industrial enterprises might not have been essential, but their co-operation with them was of crucial importance. Fortunately for England, her landed classes at this time made the decision to work on the closest and friendliest of terms with the emerging class of professional entrepreneurs. Other parts of Europe were not so fortunate and, in consequence, trailed far behind this country in terms of industrial development. Had the landed classes of England emulated the attitudes of some of their foreign contemporaries, the Industrial Revolution, not only in Shropshire but in other regions too, could very easily have been stifled at birth.[80]

Appendix I

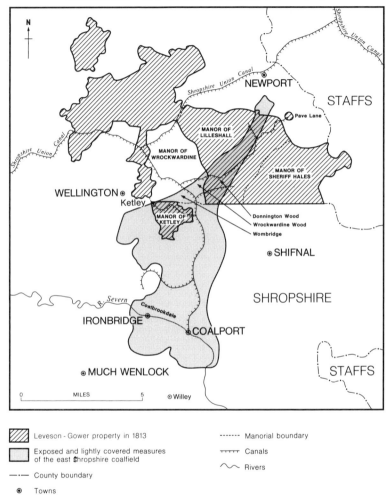

**THE INDUSTRIAL REGIONS OF SHROPSHIRE AND
LEVESON - GOWER PROPERTY IN 1813**

Map 9.1   The industrial regions of Shropshire and Leveson-Gower property in 1813. Reconstruction by J. R. Wordie.

Notes

1   B. Trinder, *The Industrial Revolution in Shropshire*, 2nd edn (London, 1981), p. 34;
and P. Deane and W. A. Cole, *British Economic Growth, 1688–1959* 2nd edn (Cambridge, 1969), p. 225.

2   Deane and Cole, op cit., p. 216; Trinder, op. cit., 1st edn (1973), p. 15; R. Townson, "A sketch of the mineralogy of Shropshire", in his book, *Tracts and Observations in Natural History and Physiology* (London, 1799), p. 179.

3   T. S. Ashton and J. Sykes, *The Coal Industry in the Eighteenth Century* (Manchester, 1964), p. 153; A. Raistrick, *Dynasty of Ironfounders: The Darbys of Coalbrookdale* (London, 1953), pp. 37–42, 193–200; J. Plymley, *A General View of the Agriculture of Shropshire* (London, 1803), pp. 290–2; H. W. Dickinson, *John Wilkinson, Ironmaster* (Ulverston, 1914), p. 23.

4   Trinder, op. cit., 2nd edn, pp. 35–8.

5   ibid., p. 115.

6   See Appendix I, Map 9.1: "The industrial regions of Shropshire and Leveson-Gower Property in 1813".

7   Townson, op. cit., pp. 164–76.

8   See *Dictionary of National Biography* (Leveson-Gower); GEC (under titles); Burke's Peerage (Sutherland); O. Browning (ed.). *Despatches of Earl Gower, English Ambassador at Paris, June 1790 to August 1792* (London, 1885); C. Granville (ed.), *Lord Granville Leveson-Gower, Private Correspondence, 1781–1821* (London, 1917); H. Walpole, *Memoirs of the Reign of King George II* (London, 1846), pp. 12–15. In the heady days of March 1783, as George III thrashed about desperately in his efforts to avoid calling Fox and North to power, Earl Gower was offered the post of Prime Minister. However, he wisely declined the invitation: J. Fortescue (ed.), *The Correspondence of King George III, 1760–1783*, 6 vols (London, 1928), Vol. 6, pp. 263–71.

9   See J. R. Wordie, *Estate Management in Eighteenth-Century England* (London, 1982), pp. 95–102.

10   *Victoria County History of Shropshire*, Vol. 11 (1985), pp. 181, 192–3, 310–11, 328.

11   Staffordshire Record Office (hereafter cited as Staffs RO) D593/P/16/3/14, Barbor to Hill, 4 August 1747.

12   Staffs RO D593/I/1/39/1. The rent agreed upon was £210 p.a.

13   *Victoria County History of Shropshire*, op. cit., p. 329, and *Kelly's Directory of Shropshire* (London, 1900), p. 296.

14   Staffs RO D593/F/3/5/6–11, Mining Accounts 1748–54.

15   See Wordie, op. cit., pp. 238–52.

16   Staffs RO D593/I/1/16/1, Schedule of tools, engines, materials, and utensils in and by this indenture granted, 23 January 1715.

17   Staffs RO D593/V/3/38–58, Copies of local Turnpike Acts, 1729–1823.

18   A. L. Thomas, "Transport and communications in north Staffordshire during the eighteenth century" *HCS* (Collections for the History of Staffordshire) (1934), pp. 57–119.

19   L. E. Stephens, *The Clerks of the Counties, 1360 to 1960* (Warwick, 1961), p. 159.

20   Staffs RO D593/B/Tittensor, Box 2, Bundle 10. Will of Robert Barbor, 1761.

21   Staffs RO D593/I/1/16/3, Lease of 1734.

22   Staffs RO D593/I/1/39, Terms of Henry Barbor's lease, 28 October 1756, and Ironbridge Gorge Museum Trust Library (hereafter cited as IGMTL) Lilleshall Company Collection, Box 1, item 42, Henry Barbor of Honnington to Abraham Darby of Coalbrookdale.

23   Staff RO D593/I/1/39/2–6, Transactions of the Lilleshall partners, 1761–4. The document of 1764 noted, "it was apprehended that the mines, quarries, and land were being mismanaged and spoiled by the said lessee".

24   Staffs RO D593/I/3/22, Grindon copper and lead leases, 1736–7, and H. Malet, *Bridgewater, the Canal Duke, 1736–1803* (Manchester, 1977), p. 36.

25   Wordie, op. cit., pp. 250–1.

26   W. H. Chaloner, *People and Industries* (London, 1963), p. 34; Malet, op. cit., p. 38.

27   Malet, op. cit., pp. 37–8.

28   See B. Falk, *The Bridgewater Millions* (London, 1942), pp. 79–112.

29   Malet, op. cit., pp. 39–41, 96–8.

30   ibid., pp. 94–5.

31   IGMTL, Lilleshall Company Collection, Box 1, item 55, Box 2, items 56–7; Staffs RO D/593/T/1/35, List of shareholders in the Trent and Mersey canal, 1770.

32   Staffs RO D593/G/4/3/32, D593/F/3/5/57.

33 Staffs RO D593/H/9/1–2 consists of maps and plans of several proposed canal routes, commissioned by the second Earl and drawn by James Brindley between 1759 and 1769.

34 Thomas, op. cit., pp. 104–6.

35 Staffs RO D593/t/1/35.

36 Staffs RO D593/I/1/33 is an agreement dated 8 June 1765, between Earl Gower and James Cotes of Woodcote, Esq., for a right of way for the Pave Lane canal across the latter's land. In the Leveson-Gower Collection at the Shropshire Record Office (hereafter cited as Salop RO) may be seen at 972/1767 a plan of "Lord Gower's Navigable Canal from Donnington Wood to Pave Lane".

37 See Map 9.1. Appendix I.

38 Staffs RO D593/G/4/3/32, Accounts of 1774.

39 Staffs RO D593/G/1/1/41–56. Estate rentals, 1698–1712, and D593/B/1/20/5, purchase deed of Meir Heath land.

40 Staffs RO D593/G/2/24, Salop rents for 1773.

41 Staffs RO D593/I/1/21a.

42 Trinder does, however, mention other farms occupied by the Darbys. "Abraham Darby II and his son purchased the Hay Farm in 1757, and by 1784 controlled Madeley and Sunniside farms as well": Trinder, op. cit., 2nd edn, p. 36. On 30 August 1785, Thomas and John Gilbert took out a lease for lives on additional farm land near to Pave Lane, in the manor of Lilleshall. IGMTL Lilleshall Company Collection, Box 2, item 91.

43 Salop RO, Leveson-Gower Collection, 972/1, Survey of Shropshire estate in 1813.

44 Staffs RO D593/G/4/3/42–63.

45 IGMTL Lilleshall Company Collection, Box 3, item 109.

46 IGMTL Lilleshall Company Collection, Box 4 item 175, Assignment of 1802, and Staffs RO D593/T/4/11, Lease of 1807.

47 IGMTL Lilleshall Company Collection, Box 4 item 175, Box 5 items 177 and 179. See also W. K. V. Gale and C. R. Nicholls, *The Lilleshall Company Limited: A History* (Ashbourne, 1979), p. 21.

48 Staffs RO D593/F/3/2/69–74.

49 Staffs RO D593/L/4/3 Appointment of John Bishton.

50 Salop RO Shropshire Parish Registers, Lichfield Diocese, Vol. 3, pp. 286–333. See also J. Bishton, *A General View of the Agriculture of Shropshire* (London, 1794).

51 IGMTL Lilleshall Company Collection Box 3, items 112, 117, 119, 120, 126–7, 131.

52 IGMTL Lilleshall Company Collection Box 3 items 147–8. From 1796 onwards it is noticeable that leases, licences to assign and the like were granted to Leveson-Gower tenants not simply by the Marquis of Stafford alone, but by the Marquis *and Earl Gower*, the courtesy title given to George Granville, his son and heir. In 1796 the Marquis was 75 years of age, and his son had in effect been managing the estates and the family's industrial interests since his return from Paris in 1792. From June 1790, Earl Gower had held the important and dangerous post of British ambassador to France.

53 Although John Bishton snr had taken on sole responsibility for Reynold's Lilleshall enterprises on 6 February, he quickly assigned a one-eighth share each to John Onions and William Phillips on 8 February, and a further one-eighth share to James Birch on 3 December 1798. Meanwhile, on 6 June 1797, John Bishton jnr had assigned his quarter share in the Snedshill coal and ironworks to his father. IGMTL Lilleshall Company Collection, Box 3 item 149, Box 4 items 150, 155, 160.

54 See Wordie, op. cit., pp. 120–9, and Gale and Nicholls, op. cit., pp. 21–38.

55 Staffs RO D593/G/1/1/41–60, D593/I/1/16/1.

56 Staffs RO D593/I/1/21–2.

57 Staffs RO D593/G/4/3/1–20. A good deal has already appeared in print on the closely related histories of the Darby and Reynolds families. See *Dictionary of National Biography*; Raistrick op. cit.; H. M. Rathbone, *Letters of Richard Reynolds, with a Memoir of his Life* (London, 1852); E. T. Wedmore, *Richard Reynolds, Philanthropist, 1735–1816* (Bristol, 1907).

58 IGMTL Lilleshall Company Collection Box 2 item 66 a (lease of 1775), Box 3 item 132 (lease of 1796) and items 147–8 (6 February 1798) for details of the background to these agreements.

59   B. R. Mitchell and P. Deane, *Abstract of British Historical Statistics* 2nd edn (Cambridge, 1971), pp. 482, 492.

60   Staffs RO D593/G/4/3/35–63, D593/F/3/7/6/1–2.

61   IGMTL Lilleshall Company Collection, Box 2 items 76–82.

62   Trinder, op. cit., 2nd edn, p. 42.

63   Staffs RO D593/F/3/7/6.

64   In 1785 and 1787 the first marquis supported the petitions of William Reynolds and others against the imposition of additional taxes upon coal and iron. J. Randall, *The History of Madeley* (Madeley, 1880), p. 62; T. S. Ashton, *Iron and Steel in the Industrial Revolution* (Manchester, 1924); Rathbone, op. cit., pp. 256–62, 279–85.

65   Staffs RO D593/L/4/3/2, Bishton to first Marquis, 21 October 1789.

66   IGMTL Lilleshall Company Collection Box 3 items 147–8.

67   Staffs RO D593/T/4/11/26.

68   *Dictionary of National Biography* (Richard Reynolds) and Staffs RO D593/T/4/11/3.

69   Staffs RO D593/I/1/21a.

70   Salop RO, Leveson-Gower Collection, 972/1, Survey of Shropshire Estates, 1813.

71   See A. H. John, *The Industrial Development of South Wales, 1750–1850* (Cardiff, 1950), pp. 7–9, 37; H. J. Habakkuk, "Economic functions of English landowners in the seventeenth and eighteenth centuries", *Explorations in Entrepreneurial History*, vol. 6, no. 2 (1953), pp. 92–102; J. D. Chambers, "The Vale of Trent, 1670–1800", *Economic History Review*, supplement no. 3 (1957), pp. 6–9, 11, 13; E. Hughes, *North Country Life in the Eighteenth Century*, Vol. 1 (Oxford, 1952), pp. 11–13, 151–200; Vol. 2 (Oxford, 1965), pp. 133–79; T. J. Raybould, "The development and organization of Lord Dudley's mineral estates, 1774–1845", *Economic History Review*, 2nd ser., vol. 27, no. 3 (1968), pp. 529–44; T. W. Beastall, *A North Country Estate: The Lumleys and the Saundersons as Landowners, 1600–1800* (London, 1975), pp. 11–46; G. Mee, *Aristocratic Enterprise: The Fitzwilliams' Industrial Undertakings, 1795–1875* (London, 1975), pp. 1–47; J. V. Beckett, *Coal and Tobacco: The Lowthers and the Economic Development of West Cumberland, 1660–1760* (Cambridge, 1981), pp. 119–55.

72   J. U. Nef, *Industry and Government in France and England, 1540–1640* (Philadelphia, 1940), p. 4.

73   J. W. Gough, *The Rise of the Entrepreneur* (London, 1969), p. 20.

74   ibid., pp. 66–8, 177–81.

75   E. Richards, "The industrial face of a great estate: Trentham and Lilleshall, 1780–1860", *Economic History Review*, 2nd ser., vol. 27, no. 3 (1974), p. 430.

76   Wordie, op. cit., p. 150, and J. R. Wordie, "Rent movements and the English tenant farmer, 1700–1839", *Research in Economic History*, vol. 6 (1981), p. 238.

77   See E. L. Jones, "Industrial capital and landed investment: the Arkwrights in Herefordshire, 1809–1843"; in E. L. Jones and G. E. Mingay (eds), *Land, Labour, and Population in the Industrial Revolution* (London, 1967), pp. 48–71, and W. H. Chaloner, "The agricultural activities of John Wilkinson, ironmaster", *Agricultural History Review*, vol. 5, pt. 2 (1957), pp. 48–51.

78   H. Heaton, "Financing the Industrial Revolution", *Bulletin of the Business History Society*, vol. 11, no. 1 (1937), pp. 1–10; T. S. Ashton, *The Industrial Revolution, 1760–1830* (Oxford, 1948), pp. 95–6; P. Deane, "Capital formation in Britain before the railway age", *Economic Development and Cultural Change*, vol. 9, no. 3 (1961), pp. 352–68; S. Pollard, "Fixed capital in the Industrial Revolution in Britain", *Journal of Economic History*, vol. 24, no. 3 (1964), pp. 299–314; L. S. Pressnell, *Country Banking in the Industrial Revolution* (Oxford, 1956), pp. 322–43.

79   F. M. L. Thompson, "The social distribution of landed property in England since the sixteenth century", *Economic History Review*, 2nd ser., vol. 19, no. 3 (1966), pp. 505–17.

80   See A. Goodwin (ed.), *The European Nobility in the Eighteenth Century* (London, 1953), pp. 53–9, 105–7, 183–5; H. J. Habakkuk and M. Postan (eds), *The Cambridge Economic History of Europe*, Vol. 6 (Cambridge, 1962), pp. 407–8; D. Spring (ed.), *European Landed Elites in the Nineteenth Century* (Baltimore, 1977), pp. 1–18.

Index

figures in *italics* refer to illustrations